THE TRIUMPH SPEED TWIN & THUNDERBIRD BIBLE

All 5T 498cc & 649cc models 1938 to 1966

Speedpro Series
Harley-Davidson Evolution Engines, How to Build & Power Tune (Hammill)
Motorcycle-engined Racing Car, How to Build (Pashley)

RAC handbooks
Caring for your scooter – How to maintain & service your 49cc to 125cc twist & go scooter (Fry)
How your motorcycle works – Your guide to the components & systems of modern motorcycles (Henshaw)
Motorcycles – A first-time-buyer's guide (Henshaw)

Enthusiast's Restoration Manual Series
Beginner's Guide to Classic Motorcycle Restoration, The (Burns)
Ducati Bevel Twins 1971 to 1986 (Falloon)
How to Restore Classic Off-road Motorcycles (Burns)
How to restore Honda CX500 & CX650 – YOUR step-by-step colour illustrated guide to complete restoration (Burns)
How to restore Honda Fours – YOUR step-by-step colour illustrated guide to complete restoration (Burns)
Triumph Trident T150/T160 & BSA Rocket III, How to Restore (Rooke)
Yamaha FS1-E, How to Restore (Watts)

Essential Buyer's Guide Series
BSA 350 & 500 Unit Construction Singles (Henshaw)
BSA 500 & 650 Twins (Henshaw)
BSA Bantam (Henshaw)
Ducati Bevel Twins (Falloon)
Ducati Desmodue Twins (Falloon)
Ducati Desmoquattro Twins – 851, 888, 916, 996, 998, ST4 1988 to 2004 (Falloon)
Hinckley Triumph triples & fours 750, 900, 955, 1000, 1050, 1200 – 1991-2009 (Henshaw)
Honda CBR FireBlade (Henshaw)
Honda CBR600 Hurricane (Henshaw)
Honda SOHC Fours 1969-1984 (Henshaw)
Kawasaki Z1 & Z900 (Orritt)
Moto Guzzi 2-valve big twins (Falloon)
New Mini (Collins)
Norton Commando (Henshaw)
Royal Enfield Bullet (Henshaw)
Triumph 350 & 500 Twins (Henshaw)
Triumph Bonneville (Henshaw)
Triumph Thunderbird, Trophy & Tiger (Henshaw)
Velocette 350 & 500 Singles (Henshaw)

Biographies
Edward Turner – The Man Behind the Motorcycles (Clew)
Jim Redman – 6 Times World Motorcycle Champion: The Autobiography (Redman)
'Sox' – Gary Hocking – the forgotten World Motorcycle Champion (Hughes)

General
BMW Boxer Twins 1970-1995 Bible, The (Falloon)
BMW Cafe Racers (Cloesen)
BMW Custom Motorcycles – Choppers, Cruisers, Bobbers, Trikes & Quads (Cloesen)
Bonjour – Is this Italy? (Turner)
British 250cc Racing Motorcycles (Pereira)
British Café Racers (Cloesen)
British Custom Motorcycles – The Brit Chop – choppers, cruisers, bobbers & trikes (Cloesen)
BSA Bantam Bible, The (Henshaw)
BSA Motorcycles – the final evolution (Jones)
Ducati 750 Bible, The (Falloon)
Ducati 750 SS 'round-case' 1974, The Book of the (Falloon)
Ducati 860, 900 and Mille Bible, The (Falloon)
Ducati Monster Bible (New Updated & Revised Edition), The (Falloon)
Ducati 916 (updated edition) (Falloon)
From Crystal Palace to Red Square – A Hapless Biker's Road to Russia (Turner)
Funky Mopeds (Skelton)
Italian Cafe Racers (Cloesen)
Italian Custom Motorcycles (Cloesen)
Japanese Custom Motorcycles – The Nippon Chop – Chopper, Cruiser, Bobber, Trikes and Quads (Cloesen)
Kawasaki Triples Bible, The (Walker)
Kawasaki Z1 Story, The (Sheehan)
Lambretta Bible, The (Davies)
Laverda Twins & Triples Bible 1968-1986 (Falloon)
Moto Guzzi Sport & Le Mans Bible, The (Falloon)
Motorcycle Apprentice (Cakebread)
Motorcycle GP Racing in the 1960s (Pereira)
Motorcycle Road & Racing Chassis Designs (Noakes)
MV Agusta Fours, The book of the classic (Falloon)
The Norton Commando Bible – All models 1968 to 1978 (Henshaw)
Scooters & Microcars, The A-Z of Popular (Dan)
Scooter Lifestyle (Grainger)
SCOOTER MANIA! – Recollections of the Isle of Man International Scooter Rally (Jackson)
Singer Story: Cars, Commercial Vehicles, Bicycles & Motorcycle (Atkinson)
Triumph Bonneville Bible (59-83) (Henshaw)
Triumph Bonneville!, Save the – The inside story of the Meriden Workers' Co-op (Rosamond)
Triumph Motorcycles & the Meriden Factory (Hancox)
Triumph Speed Twin & Thunderbird Bible (Woolridge)
Triumph Tiger Cub Bible (Estall)
Triumph Trophy Bible (Woolridge)
TT Talking – The TT's most exciting era – As seen by Manx Radio TT's lead commentator 2004-2012 (Lambert)
Velocette Motorcycles – MSS to Thruxton – New Third Edition (Burris)
Vincent Motorcycles: The Untold Story since 1946 (Guyony & Parker)

www.veloce.co.uk

For post publication news, updates and amendments relating to this book please visit www.veloce.co.uk/books/V4982

First published in 2004 by Veloce Publishing Limited, Veloce House, Parkway Farm Business Park, Middle Farm Way, Poundbury, Dorchester DT1 3AR, England. Fax 01305 268864 / e-mail info@veloce.co.uk / web www.veloce.co.uk and www.velocebooks.com.
Reprinted April 2010, July 2016, and October 2016. ISBN: 978-1-845849-82-5 UPC: 6-36847-04982-9.
© 2004, 2010 and 2016 Harry Woolridge and Veloce Publishing. All rights reserved. With the exception of quoting brief passages for the purpose of review, no part of this publication may be recorded, reproduced or transmitted by any means, including photocopying, without the written permission of Veloce Publishing Ltd. Throughout this book logos, model names and designations, etc, have been used for the purposes of identification, illustration and decoration. Such names are the property of the trademark holder as this is not an official publication. Readers with ideas for automotive books, or books on other transport or related hobby subjects, are invited to write to the editorial director of Veloce Publishing at the above address. British Library Cataloguing in Publication Data – A catalogue record for this book is available from the British Library. Typesetting, design and page make-up all by Veloce Publishing Ltd on Apple Mac.
Printed and bound by CPI Group (UK) Ltd, Croydon, CR0 4YY.

THE TRIUMPH SPEED TWIN & THUNDERBIRD BIBLE

All 5T 498cc & 649cc models 1938 to 1966

Harry Woolridge

VELOCE PUBLISHING
THE PUBLISHER OF FINE AUTOMOTIVE BOOKS

Contents

Publisher's note: Unfortunately, due to the age and condition of the source material, some of the image reproductions in this volume are not to our usual high standard; nevertheless, these pictures do add to the completeness of the book.

Acknowledgements & About the Author 5

Chapter 1. A brief history of the company 6

Chapter 2. The Speed Twin 9
   Institutional machines 9
   Identification by frame and engine number 10
   1938 Model 5T Speed Twin 11
   1938 Model 5T Speed Twin technical data 14
   1939 Model 5T Speed Twin 18
   The Maudes Trophy 22
   1939 successes 24
   1940 Model 5T Speed Twin 24
   Future design 25
   Speed Twin 1941-1944 28

Chapter 3. A new era dawns 29
   1945 Model 5T Speed Twin 29
   1945 Model 5T Speed Twin 30
   Thoughts and comments about the 1947 models 32
   1946 Model 5T Speed Twin 34
   1946 Speed Twin road tests 35
   1947 Model 5T Speed Twin 36
   1948 Model 5T Speed Twin 38
   The Speed Twin in the 1948
      International Six Days Trial 40
   1949 Model 5T Speed Twin 40
   1949 Speed Twin road test 43
   1950 Model 5T Speed Twin 44
   1951 Model 5T Speed Twin 46
   1952 Model 5T 1954 Speed Twin 47
   1953 Model 5T Speed Twin 49
   1953 Speed Twin road tests 51
   1954 Model 5T Speed Twin 52
   1955 Model 5T Speed Twin 54
   1956 Model 5T Speed Twin 56
   1957 Model 5T Speed Twin 58
   1958 Model 5T Speed Twin 59

Chapter 4. Excitement & demise 63
   The Model 5TA Speed Twin 1959-1966 63
   Technical details 65
   1959 Model 5TA Speed Twin 68
   1959 Speed Twin road test 68
   1960 Model 5TA Speed Twin 69
   1961 Model 5TA Speed Twin 70
   1962 Model 5TA Speed Twin 71

   1963 Model 5TA Speed Twin 72
   1964 Model 5TA Speed Twin 72
   1965 Model 5TA Speed Twin 75
   1966 Model 5TA Speed Twin 76
   The end of the line 77
   Performance figures: 500cc 78
   Speed Twin notable registration numbers 78
   Speed Twin colours 1938 - 1966 79
   Amal carburettor settings 80
   Overall gear ratios 81
   Chains 82
   5T Show Models 82
   Parts serviceability 86

Chapter 5. The launch of the Thunderbird 87
   3 x 90 x 500 Montlhéry demonstration 87
   The economy run 90
   Sporting achievements 90

Chapter 6. Technical development 92
   1950 Model 6T Thunderbird 92
   1950 Model 6T Thunderbird technical data 95
   1951 Model 6T Thunderbird 100
   1952 Model 6T Thunderbird 101
   1953 Model 6T Thunderbird 104
   1954 Model 6T Thunderbird 104
   1955 Model 6T Thunderbird 107
   1956 Model 6T Thunderbird 108
   1957 Model 6T Thunderbird 109
   1958 Model 6T Thunderbird 111
   1959 Model 6T Thunderbird 113
   1960 Model 6T Thunderbird 115
   1961 Model 6T Thunderbird 119
   1962 Model 6T Thunderbird 120
   1963 Model 6T Thunderbird 124
   1964 Model 6T Thunderbird 127
   1965 Model 6T Thunderbird
      & 6TP police model 131
   1966 Model 6T Thunderbird 132
   Thunderbird 6TP 134
   1966 6TP specification 135
   Colour chart Thunderbird 6T 140
   Thunderbird paint substitutes 141
   Thunderbird show models 142
   Thunderbird 6T carburettor specifications 142

Index 143

Acknowledgements & About the Author

Acknowledgements

I would like to thank all those who have helped in compiling this book. I was fortunate that many of my friends were also my workmates at Triumph so the pooling of knowledge was very useful.

Special thanks to John Nelson for the use of his photographic library, and to Miss Louise Betteridge for her patience in setting out and typing the original manuscript.

About the Author

Always a keen motorcyclist, I actually began my working life at Jaguar and Singer Cars in Coventry, before getting called up for National Service in the Royal Air Force. Posted to Egypt as a vehicle fitter, my motorcycling was curtailed somewhat, since the only bikes available were Norton 16H side valves (not the ideal mount for desert riding ...).

Released from the RAF, I worked as a fitter for British Road Services, mainly on Foden, Sentinel and AEC diesel trucks. Being an enthusiastic motorcyclist, however, I soon applied for a job in the Service Department at the Triumph Engineering Company, and was lucky enough to be selected. Thus began a relationship with Triumph and its motorcycles that lasted thirty years, and, in retrospect, is one I would not have missed at any price.

After a few years in the Service Department, I joined the team in the Experimental Department where I remained for five glorious years, and was eventually promoted to the position of Assistant Quality Control Manager. Later, in a reshuffle of titles, I became Inspection Foreman for Motorcycle Assembly and Production Development.

With the formation of the Meriden Co-operative, I served as Warranty/Service Manager until its closure in 1983.

Harry Woolridge
Nuneaton

Chapter 1
A brief history of the company

The origins of the Triumph motorcycle company go back to 1885, when a young German, Siegfried Bettmann, moved to London and started an import/export business selling pedal cycles branded with his name.

In 1886, Bettmann changed the company name to Triumph, reasoning that its meaning was self-explanatory, and also because it translated well into many European languages. During 1887, Bettmann was joined by Mauritz Shulte, a young German engineer. A year later they moved to Coventry and rented a small factory with the intention of manufacturing their own machines. Bettmann and Shulte reasoned that Coventry, being the centre of the cycle industry, would be an ideal manufacturing base since it was close to suppliers and boasted a plentiful supply of skilled labour.

In 1902, the company produced its first motorcycle, using a Belgian 2¼hp Minerva engine clipped to a bicycle frame. It was not long, however, before a Shulte-designed engine was built, and 1905 saw a totally in-house Triumph of 3hp (363cc) offered for sale.

By 1915, the engine capacity had increased to 550cc, and the machine now looked like a proper motorcycle (gone were the pedals of previous years). The machine was fitted with a three-speed gearbox, though a belt was still used for the final drive. This motorcycle, the Model H, was supplied to despatch riders during WWI, and soon gained a reputation for quality and reliability in the mud of the Western Front. The term 'trusty Triumph' originated in this period, and the company used it when advertising the model.

Triumph had experimented with a 600cc vertical twin as early as 1913, but the 1914-18 war halted development. This was the first known vertical twin from Triumph. Later, in 1933, a Val Page-designed 633cc vertical twin was produced. Unfortunately, being rather old fashioned in appearance, it did not win public acclaim.

1935 saw the company fall into financial difficulty, like so many others during the depression of the 1930s. So serious were the problems, in fact, that the company went into bankruptcy, and closed completely in 1936.

The pedal cycle part of the company was sold to Raleigh Cycles, Nottingham, and the motorcar side to the Standard Motor Company, Coventry. Most of the motorcycle manufacturing business was purchased by Mr Jack Sangster, then owner of Ariel Motors, Birmingham, for the reputed figure of £30,000. The factory and the plant were leased from a Mr Graham, the official receiver appointed by Lloyds Bank, and spares were sold on commission, thus reducing the original outlay.

It didn't take long for the newly formed 'Triumph Engineering Company Limited' to start motorcycle production. This was largely because Sangster had sent one of his most competent Ariel men, Edward Turner, to Coventry to be General Manager and Chief Designer.

This appointment was to prove inspirational, and, as we now know, the company went on to become one of Britain's most successful motorcycle firms. It wasn't long before the youthful, 35 year old Edward had designed a vertical twin which would determine the course of motorcycle design for the next three decades. Although the vertical twin concept was copied by most of the British manufacturers, good as they were, the Triumph stayed pre-eminent.

When the first Triumph twins arrived in the USA, just prior to WWII, they were an outstanding success; taking on and beating the Indians and Harleys, which were often twice the engine capacity of the Triumph, and winning races on the speedway tracks and in hill climbs. Edward Turner, who regarded himself as chief salesman as well as designer and financial director, soon saw a potential sales outlet in the USA. To this end he had started corresponding with a Mr Bill Johnson of Pasadena, a lawyer and keen motorcyclist. This correspondence soon blossomed into a strong personal and business relationship and, when Johnson wanted to open a motorcycle store, the Triumph marque was a natural choice.

Having set up a successful West Coast sales outlet, Triumph now looked to the East Coast. The company engaged the services of Mr Dennis McCormack,

A brief history of the company

a 48 year old mechanical engineer who, before becoming an American citizen, had actually been born in Coventry. McCormack took a lease on premises in Joppa Road, Towson, near Baltimore in Maryland, and set up the Triumph Corporation, subsequently known as Tri-Cor. This East Coast outlet soon began to rival Jomo in terms of sales and service.

Turner was not slow to capitalise on the US setup, and spent many months each year visiting the two distributorships.

Everything seemed to be pointing to a very rosy future for Triumph, but a certain Herr Hitler was soon going to change this. One cold November night in 1940, the Coventry factory was completely destroyed in one of the worst bombing raids the city had experienced. However, with true Coventrian grit and determination, the remains were sifted through and anything that could be of use was transported to the nearby town of Warwick. Spares were soon being produced from the tin shed that served as a factory and, by mid 1941, complete motorcycles were being manufactured for the allied armed forces.

A completely new factory was built in 1942 just outside Coventry, near Meriden Village (allegedly the centre of England). Up until 1945, however, the factory only produced machines for the War Department (these were the 3SW and 5SW 350 and 500cc side valves, and the 3HW 350cc overhead valve).

On the cessation of hostilities, Triumph was in an enviable position. The post-war twins were in great demand and the company had a nearly new factory in which to produce them. With telescopic front forks replacing the old girder units, a spring hub at the rear wheel, and a few engine modifications, Triumphs were ready for the post-war boom.

Despite this apparently bright future, though, there were many frustrations to overcome in the immediate post-war years. Steel rationing was in force, with priority being given to exporters (luckily, though, Triumph was one of these). Petrol and raw materials like rubber were also in short supply. Even electricity was rationed, being available only on certain days of the week. Triumph's answer to this was to install its own generator.

Although motorcycles were produced despite these problems, the demand was so great that it couldn't be satisfied, and waiting lists grew ever longer. There were even waiting lists in the 1950s and 1960s, and it was suggested that Edward Turner kept the market short intentionally, thereby boosting demand.

In 1951, Jack Sangster sold his interest in the Triumph Engineering Co. Ltd. to the Birmingham Small Arms Company (BSA), whilst Turner stayed on at Triumph as Managing Director. Although the rivalry between Triumph and BSA didn't diminish, the profits, which had previously stayed with the Triumph company and its shareholders, would in future go into the BSA group purse.

Jack Sangster and Edward Turner were on the BSA board of directors, but the Triumph company was left to run with very little BSA interference, possibly due to the fact that profits at Meriden were so good.

During May 1961, Bert Hopwood rejoined the Triumph company as Director and General Manager. Jack Sangster resigned as Chairman of BSA, and Mr Eric Turner (no relation to Edward) was appointed in his place.

In 1964, Edward Turner announced his retirement as Divisional Executive Director, but remained on the BSA group board in a non-executive capacity. By mid-1964, Mr Harry Sturgeon had been appointed Chief Executive of the BSA Motorcycle Division, and Bert Hopwood gained the title of Engineering Director and Deputy Director of the Division. Unfortunately, Harry Sturgeon became ill and died of a brain tumour in 1966. His short time as Chief Executive, however, had seen the motorcycle group's turnover increase by nearly 40%. This was a welcome rise in production, since all the group's models had been in great demand, especially in the USA.

One might have assumed that, as Deputy Director, Bert Hopwood would have been promoted, but this was not the case. Instead, a Mr Lionel Jofeh was appointed by Eric Turner, and given the title of Managing Director of the group's Automotive Division, the inept management of which hastened the eventual downfall of the group. For some reason Jofeh took a great dislike to the Triumph setup, and detested any successes achieved by the company, even threatening to dismiss anyone who was seen to be favouring Triumph over BSA!

Jofeh soon established a group engineering centre at Umberslade Hall, an old country mansion near Hockley Heath, midway between the Triumph and BSA factories. Mr Mike Needham, who came from the aircraft industry, took up the post of Deputy Engineering Director and undertook to set up Umberslade. He collected the design and development staff, which would ultimately number over three hundred, from the three existing factories. A couple of men were left in the design department at Triumph to cover day to day anomalies, and to liaise with Umberslade should the need arise.

It seemed that all was not going well with the motorcycle group, as high level jobs with fancy titles (and attendant high salaries) were being created almost daily. Departments, which had previously been housed in one factory, were split up, and duplication of functions was commonplace. The latter became apparent when the engineering meetings, which had previously taken place in ordinary-sized offices, had become so well attended that BSA had difficulty finding locations large enough to accommodate everyone.

'Critical path analysis' and 'production evaluation' were the 'in things' at Triumph. Even though they did little to aid production, the motions still had to be gone through. This caused much frustration and ill feeling amongst the workforce.

The Research and Development department at Umberslade Hall was becoming a luxury that the motorcycle division couldn't afford. It certainly seemed to the folk at Meriden that there was a lot of input to the department, in terms of staff and resources, but little to show for it (unless one took into account the increase in the number of peacocks around the grounds).

For the 1971 season, the Triumph factory was supposed to be building a new 650cc motorcycle designed by the Research and Development department at Umberslade Hall. The production build dates came and went, with the factory yet to see any drawings, so no jigs and fixtures could be produced which would have enabled production to commence. Eventually, the new 650 reached Triumph some three months late. Unfortunately, however, it was found that an assembled engine unit could not be fitted into the frame. Numerous modifications were made by the Meriden design staff, much to the chagrin of the Umberslade team.

Another design error concerned the height of the seat on the completed machine. At 34in from ground level it was simply too high for most people. Triumph complained at this, only to be told by Umberslade that the frames had not been made correctly, as per the drawings, so it was Triumph's problem. To counter this accusation, Triumph had the frames independently inspected and, although the report did indeed show that the frames were taller than the drawings specified, it was only by 1/32 inch). Triumph was completely vindicated.

By now, as one can imagine, feelings between Meriden and Umberslade were getting quite bitter, and various derogatory names were found for the mansion (Slumberglades was the favourite).

In July 1971, due to the financial state of the group, Jofeh agreed to resign his post as Managing Director and his contract was bought out. A new Chief Executive, Mr Brian Eustace, was appointed in November, replacing Eric Turner who stayed on in an advisory capacity. It was announced that the Motorcycle Division's losses amounted to over £8 million. Share value fell to just 7½p, from a 1971 figure of 87p. One London newspaper commented that "BSA had managed to snatch disaster from the jaws of success."

The Research and Development centre at Umberslade Hall was closed down early in 1972, and selected staff were drafted back to Meriden. By this time, Lord Shawcross had become Chairman of the Board, and announced that all of the group's 500 and 650cc motorcycles would now be built at Meriden, with all other projects shelved for the time being. Unfortunately, this directive was never implemented, and the two factories struggled on with a redundancy-depleted workforce.

Late in 1972, Mr Dennis Poore, Chairman of Norton Villiers Ltd., started discussions with BSA/Triumph and the government in an attempt to save the motorcycle industry. In March 1973, the government was informed by the Minister of State that proposals for a new motorcycle company, comprised of Norton Villiers and BSA/Triumphs, had been accepted. By the middle of the year, the new company, Norton Villiers Triumph Ltd., had been formed, with the Department of Trade and Industry (DTI) injecting £4.8 million into the venture. As the Triumph factory closed for the annual two-week holiday, everyone looked forward to a secure future.

All was not what it seemed, though. Bert Hopwood, who had been appointed responsible for the final design at Meriden, resigned within one month of his appointment, and Poore announced that the Triumph factory was to close, and that all motorcycle production would be at BSA's Small Heath site. This announcement led to the workers taking over the Meriden factory from September 14, 1973.

The Triumph factory remained closed for eighteen months until the workers' co-operative was set up, and Triumph motorcycles were produced again at Meriden.

Unfortunately, the Triumph Engineering Co. Ltd. brand name had been sold off separately, so the new title, Meriden Motorcycles, had to be registered by the co-operative.

Meriden Motorcycles operated until 1983 but was never well funded, working very much on a day-to-day basis with no money for development.

Finally, in 1983, Meriden Motorcycles was wound up by the liquidators, and all remaining stock, machine tools, jigs and fixtures went under the hammer. The site was sold separately and is now a desirable housing estate. The Triumph name lives on, however, as the avenues are called Bonneville Close and Daytona Drive!

Chapter 2
The Speed Twin

The Speed Twin was first unveiled to the motorcycle press at the end of July 1937, and it later graced the Triumph stand at the 1937 Motorcycle Show at Olympia, London. It was acclaimed by the media as one of the outstanding models of the whole show.

Its initial acceptance by the (very conservative) motorcycling public, was undoubtedly due to the fact that it looked very similar to the earlier twin port, single cylinder design with which everyone was familiar. However, the Speed Twin had a number of advantages over the single cylinder, including better, more even torque, and better pull at lower engine speeds. The Speed Twin also offered better acceleration and easier starting.

As originally conceived and produced, the Speed Twin didn't produce much more power than the single cylinder models (approximately 28bhp as opposed to the earlier machine's 24), but it felt more responsive due to its twin cylinders. One of the first road test reports gave a glowing account of its performance and, with a mean speed of 94mph and a maximum of 107mph over a measured quarter-mile, it was considered very fast for a touring machine.

Priced at £74.00, the Speed Twin was a sure-fire winner being, at the time, the only 500cc OHV twin in quantity production. The Speed Twin brought mass-produced, multi-cylinder motorcycling to the pre-war motorcyclist at a price which, whilst not cheap, was within reach of a good many prospective purchasers.

The Speed Twin started a trend that almost every other motorcycle manufacturer followed worldwide, and it made Triumph Engineering into a company which, post-war, probably made more profit per pound invested than any other similar company.

Proof of the quality of Turner's design for the Speed Twin came in October 1938 when, with a supercharger, a Speed Twin broke the lap record at Brooklands with a speed of 118.02mph. Incidentally, this record still stands, as the circuit was not used after World War II.

Institutional machines

Right from its introduction, the Speed Twin immediately found favour with the authorities for institutional use (particularly the police and army). The Metropolitan Police set the scene, and police forces throughout the world followed its lead. In time, the 650cc 6T would take over the Speed Twin's role, but not before the Speed Twin had made its mark and shown to the world the capability of an up-to-date modern motorcycle.

Some of the total mileages covered by the Metropolitan Police and the Automobile Association were, by motorcycle standards, astonishing. In 1946, 'Torrens' wrote in *The Motor Cycle* "The Metropolitan Police have forty-two machines, of which the average mileage is 98,000 and six have covered 150,000, whilst the largest single mileage is 161,000, and this last one will still do 75mph."

The AA machines were always equipped with a fairly well-laden sidecar, but even these Speed Twins used to cover between 80,000 and 100,000 miles before they were put into the Triumph Service Department for overhaul.

The Triumph Engineering Company devised a standard police specification but, of course, various forces required additional and special items. The Metropolitan Police, for example, often required Speed Twins with both a dynamo and an alternator, and previously laid down specifications were often adhered to long after the civilian model had changed. A perfect example of this is the use of a magneto on Metropolitan Police models in 1955, when coil ignition had been standard for two years.

On quite a number of Metropolitan Police models, the dynamo was geared up to run faster, and featured a slipping clutch in the drive to prevent damage during a kickback whilst starting.

The Triumph Speed Twin & Thunderbird Bible

Identification by frame and engine number

Year	Engine number	Frame number	Dates built	Quantity	Remarks
1938	8-5T	TF or TH	Nov 1937 Oct 1938		
1939	9-5T	TF	Nov 1938 Oct 1939		
1940	40-5T	TF	Nov 1939		Possibly only small quantity made
1945	5-5T	TF	Nov 1945		
1946	6-5T	TF	Nov 1945 Oct 1946		
1947	7-5T	TF	Nov 1946 Sep 1947		
1948	8-5T 89214 8-5F 100688	TF 15001 TF 23714	4.9.1947 3.9.1948	6205	
1949	5T9 102603 5T9 113386	TF 25115 TF 33615	2.11.1948 6.10.1949	6850	End of TF series
1950	5T 1009N 5T 16 OON	3618 16 1 OON	18.10.1949 2.11.1950		End of N series
1951	5T 840NA 5T 15192NA	840NA 15192NA	20.11.1950 18.10.1951	3625	End of NA series
1952	5T 26096 5T 31901	26096 31901	24.3.1952 20.8.1952	1831	Common engine and frame numbers
1953	5T 33868 5T 44774	33868 44774	18.10.1952 14.9.1953	3620	
1954	5T 45177 5T 55493	45177 55493	28.9.1953 7.7.1954	2305	
1955	5T 55494 5T 70235	55494 70235	7.7.1954 9.8.1955	2760	
1956	5T 71747 5T 82443	71747 82443	19.9.1955 27.6.1956	2187	Figures would reach six digits so new numbers commenced
1956	5T 0602 5T 02077	0602 02077	18.7.1956 25.9.1956		
1957	5T 02868 5T 010253	02868 010253	18.10.1956 20.8.1957	1349	
1958	5T 011116 5T 020074	011116 020074	20.9.1957 28.8.1958	1083	
1959	5T 023699 5T 023705	023699 023705	6.1.1959	6	Last pre-unit 5T
	5TA H 5785 5TA H 11035	H 5785 H 11035	25.9.1958 21.8.1959	2679	First unit construction
1960	5TA H 11962 5TA H 18626	H 11962 H 18626	8.10.1959 1.9.1960	2207	
1961	5TA H 19215 5TA H 24757	H 19215 H 24757	10.11.1960 22.8.1961	340	
1962	5TA H 25904 5TA H 29727	H 25904 H 29729	26.9.1961 24.9.1962	375	
1963	5TA H 30291 5TA H 32361	H 30291 H 32361	23.10.1962 1.8.1963	334	
1964	5TA H 32918 5TA H 35986	H 32918 H 35986	13.10.1963 6.7.1964	530	
1965	5TA H 37320 5TA H 39838	H 37320 H 39838	3.12.1964 1.6.1965	413	
1966	5TA H 42227 5TA H 46431	H 42227 H 46431	8.9.1965 25.5.1966	590	Speed Twin production ended

The Speed Twin

The Speed Twin found a ready market with many police forces. This picture shows 1938 models on parade.

1938 Model 5T Speed Twin

Engine prefix: 8-5T

Engine The vertical twin overhead valve gear was operated by high camshafts working in phosphor bronze bushes inside an aluminium crankcase.

The crankshaft consisted of a left and right crankweb bolted to a central flywheel by six high-tensile bolts. The assembly was supported on two ball races, one each side.

Plain bearings were used for the big ends, with white metal fused to the lower steel end caps, whilst the upper half of the bearing was machined directly onto the hiduminium alloy conrod.

The conrods were of H-section and were fitted with a bronze bush in the small end to act as a bearing for the gudgeon pin.

Cylinder material was best grade cast iron, as was the cylinder head. Two alloy rocker boxes, housing the rockers and spindles, were bolted onto the cylinder head, giving full enclosure and lubrication to all moving parts.

The oil feed to the rockers was supplied from the timing cover via a small bore metal pipe, as was the pressure gauge mounted in the tank panel. A dry sump lubrication system was maintained by a twin piston plunger pump, and the pressure was controlled by a ball-type release valve.

Ignition was supplied by a platform-mounted, MN2 R03 anti-clockwise Lucas Magdyno situated to the rear of the cylinders and driven by gears from the inlet camshaft.

11

Edward Turner's 1937 prototype Model T restored by Dave Jenkin of Yeovil, Somerset.

The dynamo was a separate unit mounted on top of the magneto, as was customary practice at that time. Ignition advance and retard control was operated, via a cable, by a left hand handlebar control lever.

An Amal Type 276 carburettor of $^{15}/_{16}$in bore supplied the combustible mixture with the float chamber mounted on the right hand side (this was due to the proximity of the dynamo). The choke was cable-operated from the right hand handlebar lever. The twistgrip, which was Triumph's own design, featured a novel friction device consisting of a spring-loaded plunger contacting a finely serrated spool on the twistgrip drum. This gave a slightly notchy feel to the operation but was guaranteed to stay in place.

Gearbox The gearbox, again Triumph's own design and manufacture, had four speeds with well chosen ratios, and was operated through a positive stop right hand foot control.

Shafts and gears were of nickel chrome steel housed in a separate alloy casing. Pivoting the gearbox case from the bottom gave provision for primary chain adjustment.

The mainshaft and high gear ran on ball journal races while the layshaft ran on a combination of cast iron and phosphor bronze bushes.

Primary transmission This was a 0.305 x ½in chain, from the engine sprocket to the clutch sprocket, housed in an oil bath of polished cast alloy.

The shock absorber was incorporated in the engine sprocket/mainshaft assembly and consisted of a spring-loaded face cam.

The clutch was a multi-plate affair, with alternating steel and corked plates, and four pressure springs controlled the drive. The clutch was operated via a rod through the mainshaft from a lever on the right side of the gearbox. This rod was connected by a cable to the left handlebar lever. The small rubber cover over the cable nipple at the gearbox lever was retained for many years.

Frame The frame was a full cradle pattern and featuring forged lugs into which the frame tubes were pinned and brazed. The main frame consisted of the tank and seat tubes and a tapering front downtube. Twin tubes running under the engine and gearbox were joined by a pair from the saddle nose at the rear wheel spindle.

The rear stand, pivoting just below the rear wheel spindle, was retained in the up position by a large spring anchored to the pillion footrest.

Suspension The front forks were of the girder type, with tapering tubes for strength. Movement was controlled by a single central spring, and hand-controlled friction dampers were built into the forward ends of the lower links. These dampers could be adjusted from the saddle, and the rider could choose the setting according to his needs. A central steering damper was controlled by a large bakelite knob at the top of the steering tube.

Petrol tank An all-welded affair with a capacity of 3¼ gallons and a quick-release hinged filler cap, opened and closed by rotating a cross lever. The centre of the tank was deeply recessed to accommodate a switch panel, housing a pressure gauge, a lighting switch, an ammeter and an inspection lamp with extension lead.

Exhaust system Two 1¾in down pipes, one on each side, terminated in parallel tubular silencers – all chrome plated.

Oil tank An all-welded steel tank with a capacity of 6 pints. It was fitted with a screwed aluminium filler cap.

Handlebars and controls 1in diameter tube swaged down at the right hand end to $^{15}/_{16}$in to accommodate the Triumph twistgrip. Large rubber bushes were used on the handlebar mounting to insulate the rider from road shocks. The clutch and brake levers were of the solid forged type. Ignition and air control levers were of the round pattern, left and right handed. Horn and ignition cut out buttons were placed right and left, respectively, with the dipper switch sited on the left.

Mudguards Steel, with a raised central band. The front mudguard had front and centre stays attached by rivets; the lower rear stay also acted as a front stand. The rear mudguard was a two part affair, the rear part being detachable just above the number plate top fixing to aid rear wheel removal. Two loop stays were riveted to the main part of the mudguard, and one was bolted to the detachable part. The main guard stays had threaded bosses to which were fitted two curved lifting handles.

Toolbox A triangular toolbox was fitted between the rear chain stays on the right side. The lid was hinged on the lower edge and was retained in the closed position by a lever screw. Early toolboxes had a rubber weatherproof band.

Wheels Triumph designed and manufactured WM2 size. The front was fitted with a 3.00 x 20in ribbed tyre, while the rear was fitted with a 3.50 x 19in Dunlop Universal tyre (Dunlop tyres and tubes were fitted as standard). Both brakes were 7in diameter, the front drum was ribbed to prevent distortion. Both drums were made from best grade cast steel. The front anchor plate was polished cast alloy and the rear was pressed steel. Front brake operation was part cable and part rod, the rear was rod-operated. The rear brake was adjusted by a large knurled nut, the front by a cable adjuster.

Seat The seat was of De Luxe pattern, usually made by either Lycett or Terry, and featured long parallel chrome springs, adjustable for height.

Electrical The electrical system was 6-volt negative earth. Charging was by a Lucas E3HM dynamo via an automatic compensating Type MCR 14 voltage control box. A Lucas D142F 8in diameter chrome-plated headlamp with fluted domed glass provided the front light, the rear was provided by a Lucas MT 110.

The horn was a Lucas HF934 Altette device with chrome outer ring, and was attached to the left hand seat spring bolt. A Lucas RS 39/Ll switch control was mounted in the petrol tank panel.

Speedometer The 120mph speedometer was mounted on top of the front forks, and was driven from the front wheel through a right-angle gearbox mounted in the front anchor plate. As an alternative, a 180kph speedometer was available at no extra cost.

Finish All painted parts, with the exception of the following, were finished in Amaranth Red:

Number plates	Black
Pillion footrests	Black
Electric horn	Black
Brake return springs	Black
Rear stand return spring	Black
Instrument panel	Black
Voltage control box	Black – semi matt
Speedometer body	Black
Speedometer angle drive	Black – semi matt
Seat frame	Black
Mudguards	Amaranth Red with a gold line (approximately ⅛in wide) on both sides of the raised centre band.
Petrol tank	Amaranth Red side and top panels on a chrome base with twin outer gold lines (approximately ³⁄₃₂in), a ³⁄₃₂in chrome band and a ⁵⁄₃₂in inner line.
Wheel rims	Amaranth Red centre with a gold line (approximately ⅛in wide) on the flat of the rim.

Many queries were raised regarding the Speed Twin Amaranth Red, the official Triumph explanation went thus: "The amaranth is a plant found mostly in tropical countries. It has a flower which is red in colour with a slight tinge of purple. A more common plant in British gardens is called Amaranth Caudatus by experts, but Love Lies Bleeding is good enough for most people. The flowers keep their colour even when picked and dried, thus the excellent service given by the Triumph Speed Twin is reflected in its colour."

Most nuts and bolts were cadmium-plated, with only headlamp fixing bolts, rocker spindle dome nuts, fork spindle locknuts and handlebar fixing bolts being chrome plated.

Transfers

Oil tank	
Minimum oil level:	Gilt
Drain refill, etc.	Gilt
Recommended lubricants	Gilt

The Triumph Speed Twin & Thunderbird Bible

1938 Speed Twin which, with the aid of the artist's brush, has had such items as the HT leads, electrical cables, and rear detachable mudguard joint removed, as instructed by Edward Turner.

The drain and refill transfers were on the front face of the oil tank, the recommended lubricants transfer was situated across the tank. The minimum oil level transfer was approximately halfway up the tank.

Rear number plate Registered design — white/gilt. Positioned between the bottom fixing bolts. Approximate length 3in.

Extras

Quickly detachable rear wheel	£2 0s 0d
Valanced front and rear mudguards	£0 12s 6d
Prop stand assembly	£0 10s 0d
Pillion footrest assembly	£0 15s 0d
Pillion seat	£0 12s 6d
Speedometer	£2 16s 0d
Carrier assembly	£0 9s 3d
Air filter assembly	£0 8s 0d

1938 Model 5T Speed Twin technical data

Engine
Bore	63mm/2.480in
Stroke	80mm/3.15in
Capacity	498cc/30.40in³
bhp (max)	28 at 6000rpm
Compression ratio	7.0:1

Cylinder head
Material	Cast iron
Valve seat angle	45°
Valve seat width	
Inlet	0.050/0.060in
Exhaust	0.060/0.080in
Valve guide bore	0.4980/0.4985in

Valves
Stern diameter	
Inlet	0.3095/0.3100in
Exhaust	0.3090/0.3095in
Head diameter	1⁵⁄₁₆in
Valve overall length	Inlet and exhaust 3⁵⁵⁄₆₄in

Valve guides
Material	Chilled cast iron
Bore diameter	0.312/0.313in
Outside diameter	0.5005/0.5010in
Length	
Inlet	1³¹⁄₃₂in
Exhaust	2¹¹⁄₆₄in

Valve springs
Free length	nominal
Inner	1⅝ ± 1⁄16in
Outer	2¹⁄₃₂ ± 1⁄16in

Fitted length
Inner	1.187in
Outer	1.281in

Cam follower
Foot radius	0.750in
Stem diameter	0.3110/0.3115in

The Speed Twin

Valve clearance — cold
    Inlet and exhaust   0.001in

Valve timing
    IYO   21°   BTDC
    IVC   75°   ABDC
    EVO   75°   BBDC
    EVC   21°   ATDC
Nil clearance for checking

Push rods
    Material   Tubular steel
    Overall length   6.300/6.325in

Rockers
    Bore diameter   0.5002/0.5012in
    Spindle diameter   0.4990/0.4995in

Camshafts and bearings
    Journal diameter
        Left hand   0.8100/0.8105in
        Right hand   0.8730/0.8735in
        End float   0.013/0.020in
        Lobe height   1.047/1.055in
    Bush diameter
        Left hand bore   0.8125/0.8135in
        Right hand bore   0.874/0.875in
        Left hand outer   1.0010/1.0015in
        Overall length LH exhaust   0.932/0.942in
        LH inlet   0.932/0.942in
        RH inlet and exhaust   1.010/1.020in

Cylinder barrel
    Material   Cast iron
    Cylinder bore diameter   2.4800/2.4805in
    Tappet guide bore   0.9985/0.9990in
    Max tolerable wear   0.007in

Tappet block
    Outer diameter   0.9995/1.000in
    Bore diameter   0.312/0.3125in

Piston rings
    Ring gap in cylinder bore
        Compression ring   0.008/0.010in
        Scraper ring   0.010/0.012in
    Thickness (top to bottom face)
        Compression ring   0.062in
        Scraper ring   0.124in
    Clearance in piston groove
        Compression ring   0.002/0.003in
        Scraper ring   0.002/0.003in

Pistons
    Clearance in cylinder bore
    at maximum diameter
    (90° to gudgeon pin)   0.004in
    Crown height from
    gudgeon pin centre   1⅜in
    Gudgeon pin diameter   0.6840in

Connecting rods
    Small end diameter   6.841/0.6843in
    Big end diameter   1.4375/1.4385in
    Side clearance (fitted)   0.012/0.030in
    Length between centres   6.499/6.501in

Crankshaft
    Crankpin diameter   1.4360/1.4365in
    Main bearing journal diameter
        Drive side   1.1247/1.1250in
        Timing side   0.9997/1in
    Crankshaft end float   0.003/0.017in
    Oil feed journal diameter   0.622/0.623in
    Balance factor   52%

Crankshaft bearings
    Drive side   1.125 x 2.812 x 0.812in
    Timing side   1.00 x 2.50 x 0.750in
    Oil feed bush   0.6245/0.6255in
    Bearing   Ball t/s and d/s

Oil pump
    Bore diameter
        Feed   0.31270/0.31290in
        Scavenge   0.4375/0.4377in
    Plunger diameter
        Feed   0.3121/0.3125in
        Scavenge   0.4371/0.4374in
    Feed bore   0.31225/0.31275in
    Scavenge bore   0.43725/0.43775in

Carburettor
    Manufacture   Amal
    Type   276/132 LH
    Bore   15/16in
    Main jet   140
    Needle jet   0.107
    Needle   No 6
    Needle position   3
    Throttle valve   6/3
    Float chamber   64/195 RH

Ignition
    Magdyno   Lucas
    Timing   37° or ⅜in BTDC
         fully advanced
    Points gap   0.012in
    Spark plug   KLG 831
    Plug gap   0.018in
    Thread size   14mm
    Reach   ½in

Clutch
    Corked plates   4
    Plain plates   5
    Pressure springs   4
    Spring free length   1½in
    Bearing rollers   20
    Roller size
        Diameter   0.2495/0.250in
        Length   0.231/0.236in

Hub bearing diameter 1.3733/1.3743in
Sprocket bore diameter 1.8745/1.8755in
Clutch rod diameter 7/32in
Clutch rod overall length 11¾in (Nominal)

Kickstart mechanism
Case bore diameter LH 0.6245/0.6255in
Bush bore diameter RH 0.751/0.752in
K/S spindle diameter RH 0.748/0.749in
K/S spindle diameter LH 0.6215/0.6225in
Ratchet sleeve o/d 0.8747/0.8752in
Ratchet spring free length ½in

Gearchange mechanism
Quadrant plunger
  Outer diameter 0.4315/0.4320in
  Plunger bore 0.4325/0.4330in
Plunger spring
  No. of coils 12
  Free length 1¼in

Footchange spindle
Diameter LH 0.6215/0.6235in
Diameter RH 0.747/0.749in
Bush LH bore diameter 0.6245/0.6255in
Bush LH outer diameter 0.8755/0.8765in
Bush RH bore diameter 0.7495/0.7505in
Bush RH outer diameter 0.8755/0.8765in

Quadrant springs
Free length 1¾in
No. of coils 12

Camplate plunger
Plunger diameter 0.436/0.4365in
Housing bore 0.4375/0.438in
Spring length 2½in
No. of coils 19

Mainshaft
Bearing LH 1¼ x 2½ x ⅝in ball
Bearing RH ¾ x 1⅞ x 9/16in ball
Mainshaft diameter LH 0.8120/0.8125in
Mainshaft sleeve bush
  Inside diameter 0.8135/0.8145in
  Outer diameter 0.909/0.910in
  Overall length 2¼in

Layshaft
Bearing diameter LH/RH 0.560/0.5605in
Bush bore diameter LH/RH 0.562/0.563in
Bush outside diameter
  LH/RH 0.688/0.689in
Layshaft sleeve bush 1⅜ x 0.7498/0.7505in
Layshaft lowgear bush
  Inside diameter 0.7493/0.7500in
  Outside diameter 0.8444/0.8454in

Number of teeth on pinions

Layshaft		Mainshaft	
19	4th	25	
21	3rd	23	
25	2nd	19	
29	1st	15	

Sprockets
	Solo	Sidecar
Engine	22	19
Clutch	43	43
Gearbox	18	18
Rear wheel	46	46

Gear ratios — internal
4th 1.00
3rd 1.20
2nd 1.73
1st 2.54

Overall ratios
	Solo	Sidecar
4th	5.00	5.8
3rd	6.00	6.95
2nd	8.65	10.00
1st	12.7	14.70

rpm at 10mph top gear 646

Chains
Primary
  Solo 5/16 x ½in x 78 link
  Sidecar 5/16 x ½in x 77 link
Secondary ⅜ x ⅝in x 92 link

Electrical
Dynamo E3HML0 40W
Voltage regulator MCRL4
Voltage 6V
Earth Negative
Bulb, main 6V 24/30W
Bulb, pilot 6V 3W
Bulb, speedometer 6V 2.5W
Bulb, tail 6V 3W
Bulb, inspection 6V 3W
Battery Lucas 6V 12Ah

Wheels
Rims
  Front WM2 x 20in
  Rear WM2 x 19in

Tyres
Front 3.25 x 20in ribbed
Rear 2.50 x 19in Universal

Brakes
Diameter 7in
Width 1⅛in

Bearings
Front — taper roller 7/16 x 1 7/16 x 11/16 x 7/16in outer
Rear — taper roller 9/16 x 1¾ x 13/16 x 9/16in outer

Spokes
Front
  RH 10 x 9G 80° x 9 1/16in

NEW TRIUMPH DESCRIBED

An Interesting o.h.v. Vertical Twin Engine

BECAUSE it is well known that Mr. Edward Turner, managing director of the Triumph Engineering Co., Ltd., was the designer of that very ingenious and unconventional engine, the Ariel Square Four, it has been freely supposed that the new Triumph "multi" also would have four cylinders arranged in some novel but practical way. However, Mr. Turner, as those who know him well are quite aware, has anything but a single-track mind and in actual fact this interesting Triumph newcomer has two cylinders and a very simple general arrangement.

Nevertheless it does contain ingenious and unusual features and it would be highly inaccurate to think of this new model as simply a later and smaller edition of the old 650 c.c. twin. In fact none of the parts is the same as those of the earlier engine.

Compact and Light.

Up to a point it is true there is similarity. The two cylinders are vertical in one casting and the crankshaft lies across the machine. Moreover, both pistons rise and fall together. There the likeness ends.

The new engine is complete in itself and is not combined with a gearbox. It fits into a frame which is for most practical purposes the same as that of the Tiger "90," and, apart from the fact that the twin engine is a trifle lighter, the weight distribution of these two motorcycles is identical.

It has already been mentioned that the cylinders are vertical and are formed in a single casting. This is mounted on a crankcase of conventional style which is only slightly broader than that of a single. It carries on two bearings as usual a crankshaft which consists of three parts.

At the centre is a small flywheel with integral balance weights. Spigoted into each side of this is a piece which comprises a short shaft, a web, a crankpin and a circular flange which fits into the flywheel spigot and is held to it by bolts passing through the flywheel and the two flanges.

When assembled the two crankpins are in line, so that the firing intervals are evenly spaced. Because the two pistons move together and not in opposite directions, the balance is of precisely the same kind as a single. The forces involved, however, are somewhat smaller than in a single of the same capacity because the stroke is so much shorter.

Unusual Big-ends.

Actually the stroke is 80 mm. and the bores measure 63 mm., giving a total swept volume of 498 c.c. The compression ratio is about 7 to 1, a moderate figure for cylinders of this size, but the power developed is stated to be 29 b.h.p. at 6,000 r.p.m.

From what has been said of the crankshaft, students of design will have realized that rollers are not used for the big ends. Actually these are plain bearings, but not of quite the usual type. It should be explained that each connecting rod is an RR 56 Hiduminium forging. This material has excellent bearing qualities, but it lacks one feature of white metal. In an emergency such as the failure, temporary or otherwise, of the oil supply, white metal will fuse. This automatically provides additional clearance so that the bearing and shaft will not seize together to the detriment of both.

From these facts arises the big-end bearing design of this new Triumph twin. To take full advantage of the light Hiduminium rod it is arranged to bear directly on the steel crankpin. The bearing cap to complete the circle embracing the crank is, however, a steel forging lined with white metal. In this way the advantages of both metals are retained, together with a strong and rigid bearing cap.

No detailed description of the pistons is necessary because they are simple full-skirted affairs of well-tried type. Nor is there any novelty in the timing gear which consists of five wheels. A small one is mounted on the crankshaft and it drives an idler wheel above it. This in turn drives two half-speed gears arranged one on each side and slightly higher up.

The Cam Arrangement.

Each of these is mounted on a camshaft and the rear one meshes with the fifth gear which is attached to the shaft of a Lucas Magdyno placed behind the cylinders. Returning to the camshafts which are located one at the back and one at the front of the crankcase near its top, each shaft runs rather more than half-way across the engine and is mounted in two plain bearings.

On each shaft there are two cams very close together astride the centre line of the engine. The rear camshaft operates the inlet valves and the front one the exhausts, but the cam contours are identical in both cases and the two camshafts are interchangeable.

Immediately above each pair of cams is a phosphor-bronze block which carries

The new Triumph vertical twin is a remarkably good-looking machine. It has none of the bulkiness usually associated with "multis" and the engine actually weighs slightly less than a standard "90."

The Triumph Speed Twin & Thunderbird Bible

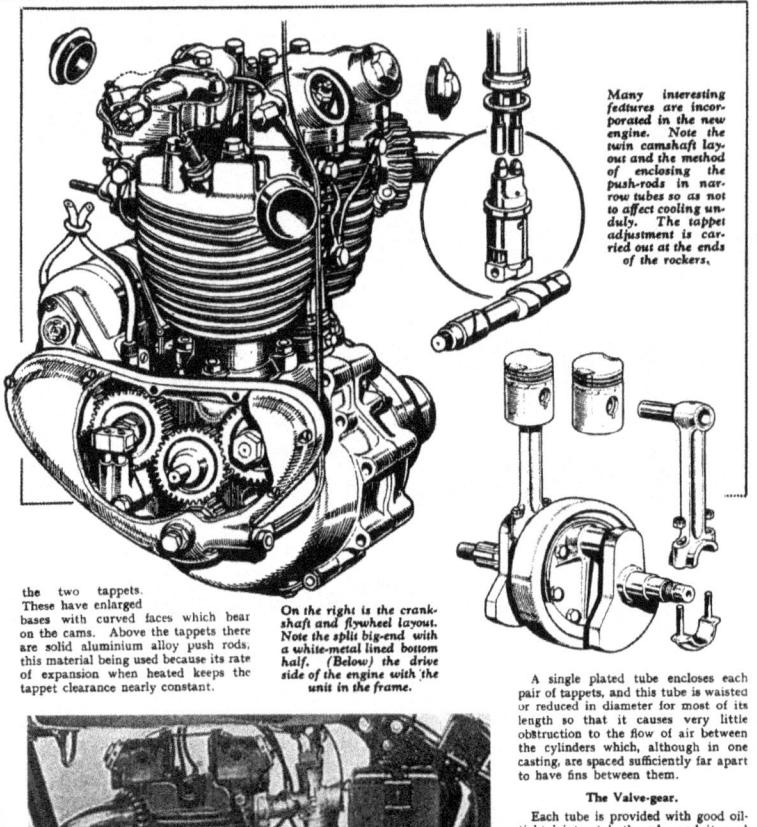

Many interesting features are incorporated in the new engine. Note the twin camshaft layout and the method of enclosing the push-rods in narrow tubes so as not to affect cooling unduly. The tappet adjustment is carried out at the ends of the rockers.

the two tappets. These have enlarged bases with curved faces which bear on the cams. Above the tappets there are solid aluminium alloy push rods, this material being used because its rate of expansion when heated keeps the tappet clearance nearly constant.

On the right is the crankshaft and flywheel layout. Note the split big-end with a white-metal lined bottom half. (Below) the drive side of the engine with the unit in the frame.

A single plated tube encloses each pair of tappets, and this tube is waisted or reduced in diameter for most of its length so that it causes very little obstruction to the flow of air between the cylinders which, although in one casting, are spaced sufficiently far apart to have fins between them.

The Valve-gear.

Each tube is provided with good oil-tight joints at both ends, and it need never be disturbed except when decarbonizing. Adjustment of tappet clearances is made at the push-rod end of each overhead rocker, there being a conventional lock-nut and set screw with a ball-end bearing in the cupped steel top of the push rod.

Both cylinder heads are formed in a single casting and the combustion spaces are hemispherical. The valves are arranged at a wide angle, the exhausts sloping forward, of course, and the inlets backward. Two light alloy castings mounted, one across the front and one across the back of the cylinder-head casting, enclose the valve stems and springs. They also carry the overhead rockers, and opposite each point of adjustment there is a screwed cap with a hexagon. The lat-

Dimensions
Wheelbase	54in
Overall length	84in
Overall width	28½in
Seat height	29½in adjustable
Weight dry	355lb
Ground clearance	6in

Torque settings
Conrod nuts	28lb/ft
Flywheel nuts	12lb/ft
Cylinder head bolts	18lb/ft
Camshaft pinion nuts	50lb/ft
Crankshaft pinion nut	50lb/ft
Engine sprocket nut	80lb/ft
Oil release valve	15lb/ft
Clutch shaft nut	50lb/ft
Kickstart ratchet nut	30lb/ft
Gearbox sprocket nut	80lb/ft

Lubrication
Engine	
Summer	SAE 50
Winter	SAE 30
Gearbox	EP 80/90
Primary chaincase	SAE 20
Grease	Castrol LM

Left hand threads Camshaft pinion nuts

Capacities
Fuel tank	3¼gal
Oil tank	6pt
Gear box	¾pt EP 90
Primary case	¼pt SAE 20

1939 Model 5T Speed Twin

Engine prefix: 9-5T
Alterations for 1939

Valve timing
IVO	26°	BTDC
IVC	69°	ABDC
EVO	61°	BBDC
EVC	35°	ATDC

Cylinder barrel The six-stud fixing at the cylinder/crankcase joint was strengthened by a change to eight-stud fixing, following T100 practice

Primary chaincase The alloy oil bath chaincase had added provision for rear chain lubrication. This took the form of a tapering screw retained by a coil spring, allowing oil through and down a small trough which, in theory, was supposed to deposit oil on the chain. It did, but it also lubricated many a girlfriend's silk stocking!

Most owners screwed the adjuster fully home and used a good, old-fashioned oil can.

RH 10 x 9G 97° x 9¹⁄₁₆in
LH 10 x 9G 80° x 9⅜in
LH 10 x 9G 97° x 9⅜in

Rear

RH 10 x 9G 76° x 9in
RH 10 x 9G 100° x 9in
LH 10 x 9G 76° x 8¾in
LH 10 x 9G 100° x 8¾in

Wheel offset
Front – dimension from drum fixing face to centre of rim: 1in
Rear – dimension from outside edge of sprocket to centre of rim: 3⁵⁄₃₂in

Frame — Steering head bearings
Top	22 x ³⁄₁₆in ball
Bottom	20 x ¼in ball

The Speed Twin

it easy to tighten the cap so as to avoid oil leaks and, of course, removal of the cap makes tappet adjustment very simple.

Each cylinder has a single exhaust port from which a nicely curved pipe leads back to a cylindrical silencer by the chain stays, the appearance being very much that of an ordinary two-port engine. The inlet ports also are separate and are connected by a small Y-piece to a slightly down-draught Amal carburetter.

Lubrication.

Finally, so far as the engine is concerned, a word about the lubrication system. In the lower part of the timing case there is a double plunger pump of the usual Triumph pattern driven by an eccentric pin and sliding block. This pump is rather larger than its predecessor, and it delivers oil at a pressure of some 50 lb. per sq. inch.

Oil is fed to the big-end bearings through passages drilled in the crankshaft. A separate supply is taken by an external pipe to the two rocker boxes and is fed direct to the rocker bearings through the fixed spindles. The surplus is carried by short pipes into the push-rod tubes and thus lubricates the tappets and cams.

This interesting and very practical engine is mounted in a machine which in all other respects resembles the Triumph Tiger "90" 500 c.c. single. In spite of its extra exhaust pipe and silencer, the complete twin motorcycle weighs a trifle less than the single, but in other respects they are alike, and even in appearance the twin might easily be mistaken for a two-port single.

Solo gear ratios are 5.0, 6.0, 8.65 and 12.7 to 1, the sidecar ratios being 5.8, 6.95, 10.0 and 14.7 to 1. Both tyres are 26 ins. by 3.25 ins. The wheelbase measures 54 ins., and the overall length is 84 ins.

This is undoubtedly an interesting machine, but it is much more than that. From the earliest drawing-board stage trouble has been notably absent, we understand, and one of the experimental models with sidecar attached has covered 10,000 miles on the road in all weather and in a comparatively short time. Speeds of 90 m.p.h. solo are spoken of.

At an early date we shall publish a full road test report, but already it seems clear that an outstanding machine has been added to the list of British motorcycles.

The off side of the new Triumph twin unit. The two hexagon-headed caps give easy access to the valve tappet adjustment; below them will be noticed the pipes which drain surplus oil from the rocker box into the push-rod tube. Incidentally, how unusual is the appearance of an o.h.v. engine's timing side without push-rods.

Lubrication Rocker oil feed pressure was reduced by the introduction of a restrictor. This took the form of a coarse threaded stud screwed into a threaded tube. Oil supply was regulated by altering the depth of the stud in the tube, as oil had to pass around the outside of the stud thread (i.e. the more thread in the tube the less oil, and vice versa).

Shock absorber The engine shaft shock absorber cam contour was changed to provide smoother operation.

Petrol tank The tank badges were changed to diecast in relief with a red background. These replaced the embossed type.

Front number plate A chrome diecast bead was added around the front number plate.

Speedometer The speedometer was reworked to show engine revolutions in each gear as well as miles per hour.

Handlebars The handlebars were reduced in width and given a more rearward angle, providing a better riding position.

Headlamp The domed headlamp glass of 1938 was replaced by a fluted and flat one.

Price The price was reduced to £74 0s 0d

Extras

120mph speedometer	£2 15s 0d
120mph speedometer 5in dial	£5 5s 0d
Rear stop light	£0 6s 0d
Pillion footrests	£0 7s 6d
Pillion seat	£0 12s 6d
Prop stand	£0 10s 0d
Quickly detachable rear wheel	£2 0s 0d
Valanced mudguards	£0 12s 6d

The Triumph Speed Twin & Thunderbird Bible

Road Tests of 1938 Models

The 497 c.c. "Speed Twin" Triumph

No one needs reminding that the new vertical-twin Triumph was one of the outstanding machines at the Earls Court Motor Cycle Show. Nor is it necessary to recapitulate the many interesting features of its design, beyond, perhaps, mentioning the high-camshaft mountings, the light-alloy connecting rods, the plain big-end bearings and the pressure-feed lubrication system.

The engine, which looks at first glance a single-cylinder, is so compact that it is housed without alteration of chain-line in the normal Triumph "Tiger 90" frame. Nor is there any need to add that it was with considerable anticipation that one of these machines was taken over for road test! It may be said right away that the machine submitted for test amply fulfilled the high claims made by its makers; its all-round performance was surprising.

No decompressor is fitted to the "Speed Twin" Triumph and none was found necessary, for the engine would start immediately under all conditions. When the engine was cold it was necessary to flood the carburettor and a fairly hearty kick was required. At all other times a gentle dig on the kick-starter would set the engine ticking over. With the ignition retarded the slow running was excellent and could be relied upon in traffic. At one period during the test the slow running disappeared, but this was quickly traced to a loose adjuster in the throttle cable.

Whether the engine was idling or on larger throttle openings, mechanical noise was very slight. At very low speeds a certain amount of mechanical noise could be heard, but this was no greater than that of a good 500 c.c. single at similar speeds. Once the machine was on the move all traces of mechanical sound disappeared and at high speeds the engine could not be heard even when the rider turned his head out of the air stream.

At no time was the exhaust noise objectionable; at low road speeds the exhaust was almost inaudible, while at speeds of 60 m.p.h. and over it developed into a pleasant low zoom.

So much then for general features of the machine. It is in the engine's performance that the real delight of the "Speed Twin" lies. So versatile did the engine prove that the machine was equally at home in the thickest traffic or on the fastest main road. In traffic it would trickle along perfectly happily at 20 m.p.h. in top gear, and would accelerate rapidly and smoothly from this speed. If need be, the engine, with the ignition retarded, could be throttled down to 12 m.p.h. in top gear without any transmission snatch. If the gears were used, acceleration well above average was available. To accelerate from 15 to 30 m.p.h. in bottom gear, for example, took only 2⅜ seconds. In second gear, the one normally used for hurried acceleration, less than four seconds was required. Even in top gear the time taken was only seven seconds.

Similarly on the open road, the acceleration was excellent, as a glance at the figures in the table shows.

On the Open Road

Much of the joy in driving the model comes, however, from the delightful way the machine will zoom from 30 m.p.h. to 60, 70 or 80 m.p.h. at the will of the rider without his having to touch any control other than the twist-grip. Some idea of the model's performance when the gears are used can be obtained from the fact that 74 m.p.h. was reached in a quarter of a mile from a standing start.

On the open road the machine was utterly delightful. Ample power for all conditions was always available at a turn of the twist-grip, and the lack of noise when the machine was cruising in the seventies was almost uncanny. Main road hills were taken in the model's stride with just a little more throttle opening, and even on very steep hills or on hills with sharp bends which necessitated a change down, the acceleration available would rapidly bring the machine back to a high cruising speed. Thus it was found that large mileages were tucked into the hour without the rider consciously hurrying, and long runs were accomplished with less mental effort than usual.

Even when the performance figures already quoted are borne in mind, the sheer maximum speed of the machine is surprising. The timed tests were carried out on a day when there was a fair breeze blowing. With the rider clad in a single-piece "International" suit and lying well down along the tank (sitting on the mudguard, there being no pillion seat) the mean speed of four runs, two with and two against the wind, was 93.75 m.p.h.

The best timed run with the wind behind gave a speed over the quarter-mile of 107 m.p.h.—truly an amazing figure for a fully equipped five-hundred. Moreover, so steady was the model at this speed that the rider found it difficult to realise that the machine was travelling so quickly. Naturally, the steering damper was tightened down for the tests of maximum speed, but at no other time was it used or found necessary.

The steering and handling of the machine on the road are excellent. The only criticism was that the rear wheel had a tendency to hop on uneven surfaces. Cornering and general manœuvrability proved to be of a very high order, and the model, with its low centre of gravity, felt more like a two-fifty than a five-hundred from the point of view of ease of handling.

It is extremely fortunate that the Triumph is so well-mannered, for owing to the smoothness and silence of the engine there was a distinct tendency for the rider to take corners at higher speeds than usual, but even on corners rounded at really high speeds the Triumph was perfectly steady and safe.

A high degree of balance has been achieved with the Triumph, and apart from a slight period around 60 m.p.h. in top gear the engine is perfectly smooth and sweet. It may even be said that the period is only noticeable because of the exceptional smoothness of the engine at all other speeds, and at no time was the vibration sufficient to cause any discomfort.

Well Chosen Ratios

The Triumph four-speed gear box was delightfully quiet on all gears. The clutch was free from drag and the gear change was light and positive.

The gear ratios are well chosen and the maximum speeds reached by the machine in the indirect gears were: Third (6 to 1), 80 m.p.h.; second (8.65 to 1), 62 m.p.h.; and bottom (12.7 to 1), 46 m.p.h. With regard to the figures for bottom and second gear, it should be mentioned that the engine at these speeds was being grossly over-revved.

For normal speeds and for persons of normal height the riding position is good. The controls are well placed and the brake and gear lever pedals are in convenient positions. For a tall rider, however, the saddle is somewhat too near the handlebars. With the saddle moved back a little way it is probable that the tendency towards rear-wheel hop at high speeds would be overcome; at the same time the riding position would be improved. These remarks apply only to fast road work. At normal speeds the riding position is comfortable and the supple saddle and wide range of movement of the front forks successfully smooth out road shocks.

The new Triumph twist-grip with internal ratchet is pleasant in use, and all feeling of the ratchet is lost when the machine is on the road, yet the grip remains positive in action. On the model tested there was a tendency for the throttle to close if the hand was removed from the grip at high speeds.

Clean and Smart

As is to be expected with a machine of such a high general standard as the Triumph, the brakes proved to be first class. Both were extremely powerful and smooth, and applied together they would bring the model to rest from 30 m.p.h. in a fraction less than 30ft.

In economy the Triumph also scored, for at a maintained speed of 40 m.p.h. the petrol consumption was 82 m.p.g. A small trouble that occurred in the course of the test was the fracture of the angle bracket used for the attachment of the front end of the fuel tank.

Finally, mention must be made of the machine's appearance. The standard finish is amaranth red. It is a plum colour and looks extremely smart in conjunction with the chromium plating on other parts of the machine. At the conclusion of the test, which included hundreds of miles of really hard driving, the Triumph was as clean and smart as at the beginning, and apart from a very slight seep of oil from the rear end of the primary chain case, not a spot of oil had leaked from any of the joints of the power unit.

PERFORMANCE DATA

Gear	Maximum Speed	Acceleration 15–30 m.p.h.	Acceleration 30–50 m.p.h.
First (12.7)	44 m.p.h.	2⅜ secs.	—
Second (8.65)	62 m.p.h.	3⅞ secs.	6 secs.
Third (6.0)	80 m.p.h.	5 secs.	8½ secs.
Top (5.0)	93.75 m.p.h.	7 secs.	11 secs.

Speed attained over 1 mile through gears from standing start: 74 m.p.h.
Braking from 30 m.p.h. in top gear: 30 feet.
Fuel consumption at a maintained 40 m.p.h.: 82.5 m.p.g.
Minimum non-snatch speed in top gear: 12 m.p.h.

SPECIFICATION

- **TYPE:** "Speed Twin" model.
- **ENGINE:** 63 × 80 mm. (497 c.c.) vertical twin-cylinder o.h.v. Triumph with totally enclosed valve gear and dry-sump lubrication.
- **CARBURETTOR:** Amal with special Triumph twist-grip control.
- **GEAR BOX:** Triumph four-speed with enclosed foot change.
- **TRANSMISSION:** Chain with primary oil bath and double rear chain guard
- **IGNITION:** Lucas Magdyno.
- **LIGHTING:** Lucas 6-volt with voltage control and tank-top switch panel.
- **FUEL CAPACITY:** 3¼ gals.
- **TYRES:** Dunlop. 3.00—20 ribbed front; 3.50—19" Universal rear.
- **GROUND CLEARANCE:** 5in.
- **WEIGHT:** 365 lb. fully equipped.
- **PRICE:** £77 15s., with full electrical equipment and 120 m.p.h. illuminated speedometer.
- **MAKERS:** Triumph Engineering Co. Ltd., Coventry.

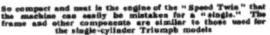

One of the first road test reports.

The Speed Twin

Sir Malcolm Campbell's Opinion

Praise from Sir Malcolm Campbell.

Sir Malcolm Campbell, three Times Holder of World's Land Speed Record.

27 Nov 1939

In my opinion, the Triumph Speed Twin has no equal. It is a machine eminently suitable for all purposes, is an extremely sound engineering job, and the workmanship is superb.

I acquired my first Triumph motor cycle in 1908, and was never without one until the outbreak of the Great War in 1914. I now own a Triumph Speed Twin, and a Tiger 100, and so long as I indulge in this pastime I shall continue to use the machines made by this eminent firm.

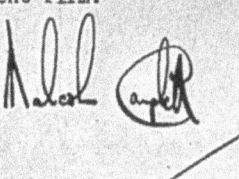

Unstinted praise from the buyers who rode the bikes.

The Maudes Trophy

The Maudes Trophy originated when Mr. George Pettyt, proprietor of Maudes Motor Mart, decided in 1923 that an event was needed to publicise the capabilities of the touring motorcycle. He presented a trophy to be awarded each year to the manufacturer whose product made the best meritorious performance in an ACU-observed test.

The first year's award went to Norton Motors, when a standard OHV model was assembled from parts selected by an ACU engineer. The machine was then subjected to a 12-hour high-speed test held at Brooklands wherein 18 World Records were set up.

The Triumph test started in February 1939, when two brand new machines, one a Speed Twin and the other a Tiger 100, were chosen completely at random from dealers' stock by the ACU observer Mr. E.B. Ware. Mr. Ware chose a Speed Twin from Messrs. Horridge & Wildgoose of Sheffield, and a Tiger 100 from Messrs. Bryant of Biggleswade. These two motorcycles were subsequently marked and then taken back to the Triumph factory in Coventry.

The test got underway at 1pm in the afternoon of Monday, February 27, 1939. The riders were Reg Ballard and Bill Nicholls, on Speed Twin and Tiger 100 respectively.

Although new, the motorcycles cruised at around 50-55mph on the way from Coventry to John O'Groats, accompanied by a Triumph Dolomite car carrying the ACU observer and Mr. Headlam of Triumph, the event controller.

The first afternoon run was from Coventry to Carlisle, some 200 miles, and, although torrential rain was encountered towards the end of the run, no problems were recorded.

Tuesday's run was from Carlisle to Inverness, some 275 miles, and this was accomplished at an average speed of 40mph, despite a diversion due to the road over Amulree being snowbound, forcing the route to go via Lockearnhead, Crianlarich, Glencoe, Fort William, and then to Inverness. The road through Glencoe proved rather tricky to negotiate due to packed snow. These conditions were endured for about 12 miles. Not long after this, the T100 picked up a nail which punctured the rear tyre. The inner tube was repaired but, unfortunately, was punctured again during refitting. The repairs were duly executed and, when the motorcycle reached Inverness, a new inner tube was fitted, mainly for safety reasons. The motorcycles had now covered nearly 500 miles, so the oil tanks were drained, refilled, and the primary cases were topped up.

The Maudes Trophy. The top picture shows the arduous conditions encountered. The bottom picture shows the Speed Twin at speed at Brooklands.

Wednesday's route took the riders from John O'Groats and then back to Inverness. This time there were only route diversions, due to snowbound roads, on the outward run as the roads had become passable by the afternoon. The average speed for the day's run was 42mph.

The run from Inverness south on Thursday was particularly unpleasant, as the riders struggled through heavy rain and sleet for hour after hour. Considering these conditions, the average speed of 43mph was very good.

At the night stop in Preston, the rear chains were adjusted (primary chains were left untouched and remained so throughout the 1800 mile journey).

On the Friday run, from Preston to Exeter, a strong wind and persistent drizzle meant that conditions were again far from ideal. After the lunchtime stop in Worcester, however, the weather improved, much to everyone's relief. However, road repairs and driving through Bristol meant that Friday's 38mph average was the lowest of the whole trip, despite some spirited riding.

Exeter to Lands End and back to Exeter was the route for Saturday, and the only incident was when the Speed Twin slipped off its stand and bent a footrest (this was replaced at the end of the day). The average speed on this run was nearly 47mph.

The final day's run (on Sunday, from Exeter to Brooklands) was only 157 miles, and this was completed at an average speed of 50mph, the motorcycles arriving at Brooklands around midday.

Apart from a rocker feed oil pipe union nut which needed to be tightened, the previously mentioned puncture, and the bent footrest, this was the only time the spanners were laid on the motorcycles outside of normal routine servicing in the whole of the 1800 miles.

It was recorded in *Motorcycling*, by Henry Laird, that, when inspected, both motorcycles were in excellent order, with no oil leaks, apart from slight smears. Total mileage was 1806, and was achieved at an average speed of 42mph. The two riders who had done such a good job, and in such adverse conditions, were relieved of the motorcycles and Freddie Clarke, Ivan Wicksteed, David Whitworth and Allan Jefferies, all speed men, took over for the 6-hour Brooklands test on Monday.

Both machines were inspected before the Brooklands endurance test: the tyres were changed to race type, in the interest of safety, the valve clearances were checked but no adjustment was required, and a new steering damper friction disc was fitted to the Tiger 100 (due to overenthusiastic greasing during one of the routine services by Tommy Wallis, the Triumph mechanic).

At 7.30am, the motorcycles were started and, during warmup, the Tiger 100 speedometer needle fluctuated erratically so the speedometer was changed. Lodge R49 racing plugs were fitted and, at 8am, the timekeeper, Mr. George Reynolds, started both motorcycles.

With Allan Jefferies on the Speed Twin and Ivan Wicksteed on the Tiger 100, both motorcycles ran steadily for several laps until the rear tyre of the Tiger 100 punctured on lap ten. A complete new rear wheel was fitted within four minutes, but this lowered the average speed so a few laps at 82.83mph were put in to re-establish a high average.

At the end of the first hour, the Speed Twin had covered 74.2 miles and the Tiger 100 70.2 miles. After 1½ hours, Whitworth took over from Wicksteed and Clarke took over from Jefferies, and the bikes were refuelled. Everything was going to plan until oil leaked from the oil pipe to the pressure gauge on the Speed Twin, all over the offside of the bike. The pipe was hammered flat to prevent the problem recurring, and Clarke returned to circle the track. In the second hour, and including pit stops, the Tiger 100 was averaging 79mph and the Speed Twin 74mph. Just before the 3-hour stage, Clarke came into the pits again with the hammered pipe seeping oil; this was resealed.

Jefferies and Wicksteed went out again and, at lap 133, a sparkplug was changed on the Speed Twin.

Records broken.

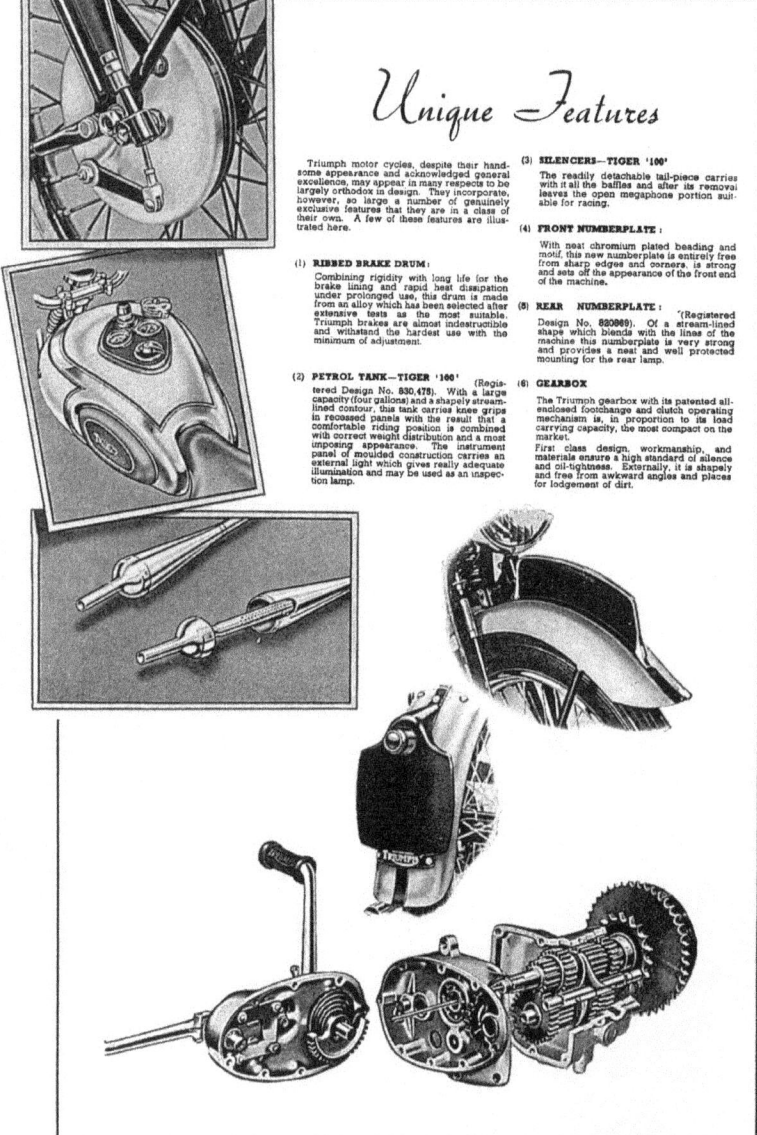

1939 features.

Ready for the off; the two machines before the high-speed trial. A. Jeffries on the Speed Twin and I. Wicksteed on the Tiger 100.

1939 successes

North West GP	1st
Enniskillen 100	1st + Fastest lap
Belfast 100	1st + Record lap
Cookstown 100	1st + Record lap
Ascot Speedway USA Gold Cup	1st + Record lap
Toronto Canada 50 Mile TT	1st

1940 Model 5T Speed Twin

Engine Prefix: 40-5T
Alterations for 1940

Engine In order to avoid loss of oil pressure, between the timing cover bush and the crankshaft, a shallow bronze piston with a tubular extension was fitted. With the extension lying within the crankshaft and the shallow

It's all over. The winning team, though they didn't know it at the time (this picture was taken in March 1939, and the award was not declared until November). Left to right: E.B. Ware (ACU observer), M.D. Whitworth (rider), I. Wicksteed (rider), A. Jeffries (rider), F. Clarke (rider), T. Wallis (Triumph fitter), E. Headlam (event controller).

Towards the end of the 6 hours, the riders increased the lap speed, with the Tiger 100 lapping at 88.45mph and the Speed Twin at 84.41mph. At the end of the 6 hours, average speeds including all stops, were Tiger 100 78.50mph and Speed Twin 75.02mph, with 471.5 and 450.25 miles covered, respectively.

The next day, Tuesday, both motorcycles were ridden back to Coventry to record a total of 2383 miles for the Tiger 100 and 2362 miles for the Speed Twin.

When the engines were stripped at the factory, it was observed that the left hand piston on the Speed Twin and the right hand piston on the Tiger 100 had picked-up slightly. Apart from this, though, everything else was in perfect order.

The Maudes Trophy was awarded to the Triumph Engineering Co. Ltd. in November, 1939.

piston against the timing cover bush, a more effective seal was achieved. This modification only applied to 1940 models

Larger clearances on the big ends resulted in increased oil flow through the crankshaft, and improved piston and cylinder wall oiling.

Because of the fuel shortages, a 23-tooth engine sprocket was fitted to aid economy. The quoted economy figure for the Speed Twin was 100mpg at 40mph.

Frame The frame head angle was changed to give more trail, bringing the Speed Twin into line with the Tiger 100.

Forks Redesigned forks had small check springs fitted each side of the main spring. These were designed so that when the bike was static, tension was at a minimum; tension then increased as the fork deflected. A lighter main spring was also used, and this gave a more sensitive action.

Petrol tank The capacity was increased to four gallons (the same as that of the Tiger 100), and the knee grips were changed to the screw fixing type (the tank was recessed to accommodate them). Colours remained as for 1938 for the Amaranth and Gold, but an option for 1940 was Black and Chrome with Ivory lining.

Switch panel The Bakelite panel was replaced by a steel one because the former tended to crack, and the steel panel was given a crystalline (crinkled) black finish.

Speedometer cable A new slimline cable was fitted similar to the later post-war pattern.

Price

Fully equipped	£80 0s 0d

Extras

120mph speedometer	£2 15s 0d
120mph speedometer with 5in dial	£5 5s 0d
Pillion footrests	£0 7s 6d
Pillion seat	£0 12s 6d
Prop stand	£0 10s 0d
Valanced front and rear mudguards	£0 12s 6d
Quickly detachable rear wheel	£2 0s 0d

A patent was taken out on February 10, 1939, in the name of the Triumph Engineering Co. Ltd. (Patent No. 524885) covering the spring hub, and it was scheduled to be included in the 1940 programme. Some development work was carried out in 1939, and testing was well under way, but prevailing circumstances prevented its inclusion into the 1940 motorcycle range. It wasn't until seven years later that the spring hub became available.

Future design

The following is an extract from a paper that Edward Turner read before the Institute of Automobile Engineers in 1943 when he was Technical Director of BSA Motor Cycles.

From it one can see that he was quite aware of all design aspects and, in some respects, rather scathing over the racing design being fed through into the standard touring motorcycles.

Although he didn't wish to see a two-wheeled car, his ideal was certainly leaning towards the totally-enclosed two-wheeler, produced on a scale that everyone could afford.

"At a time when we are all preoccupied with the earnest job in hand of winning the war, it is impossible to escape from the significance of the oft repeated expression 'Winning the Peace.' This implies building a better world for all to enjoy, and in the motorcycle world we will have an opportunity of making a useful contribution to this. It has been apparent, however, that the trend of development in the years leading up to

Overseas successes.

Triumphs escort royalty.

the present war was in the wrong direction, and tended to narrow the scope of appeal of the motorcycle.

"The TT races provided a stimulus for design and, in fact, became a major objective for many manufacturers. It is, therefore, not surprising that the design requirements of this form of activity have had great influence on the standard products.

"Logically, a vehicle, the design of which is inspired by specific activities, is bound to attract a market interested in these activities: thus we have an industry almost entirely supported by the sporting elements and consequently restricted in its appeal.

"It is not suggested that the post-war motorcycle industry should not cater for the sport; on the contrary, this section of development should and will receive considerable attention, but if motorcycle manufacture is ever to be one of Britain's staple industries, a type of motorcycle must be developed which will attract, by its utility, the ordinary pedestrian.

"What can the power-driven two-wheeler offer that will induce the pedestrian to ride one, or a portion of car and cycle owners to prefer it as a means of transport or conveyance? In defining this we are defining the aims of post-war motorcycle design development.

1) The motorcycle is the most economical form of mechanically propelled vehicle. This applies to first cost, maintenance, and running costs, such as petrol, oil and rubber.

2) Handleability. This appears to be the only word to describe the facility with which the vehicle can be moved when not under power; it also covers the fact that traffic congestion is more easily negotiated with a motorcycle than with a car, and that the vehicle needs less parking space on the road or in the home.

3) It offers a most fascinating means of enjoying the open air.

4) In underdeveloped areas abroad, it is often the only means of conveyance, due to its narrow width and ability to negotiate rough country.

5) It is the best means of training the rising generation in road sense and mechanical sense.

6) It is far and away the fastest vehicle available to man for a given capital expenditure.

"Far too much emphasis has been laid on speed in the past, and manufacturers were forced to resort to very high compression ratios, freak timing diagrams, large clearances and other undesirable expedients to provide the necessary competitive performance. Under ordinary conditions 55mph is, in the author's experience, about the maximum speed possible on a motorcycle without discomfort in good weather, and in designing a motorcycle for economical transport as distinct from sport there seems no point in making a machine capable of sustained speeds in excess of 55mph.

"It would appear that the motorcycle most likely to create a larger market must comply with the following:

1) Be economical to buy and use.

2) Have good practical weather protection.

3) Be infinitely more silent both as regards exhaust and mechanical noise than has heretofore been accepted as standard.

4) Start easily and idle with certainty.

5) Be easy to clean, maintain and have as many of the working parts enclosed as is possible.

The Speed Twin

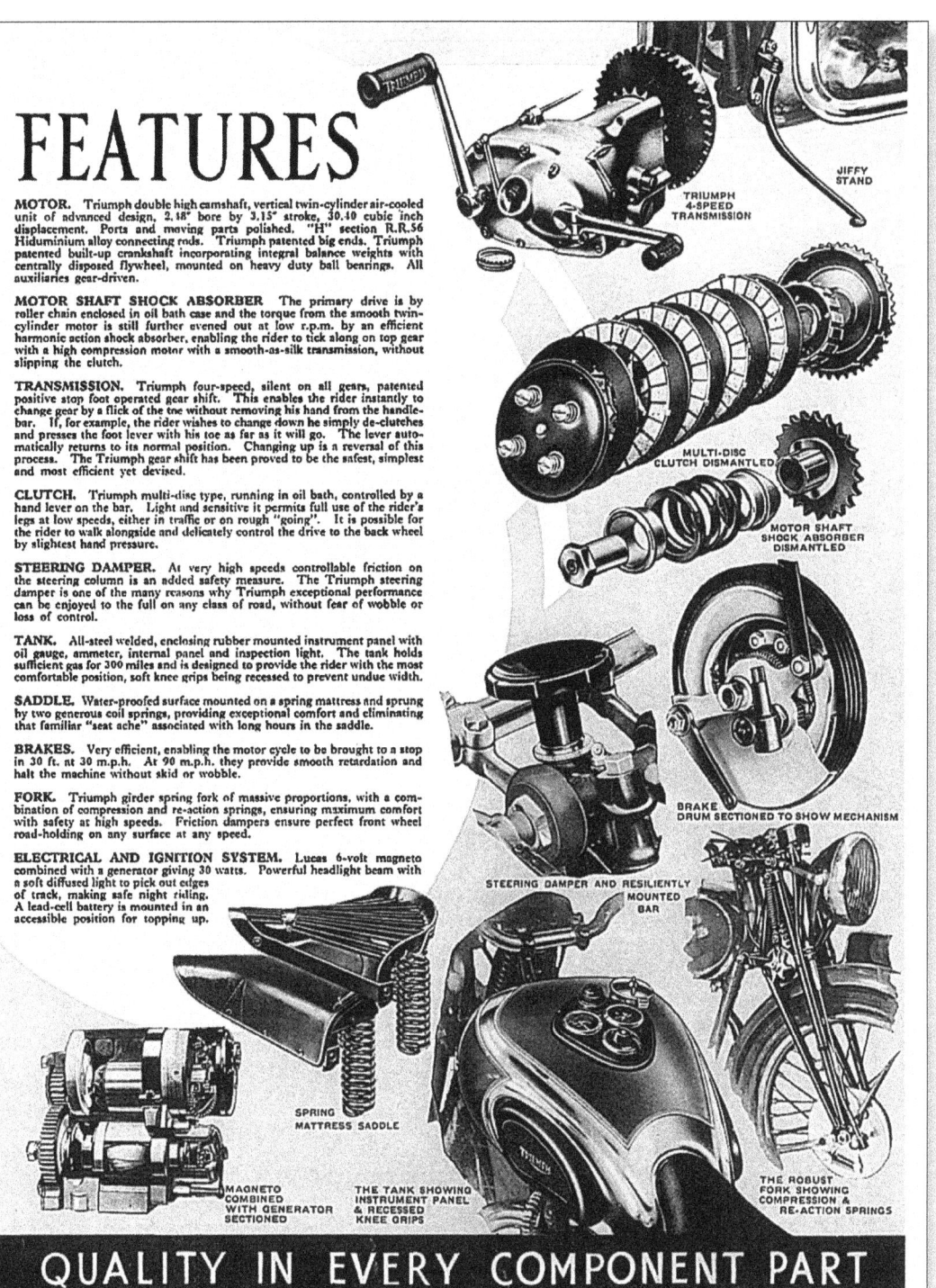

1940 Speed Twin features. British readers will have to pardon the American terms, as this leaflet was written for the US market.

The Triumph Speed Twin & Thunderbird Bible

The 1941 350xx 3TWD. Note the alternator in the timing cover and the use of the petrol tank as part of the frame. Both these innovations would be featured on the Speed Twin at a later date.

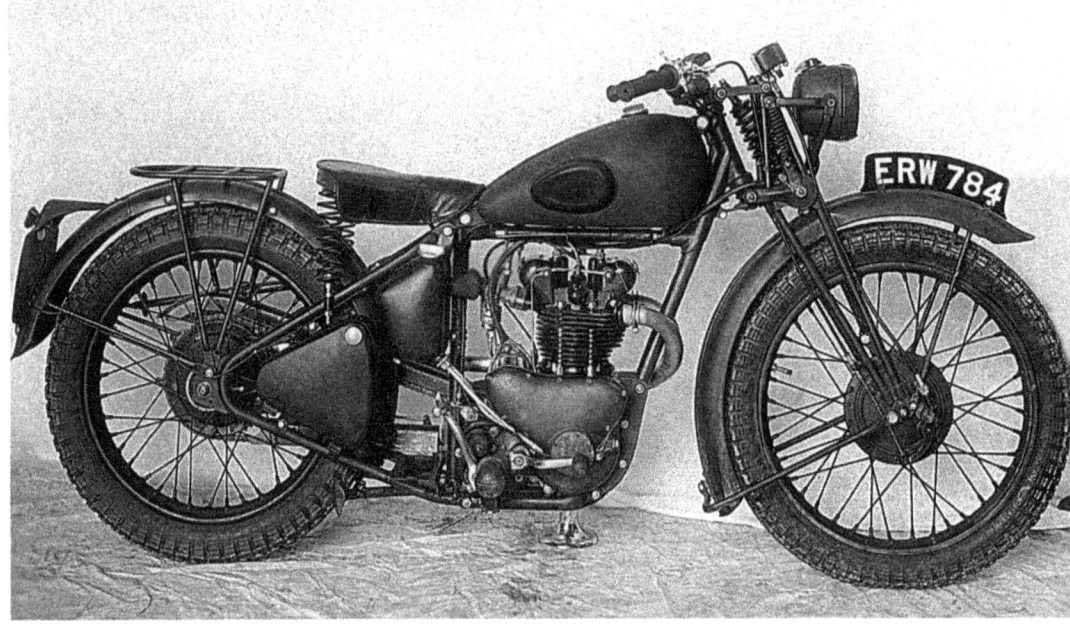

6) Conform to the reliability standard that motor cars have taught the public to expect, and the author would suggest as a minimum of 10,000 miles without overhaul or adjustment. For such a relatively cheap vehicle, 60,000 miles ought to be accepted as adequate life.

7) Handleability. The machine should be as light as it is possible to make it, consistent with reliability.

8) It should be less vulnerable and possess a maximum of stability."

He went on to discuss the merits of multi-cylinder engines and the induction problems associated with V-Twins. He also remarked that four-cylinder engines would be used in high priced machines in the sporting classes.

I think this brief resume gives a good insight into the thoughts of the Speed Twin's designer and maybe shows why, in 1959, the Speed Twin went the way of near-total enclosure.

Speed Twin 1941-1944

Because Triumph was fully engaged in the war effort producing motorcycles for the armed services and generators for the Royal Air Force, virtually no new models were introduced, and it's fairly certain that no Speed Twins were produced in these years.

However, when the War Office asked manufacturers to produce a prototype motorcycle to certain specifications, Edward Turner was quick to respond, and Triumph offered a 350cc OHV twin with a weight of only 230lb.

Approximately 25 of these machines were produced before the factory was bombed out of existence. It was said that some of the 25 got as far as the Dunkirk beaches, but the ones remaining at the factory were totally destroyed. The only remaining 3TWD 350cc twin is kept at the National Motor Museum at Beaulieu.

Chapter 3
A new era dawns

Triumph's post-war programme, consisting of the 500cc 5T and T100, plus a newcomer, the 350cc 3T, was very conservative, with nothing radical in the line-up. For the first time in its history, however, Triumph had no single cylinder motorcycles in its range. While it's true that a 350cc OHV single, the 3HW, was sold in 1945, this was essentially rebuilt or assembled from spare parts and was used to top up production when twin-cylinder assembly was held up due to material and parts shortages.

A certain amount of re-styling and tidying-up had taken place in the design, though, with the rear-mounted Magdyno giving way to a separate dynamo mounted at the front of the crankcase, and a magneto flange mounted at the rear. Both these units were driven independently by gear pinions.

New hydraulically-damped telescopic front forks (I say new, but actually Triumph had a telescopic fork on test in 1942) replaced the previous girders, making the front of the machine look much sleeker and much tidier.

A 19in front wheel was fitted in place of the previous 20in wheel.

Rear suspension, in the form of the spring wheel, was offered as an optional extra, at a cost of £20 6s 5d, though it was not until September 1947 that this actually became available and was fitted to production machines.

A footchange pedal with a flattened, spoon-shaped lever with the Triumph logo in relief was fitted. Because of the acute rubber shortage in the post-war years, though, there was no rubber covering.

1945 Model 5T Speed Twin

Engine prefix: 45-5T
Alterations for 1945

Engine New crankcases with provision for a front-mounted dynamo and a rear, flange-mounted magneto (BTH) were substituted for the original design. Automatic ignition control via a BTH unit replaced the manually-operated type. The external rocker oil drain pipes were deleted and replaced by internal drillings in the cylinder head and barrel. The rocker oil feed was also redesigned, the feed now being taken from a T-junction in the return pipe at the oil tank. The engine breather was now a timed rotary valve driven by the inlet camshaft, and it vented to the atmosphere via a flexible pipe on the left hand side. The oil pressure release valve was redesigned, a piston type replacing the ball and spring arrangement used previously.

Front forks Telescopic, hydraulically-damped front forks replaced the girders. Their total movement was 6½in.

Front wheel A 19in diameter rim replaced the earlier 20in wheel, and a 3.25 x 19in Dunlop Universal tyre replaced the 3.00 x 20in tyre used previously.

Handlebar A new handlebar bend was required to suit the telescopic forks.

Headlamp The headlamp size was reduced to 7in diameter.

Oil tank The capacity was increased to eight pints, and a 2in hinged filler cap was fitted, matching that fitted to the Tiger 100.

Electrical The electrical system was 6-volt negative earth. Charging was by a Lucas E3H-RD dynamo via an automatic compensated voltage control box, type MCR-L-4.

Carburettor The choke was operated by a spring-loaded plunger on top of the mixing chamber. A throttle cable fitted with a 90° metal elbow provided better routing out of the twistgrip.

The Triumph Speed Twin & Thunderbird Bible

A factory photograph of a 1945 Speed Twin showing the twin petrol taps and an incorrectly painted front brake anchor plate.

Price £158 15s 0d

Extras
Speedometer £4 8s 11d

1945 Model 5T Speed Twin

Engine As original specification.

Cylinder head As original specification.

Valves As original specification.

Valve guides As original specification.

Valve springs As original specification.

Cam followers As original specification.

Valve clearance — cold. As original specification.

Valve timing
IVO	26½°	BTDC
IVC	69½°	ABDC
EVO	61½°	BBDC
EVC	35½°	ATDC

0.020in clearance for checking timing

Push rod
Material　　　　Tubular steel with end caps top and bottom
Overall length　　6.3000/6.325in

Rockers As original specification.

Camshafts and bearings — As original specification.
Bush diameter
LH bore　　　　0.8125/0.8135in
RH bore　　　　0.874/0.875in
LH outer　　　　1.001/1.0015in
RH outer　　　　1.126/1.127in
Overall length LH EX　0.932/0.942in
LH IN　　　　　1.000/1.110in
RH IN & EX　　1.010/1.020in

Cylinder barrel
Material　　　　Cast iron
Cylinder bore diameter　2.4800/2.4805in
Tappet guide bore　0.9985/0.9990in
Maximum tolerable wear　0.007in

Tappet block
Outer diameter　0.9995/1.000in
Bore diameter　0.312/0.3125in

Piston rings As original specification.

Pistons
Clearance in cylinder bore at max diameter
(90° to gudgeon pin)　0.004/0.0045in
Crown height from gudgeon pin centre 7.0:1
　　　　　　　　1⅜in
Gudgeon pin diameter　0.6882/0.6885in

Connecting rods
Small end diameter　0.6905/0.6910in
Big end diameter　1.4375/1.4385in
Side clearance (fitted)　0.012/0.016in
Length between centres　6.499/6.501in
Bearing, big end　White metal

Crankshaft As original specification.

Crankshaft bearing As original specification.

Oil pump As original specification.

A new era dawns

Carburettor
Type	276 LH
Bore	15/16in
Main jet	140
Needle jet	0.107
Needle	No 6
Needle position	3
Throttle valve	6/3
Float chamber	64/192

Ignition
Magneto	BTH — anti clock
Control	BTH automatic advance control
Timing	37° or 3/8in BTDC fully advanced
Points gap	0.012in
Spark plug	Lodge H14 or Champion Ll IS
Plug gap	0.018in
Thread size	14mm
Reach	1/2in

Transmission
Clutch	As original specification
Kickstart mechanism	As original specification
Gearchange mechanism	As original specification
Footchange spindle	As original specification
Quadrant springs	As original specification
Camplate plunger	
Plunger diameter	0.4360/0.4365in
Housing bore diameter	0.4375/0.4380in
Spring length	2½in
No of coils	22
Mainshaft	As original specification
Layshaft	As original specification
No of teeth on pinions	As original specification
Sprockets	As original specification
Gear ratios — internal	As original specification
Chains	As original specification

Frame As original specification.

Front fork
Stanchion diameter	1.3025/1.303in
Top bush inner diameter	1.3065/1.3075in
Top bush outer diameter	1.498/1.499in
Top bush O/A length	0.995/1.005in
Bottom bush inner diameter	1.2485/1.2495in
Bottom bush outer diameter	1.4935/1.4945in
Bottom bush O/A length	0.870/0.875in
Fork leg bore	1.498/1.500in
Spring free length	20in ± 1/8in
Wire diameter	0.160in

Wheels
Rim size	
Front and rear	WM2 x 19in
Tyres	
Front	3.25 x 19in Dunlop Universal
Rear	3.50 x 19in Dunlop Universal
Pressures	
Front	18psi
Rear	16psi

Wheel bearings
Front ball journal	20 x 47 x 14mm
Rear taper roller	9/16 x 1¾ x 13/16 x 9/16in outer

Spokes
Front	
LH inner	10 x 8 11/32 x 10 88°
LH outer	10 x 8 11/32 x 10G 90°
RH inner	10 x 6 3/8 x 10G 83°
RH outer	10 x 6 3/8in x 10G 96°

Alex Oxley did a series of cartoons for Triumph. They were quite amusing in their day, and illustrate how gentle advertising was at that time.

The Triumph Speed Twin & Thunderbird Bible

Speedometer
Type	Smiths S464/3/L with rev dial calibrated in mph
Cable length	54in

Electrical
Dynamo	Lucas MH RD 40W
Voltage	6V
Earth	Negative
Battery	Lucas PUW7E/4 12Ah
Horn	Lucas Altette HF 1234
Headlamp	Lucas 7in D42 CPR
Tail lamp	Lucas MT 110
Bulb main	6V 24/30 or 24/24
Bulb pilot	6V 3W
Bulb speedo	6V 3W
Bulb tail	6V 3W
Bulb inspection	6V 3W

Dimensions
Wheelbase	54in
O/all length	84in
O/all width	28½in
Seat height	29½in
Weight	361lb
Ground clearance	6in

Lubrication
Engine	
Summer	SAE 4050
Winter	SAE 2030
Gearbox	EP90
Primary case	SAE 20
Telescopic fork	SAE 20 or 30
Grease	Castrol LM

Capacities
Fuel tank	4gal (18L)
Oil tank	6pt (3.5L)
Gearbox	⅔pt (400cc)
Primary case	½pt (300cc)
Telescopic fork	⅙pt (100cc)

Left hand threads
Camshaft pinion nuts

Price £139 14s 0d

Extras
Smiths 120mph speedometer: £4 8s 10d

Thoughts and comments about the 1947 models

The following is a memo from Edward Turner to his works team outlining his thoughts on the coming 1947 season. Those conversant with the design history of the Speed Twin will note that some of the items actually did get incorporated in the production machine, whilst others, sad to say, never saw the light of day (probably because of cost considerations).

Rear
LH inner	10 x 8¾in x 9G 76°
LH outer	10 x 8¾in x 9G 100°
RH inner	10 x 8¾in x 9G 76°
LH outer	10 x 8¾in x 9G 100°

Wheel offset

Front — dimension from drum edge to centre of rim: 2³⁄₁₆ in

Rear — dimension from drum edge to centre of rim: 3⁵⁄₃₂ in

A new era dawns

The time has come when we must consider 1947 improvements. The demand for our products today, fortunately, does not make radical changes essential, but it would be desirable to introduce certain modifications to increase the appeal of the machine and show an indication that we are not resting on our laurels. Any contemplated changes must not interfere with the main manufacturing equipment, neither should they increase the cost of the machine. On the other hand, any improvement that could reduce the cost of the machine without impairing its efficiency or lowering its standard would be an advantage. I would welcome any suggestions, in addition to those outlined below, which are only for consideration.

Gearbox: Modification to cam plate to provide easily found neutral, either below bottom gear or other alternative.

Clutch: Sooner or later it will be necessary to abandon the cork clutch, and experiments should be conducted once more with fabric inserts, with very much increased spring pressure, and a proportional reduction in axial pushrod movement by increasing the leverage of the operating mechanism.

Handlebar: This should be cleaner, and have two built-in switches and internal wiring. The dip switch and horn button should be on the left, and the cutout button on the right.

Horn: We must draw a small streamlined horn to mount on the front fork and try all electrical manufacturers with a view to buying this horn at a keen price.

Instrument panel: It would be a great advantage if we could remove the instrument panel from the tank completely and locate it on the crown of the fork.

Saddle: A new pan seat on a metal base with sorbo insulation should be drawn out for Dunlop's Experimental Department to pick up as a development. This they are willing to do.

Guards: The problem here is to produce new guards giving more effective mud protection without increasing the price and withal retaining an elegant appearance.

I would like to see a layout for the whole of the rear guard to be detached in one piece for wheel removal, jointing at the back stays, so as to remove the ugly gap in the guard at the back, simplify the stays, and have an entirely flush rear guard surface. Front guard - some valance which would either be in one piece with the guard, thereby not increasing the price, or alternative suggestions.

Stand: It will be absolutely vital for us to produce a quick-operating prop stand for 1947. Please obtain the stand used by AMC as a basis for discussion.

Twistgrip: A quick-opening twistgrip, on the helical principle, to enable an internal cable to go through the bar would be a neater job. The present twistgrip, though successful, is not entirely suitable for small choke carburettors, and the cable is untidy.

Petrol indicator: A simple device to enable the rider to see at a glance how much petrol there is in the tank would be an advantage.

Chain cover: Although I do not anticipate going in for an enclosed rear chain for 1947, any improvement in the present chainguard arrangements, particularly in its effect on water, should be tried out.

Carburettor: I would like to see experiments brought well forward for fitting a Zenith or Solex carburettor on our machines for 1947. I believe these could be bought at an even lower price than Amal, and they would have the advantage of enabling us to use a piano wire push/pull twistgrip.

On receipt of your further suggestions, which will have careful consideration, I will draw up a schedule for design modifications for 1947 which should be made, tested and released for production not later than the end of July for inclusion in our range early in October, although these will be publicised in the press early in September.

Signed E. Turner — Managing Director

Left-hand view of the 1946 Speed Twin

The Triumph Speed Twin & Thunderbird Bible

1946 Model 5T Speed Twin

Engine prefix: 46-5T
Alterations from 1945

Engine Compression ratio lowered to 6.5:1. Engine sprocket reverted to 22 teeth.

Carburettor Float chamber 1 AT

Gearbox From engine number 74760, a change in the dogs of the mainshaft 2nd gear to the mainshaft 4th gear was introduced to provide easier gear engagement. Providing the gears are kept as matching pairs (new or old) they are fully interchangeable.

Frame No change.

Oil tank Early models had an eight-pint oil tank, with a 2in hinged filler cap. Later models reverted to the pre-war type, i.e. six pints with screwed alloy cap.

Apart from these small changes, it was a period of marking time on modifications, with the emphasis being on trying to catch up with outstanding orders.

Price £158 15s 0d

Extras Smiths 120mph speedometer £4 8s 11d

Very little change to the specification took place for the 1947 season.

It was a very difficult time for manufacturers, as Britain had not fully recovered from the ravages of war, and no real manufacturing rhythm could be achieved due to the shortage of raw materials. Steel rationing resulted in stop-start production. It was in this difficult environment that Edward Turner issued the following statement to support his no change policy:

'We believe that the best contribution Triumphs can make to the national recovery is to supply Triumph Twins to would-be owners, and they number many thousands, with the least possible delay. We shall continue our successful range of models unchanged for 1947 in order to avoid the production hold-ups, which would be unavoidable were any other policy to be followed, especially under present day conditions'.

That he was correct in taking this route was borne out by the fact that, despite the most strenuous efforts, supply never caught up with demand.

The victory parade with the King and Queen on the saluting base as the Speed Twins pass by. London, June 8, 1946.

A new era dawns

1946 Speed Twin road tests

The first post-war test of the Speed Twin by 'Torrens', which appeared in *The Motorcycle*, praised the change to telescopic front forks, both from the point of view of rider comfort and the much tidier general appearance. The four-gallon fuel tank, which had replaced the pre-war three-gallon tank, was also praised, although this had actually been specified for 1940.

The Speed Twin engine was always tidy in appearance, but this was improved by the removal of the external oil drain pipes which used to lead from the rocker boxes. This oil return was now internal, drillings in the head and barrel carrying the oil away.

The handlebar control layout was re-arranged to reduce the number of levers. For example, the ignition lever had been dispensed with, as had the air control or choke lever. A spring-loaded plunger on top of the carburettor mixing chamber controlled the air slide, while the ignition advance and retard was looked after by an automatic centrifugal device attached to the magneto drive.

In the interests of reliability, the compression ratio was reduced from 7.0:1 to 6.5:1 to suit the 'pool' petrol available (approximately 72 octane). This didn't seem to affect the overall performance very much, and Edward Turner was quoted as saying he believed the Speed Twin had all the speed and more that the average rider needed. He was quite prepared to sacrifice speed in the interests of smoother performance (on the inferior fuel) and his ideal of efficient simplicity.

To say that 'Torrens' was taken by the Speed Twin is something of an understatement given his use of terms like "exhilarating," "sympathy with the machine," "hairline steering," and "super adequate braking" to sum up his impressions after just a few miles.

One slight criticism, however, concerned rear wheel hop, and it was thought that moving the footrests towards the rear would have alleviated this tendency.

Braking figures were good: 35 feet for the front brake alone, with 29 feet for both brakes from 30mph. Due to the leverage available, and perhaps because of the light rear end, the rear brake could lock the rear wheel under relatively light application of the pedal.

In the maximum speed and flying quarter-mile tests the new Speed Twin was slightly slower than its predecessor, but made up for this by providing remarkable flexibility and silky performance, for example, with top gear engaged and road speed as low as 17mph, the machine could be accelerated using full throttle.

This smooth power took the effort out of riding at high average speeds, and economy was quoted as 66-77mpg.

No oil leaks were visible when the test concluded, the general finish was above reproach, and all the instruments were in full working order. The tester didn't like the carburettor-mounted choke lever, though, as he couldn't reach it with a gloved hand (and it was, by its nature, either fully on or off with no progressive setting).

The tester concluded his review by saying that the Speed Twin was one of the most handsome motorcycles ever produced.

The 1947 sales brochure illustration showed the spring wheel for the first time. Note also the 'bare' footchange gear pedal.

The Triumph Speed Twin & Thunderbird Bible

Tank panel and lining detail.

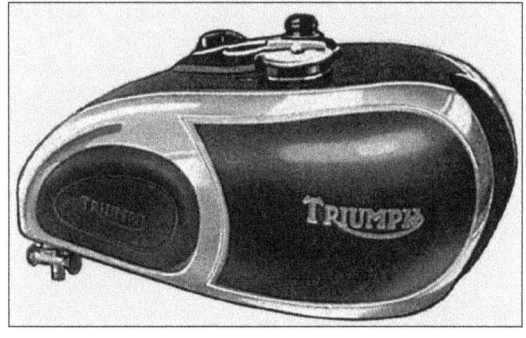

Second gear (8.65 to 1)	62mph = 6919rpm 12⅗s

Measured quarter mile
    Flying start   86.6mph
    Standing start   50.7mph

Fuel consumption
    Urban   66mpg
    Overall   77mpg

Braking from 30mph
    Front brake only   35ft
    Rear brake only   54ft
    Both brakes   29ft

1947 Model 5T Speed Twin

Engine prefix: 47-5T
Alterations from 1946

Engine No change.

Carburettor The float chamber was changed over to the left side of the mixing chamber. This entailed a new carburettor with a throttle stop screw and a pilot mixture

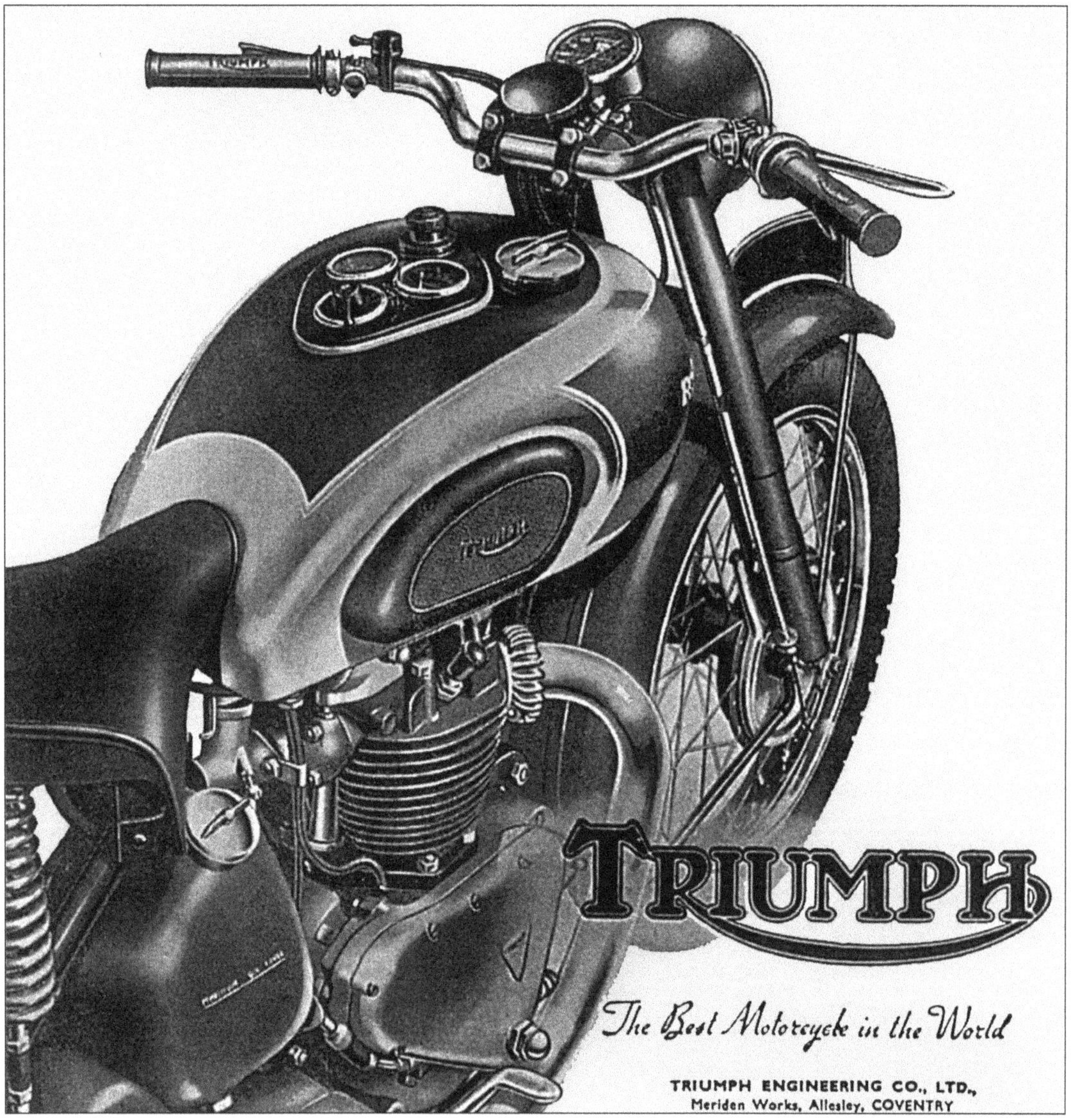

A wealth of detail here with identical horn and ignition cut-out push button switches, dip switch, and large ebonite steering damper knob.

A new era dawns

Two views of what Johnson Motors USA thought the Speed Twin should look like. Note the twin carburettor setup.

The Triumph Speed Twin & Thunderbird Bible

A 1948 Speed Twin showing the new front and rear mudguards.

screw on the right side. New carburettor No 276 BN/IAT. The mixing chamber was now No 76/132M.

Frame No change, but a prop stand was offered as a bolt on extra - to be fitted under the chaincase. The pre-war prop stand could no longer be fitted because the dynamo was now occupying the required space.

Headlamp The headlamp shell was now painted Amaranth Red, and the rim was chrome plated.

Price £180 6s 10d

Extras
Smiths 120mph speedometer   £5 1s 8d

1948 Model 5T Speed Twin

Engine prefix: 48-5T
Frame numbers: TF 15001 to TF 24765
Engine numbers: 88227 — 4.9.1947 to 102160 — 19.10.1948

Alterations from 1947

There were no engine changes for 1948, but during the season year, several changes took place to the motorcycle parts. Due to circumstances outside the company's control, these changes could not be introduced at the onset of the season, but were brought in as and when convenient.

Gearbox With the introduction of the spring wheel, an alternative to the original rear wheel-driven speedometer gearbox had to be found. The solution was to attach the speedometer gearbox to the rear of the gearbox, and drive it from the rear of the final drive gearbox sprocket. When this was specified, the cable length was reduced to 49in.

Footchange lever The footchange lever regained a rubber covering for the foot part. This, of course, had the Triumph logo moulded into it.

Speedometer cable A 49in speedometer cable was fitted from TF 15069, September 16.

A new era dawns

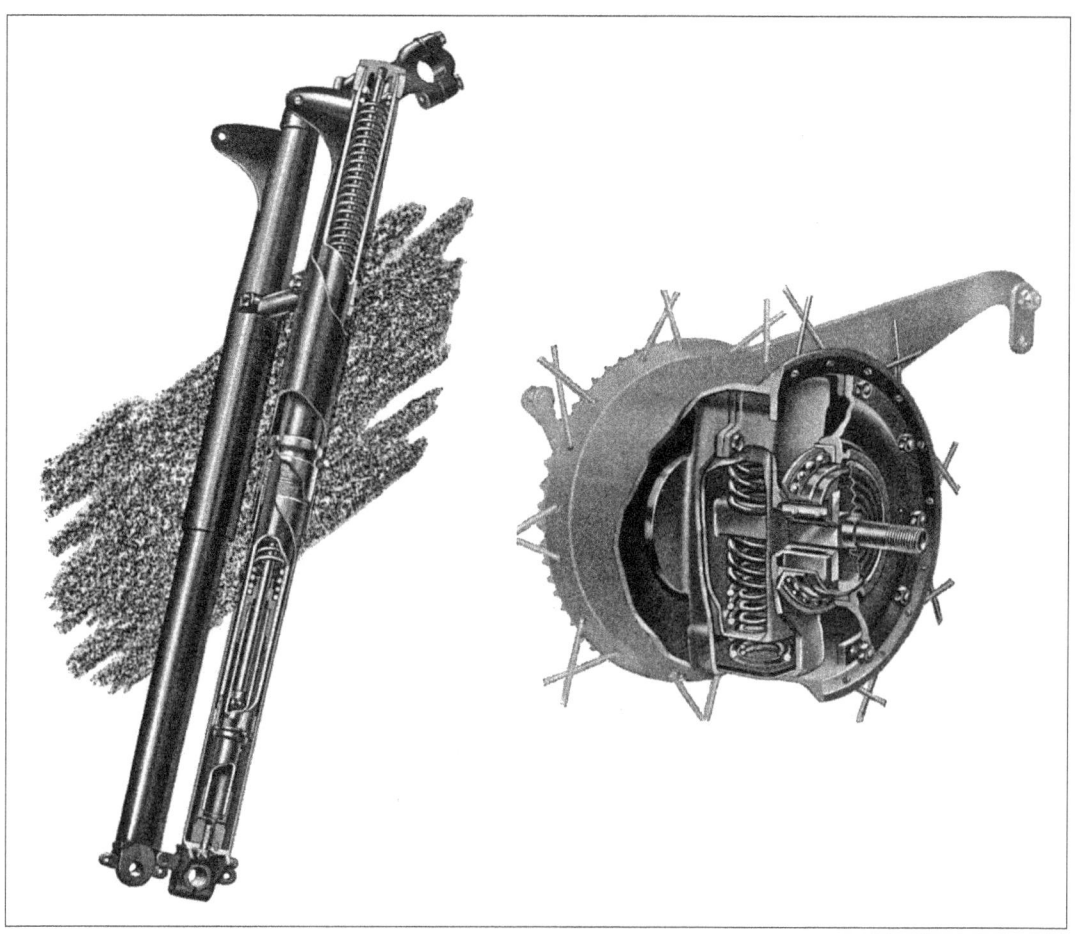

The Speed Twin suspension details.

Steering damper The front fork steering damper was reduced in diameter, and the material changed from ebonite to aluminium alloy embossed with the Triumph logo, from TF 15530, October 1.

Spring wheel The first Speed Twin to be equipped with the optional spring wheel was TF 15069, September 16.

Front mudguard A new front mudguard was fitted. This had two detachable front stays and a raised pressed front edge to aid waterproofing. It was fitted from TF 16227, November 4.

Rear mudguard The new rear mudguard was wider and had only two fixing stays on each side. It was detachable from under the seat, and was fitted from TF 17790, January 1.

Rear frame A new rear frame, to accept the above rear mudguard, was fitted from TF 17790, January 1.

Voltage control (Lucas MCR-l) The new fixing comprised a nut and bolt fitting across the rear subframe, to two small welded bracket, from TF 17790, January 1.

Rear number plate The top portion of the rear number plate was reshaped to provide a handhold whilst using the rear stand. This was necessary because the two side handles fitted to the earlier rear mudguard had been deleted.

Front number plate The front number plate incorporated a minor change, whereby the styling beading was cast onto the actual plate; prior to this, the beading had been detachable.

Carburettor The throttle valve was changed to a 6/3½ from TF 23324, August 17.

Headlamp The headlamp was fitted with a domed glass.

Ignition Plug caps were introduced as a standard fitment.

Weight With optional spring wheel fitted: 374lb.

Price £180 6s 10d

Extras
Smiths 120mph speedometer	£5 1s 8d
Prop stand	£1 11s 8d
Spring wheel	£20 6s 5d

The Triumph Speed Twin & Thunderbird Bible

The three gold medallists riding Speed Twins in 1948.

The Speed Twin in the 1948 International Six Days Trial

One of the major annual events that the Triumph company took seriously was the International Six Day Trial (ISDT). This event, as the name implies, consisted of six separate days' trials, over a different course each day. Riders rode against the clock, checking in at numerous points along the route. If a rider checked in outside his time allowance, time marks would be deducted. For a gold medal to be gained, a clean sheet at the end of the six days was required. It was usual for the trial to be run over rough mountain tracks and linking tarmacadam roads, so, as fairly high average speeds were needed to keep on schedule, a rider with stamina and a reliable machine were required. ISDT riders needed a good degree of mechanical expertise, too, as outside assistance was barred and exclusion could be the penalty if any was detected.

The first ISDT was held in Cumbria in 1913, but Triumph didn't feature largely until the mid-1930s. The introduction of the Tiger models saw Triumph taking the event seriously, with the Tiger 100 being used just prior to WWII. Post-war, the ISDT resumed with the 1947 event held in Czechoslovakia. However, as the regulations had arrived late and seemed to favour the small capacity machines (of which most of the continental teams consisted), the British manufacturers declined to take part. Of the three private entries from Great Britain two were Triumph Speed Twins, ridden by J.A. Hitchcock and A.A. Sanders. The latter retired on the first day due to numerous punctures and running out of time. Hitchcock managed to get to the last day before the bearings in the spring hub failed.

The 1948 event took place in San Remo, Italy, and Triumph built and entered a team of three, mounted on Speed Twins. These were basically standard machines but, in the interests of lightness and reliability (especially given the expected hot weather) alloy cylinder barrels and heads had been fitted (borrowed from the Triumph wartime generator set).

The riders were P.H. (Jim) Alves, A. Jefferies, and A.F. Gaymer, all works riders in trials and scrambles (Jefferies was also a road racer, and had won the British Experts Trial of 1938, Triumph-mounted of course, but not on a Speed Twin).

The San Remo event was expected to be the most difficult ISDT yet staged, with riders expected to contend with swirling dust and rocky cobbled tracks. Many competitors were forced out by these arduous conditions, but the Triumph team were obviously up to it and finished the event without losing a single mark.

Each rider received a gold medal for this achievement, and they were also presented with a manufacturer's team prize (the only one awarded to a British manufacturer).

One outcome of this success was that there was a great demand for a o Triumph competition bike. The company appraised the situation and built a suitable machine which, given the 1948 success, just had to be called the Trophy.

The registration numbers of the three ISDT Speed Twins were HHP 90, HHP 91, and HHP 92. The motorcycles were built on July 22, 1948, with the following frame, engine and gearbox numbers:

TF 22661	5T 99308	99634
TF 22662	5T 99240	99636
TF 22663	5T 99367	99635

1949 Model 5T Speed Twin

Engine prefix: 5T-9
Frame numbers: TF 25115 to TF 33615
Engine numbers: 102581 — 2.11.1948 to 113386 — 6.10.1949

The appearance of the Speed Twin got a major revision for 1949, with the introduction of the nacelle. This housed the light switch and ammeter so the tank panel was no longer required.

A new era dawns

Speed Twins for the Swedish army. The new for 1949 nacelle and petrol tank with luggage rack are well illustrated.

Engine The oil pressure release valve was modified, and fitted with an indicator button. This was necessary because the oil pressure gauge had been deleted.

The engine breather discharge pipe was relocated, and now pointed downwards from an interference fit metal pipe in the crankcase. A flexible rubber pipe was added to the discharge pipe to take the crankcase fumes into the atmosphere. Because slightly better quality fuel had become available, the compression ratio was increased back to 7.0:1.

Gearbox The speedometer drive for all models was now taken from the gearbox sprocket. Previously, this had only been the case for spring wheel-equipped models.

Carburettor The choke was now operated via a cable (rather than the spring-loaded plunger) and the control lever was situated on the left chainstay, just under the seat. Carburettor no. 276/DK/1AT.

Front forks The upper end of the fork was almost completely new for 1949. The nacelle top unit housed the light switch on the right and the ammeter on the left. The ignition cutout button was situated between the two, and the speedometer was positioned at the front. An adaptor ring was fitted to take the standard headlamp rim and glass.

Because of a shortage of steel pressings, the first 800 (5T and T100) lower nacelle units were alloy castings.

Handlebars A new handlebar bend was employed to suit the nacelle.

Controls The spring and plunger friction device on the twistgrip was dropped, and a knurled adjustable knob with a friction spring was introduced.

The dip switch was now fitted to the front brake damp bracket and had a chrome plated surround.

The horn push button was relocated, and was now screwed directly into a threaded hole in the handlebar on the left hand side.

Petrol tank The petrol tank switch panel was deleted and was replaced by a chrome-plated three-bar parcel grid, offered as an optional extra. When the parcel grid was not fitted, the threaded pommel holes were plugged by small rubber grommets.

Air filter An air filter was specified as standard, and was fitted between the battery carrier and seat downtube. The battery carrier back strap was stepped to suit.

Toolbox This remained essentially the same as before, but the threaded lid retaining knob gave way to a push and twist dzus fastener.

Footbrake pedal The rubber pad covering the foot part of the lever was deleted, leaving the bare metal with a ridged line appearance.

The new-for-1949, nacelle and instrument locations.

The Triumph Speed Twin & Thunderbird Bible

A timing side view of the 1949 model.

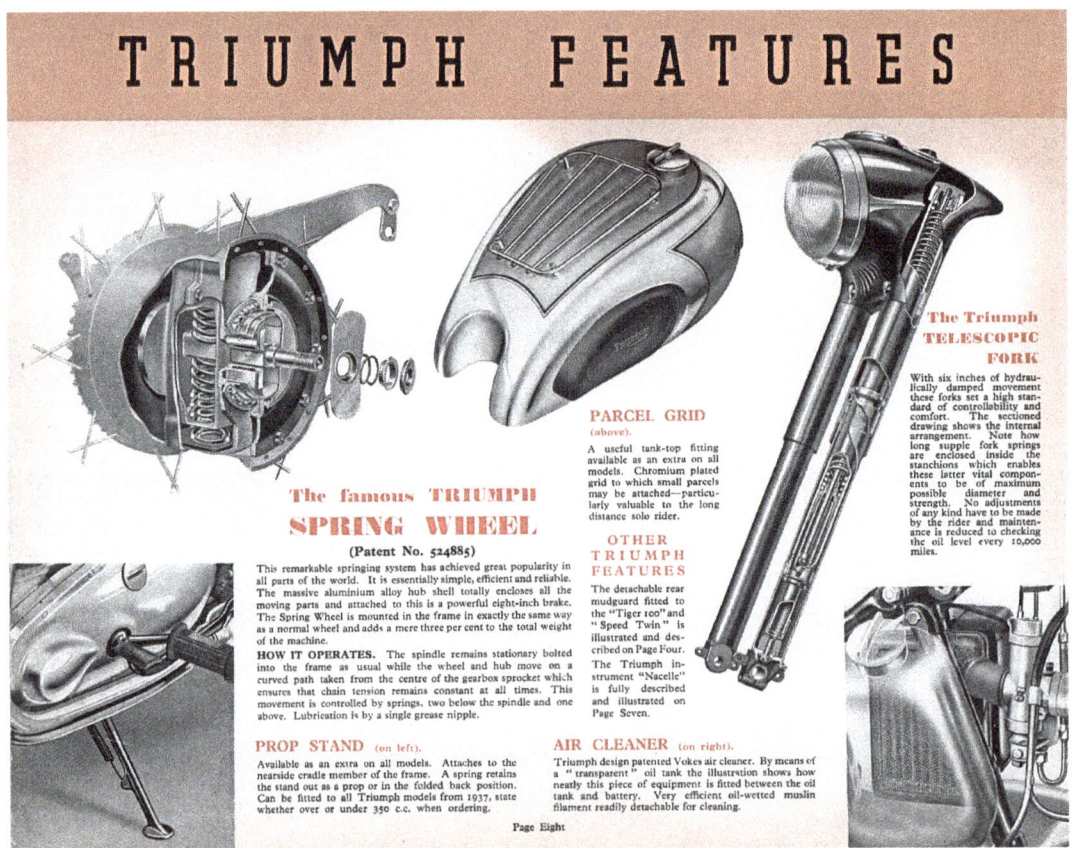

1949 features.

A new era dawns

Although this is a T100, this picture clearly shows the front fork details, and the position of the oil tank transfer.

Electrical The dynamo output was increased by the use of a 60-watt E3L-Ll-0 unit, which was longer than the previous 40-watt type. Introduction frame number was TF 29130, April 4. A new Lucas regulator box, type MCR2L, was required because of the new dynamo.

The rear light cable was armoured and, in the interests of tidying-up the rear end, was routed onto the inside of the mudguard, down the centre rib, before emerging through a grommet.

Speedometer Basically the same as before, except for a new bezel to allow fitting to the nacelle. It also had a rear, or bottom-mounted, trip control, extended so as to protrude below the nacelle.

Price £180 6s 10d

Extras

Smiths 120mph speedometer	£5 1s 8d
Prop stand	£1 11s 8d
Spring wheel	£20 6s 5d

1949 Speed Twin road test

(The following road test was originally published in *The Motorcycle* and *Motorcycling* magazines). The basic details of the 1949 Speed Twin were as those of the 1946 machine, though, of course, the newer items, such as the front fork nacelle and the spring wheel, gave the bike a new look.

The spring wheel enhanced rider comfort, and the tester found that it absorbed all but the most severe bumps, taking all the punishment itself and transmitting nothing to the rider.

Criticism of the choke location on the 1946 test had been taken on board, and the control was now located on the left, under the seat. Although much better than before, the tester remarked that it still took a little getting used to.

Starting was exceptional, with never more than two digs on the kickstart required, even on a cold morning. A small amount of throttle was required when the engine was cold, but with the engine warm it would always start on the pilot jet with the throttle shut.

Main road cruising was effortless. It was difficult to hear the exhaust note when riding at 55mph, and the new air filter arrangement completely eliminated induction hiss. A slight movement of the body was all that was necessary to negotiate main road bends. When these were sharper than anticipated, however, the Speed Twin could be heeled over with complete confidence.

The Speed Twin is essentially a 'top gear motorcycle,' the other three ratios only being required in congested traffic and/or whilst driving in town. Acceleration was of a high order, third gear taking one past baulking traffic at 70mph.

The engine and transmission were so smooth that no snatch could be felt at 20mph in top gear, and it was possible, with a little discretion, to accelerate to maximum from this speed without changing gear.

Braking was adequate, but the tester felt that a little more bite would have been advantageous. Generally, however, the brakes could be commended on the progressive way they did their job.

Gear changes were excellent and, providing a slight pause was made when changing up in the lower ratios, were noiseless. The change between third and top, however, could be made as fast as the pedal could be moved, both up and down. Clutch operation was also excellent, light in action and with no trace of slip or drag.

Even though the compression ratio had been increased again to 7.0:1, because of the air filter, there was no increase in top speed over the 1946 model, though the standing start figure had improved.

No oil leaks were apparent at the conclusion of the test and, apart from travel stains collected during a very wet period, the engine and gearbox were as clean as they had been at the beginning.

Criticisms were confined to the choke lever position, the prop stand being inaccessible to the foot when in the retracted position, and the fact that the speedometer wasn't easy to read when the needle was between 50 and 80mph.

Maximum speeds
Top gear (5 to 1)   88mph 5619rpm 39s
Third gear (6 to 1)   84mph 6670rpm 26s
Second gear (8.65 to 1)   63mph 6930rpm 12⅕s

Measured quarter mile
Flying start   84.9mph
Standing start   54.5mph

Fuel consumption
Urban   67mpg
Overall   74mpg

Braking from 30mph
Front brake only   37ft
Rear brake only   49ft
Both brakes   30ft

1950 Model 5T Speed Twin

Engine prefix: 5T
Engine and frame numbers: 1009N — 17.10.1949 to 16084N — 2.11.1950

Reference to the year of manufacture within the engine number was discontinued, as it was causing embarrassment to overseas dealers who on occasions were still selling the previous season's models.

Taking advantage of this change, an opportunity to tidy-up the numbering system was implemented which meant that engine and frame numbers were identical from this date on.

Engine The external overhead rocker oil drain pipes were reintroduced following the introduction of the 650cc 6T model (with its larger cylinder bore, there was no room left for the internal oil drain drillings).

The oil pump was modified to give increased oil flow.

The shock absorber cam contour was re-designed to give a progressive spring load.

Gearbox A completely re-designed gearbox was introduced as it was felt that the original type wouldn't be adequate for the 650 6T. This new gearbox was fitted with a much stronger live layshaft (this had been the previous box's weakness). It also had provision for the speedometer drive to be taken from the right hand end of the shaft, through a right angle drive, to emerge from the front of the inner cover. The re-design also incorporated a full garter oil seal on the final drive sprocket, to aid oil sealing.

It should be noted that the shafts and gears are not interchangeable between the two gearboxes.

The new gearboxes had the following internal ratios:

1st   2.44
2nd   1.69
3rd   1.19
4th   1.00

Gearbox gears — Number of teeth

Layshaft		Mainshaft
20	4th	26
22	3rd	24
26	2nd	20
30	1st	16

Petrol tank Because of rust problems on some overseas machines, the chrome plate was discontinued on the petrol tanks. Tanks were now all one colour — Amaranth Red. New styling bands were fitted from the forward edge of the knee grip. The raised flutes were in chrome and the background was painted red. Two chrome-plated Triumph badges, with the Triumph name and a raised painted background, were retained by the same screws.

A plain, push and twist cam action Ceandes filler cap replaced the hinged lever type.

The parcel grid, which had previously been an optional extra, became standard equipment.

Rear suspension Due to some failures of the cup and cone bearings in the spring wheel, a new design was introduced and designated the MkII.

Its main feature was the large (3½in diameter) journal ball races. It could be easily identified because of the ribbed end plates.

Seat Barrel-shaped springs were fitted to the saddle to improve the ride. The Triumph-patented Twinseat was offered as an optional extra, replacing the single saddle and pillion pad.

Electrical
Dynamo type: E3L-L1-0

A new era dawns

Many Automobile Association box sidecars were hauled along by Speed Twins such as the one shown here. This one is brand new, and is awaiting collection from the works carpark.

This picture shows the new tank badges for 1950.

The Triumph Speed Twin & Thunderbird Bible

Above and right: A radio-equipped Speed Twin. The stop light switch was an optional extra.

Twinseat	£2 4s 6d
Pillion footrests	£1 0s 4d
Spring wheel	£20 6s 5d

Price £185 8s 5d

1951 Model 5T Speed Twin

Engine prefix: 5T
Engine and frame numbers: 840NA — 21.11.1950 to 15192NA — 16.11.1951

Engine A new fully-machined crankshaft with heavier bobweights was introduced, for greater consistency.

The camwheel pinions now incorporated three keyways, bringing the Speed Twin into line with the T100 model.

The crankshaft right hand bearing was changed from a ball journal to a roller bearing which was capable of carrying higher loadings.

Cam followers with Stellite-faced tips were fitted to combat premature wear.

Taper-faced piston rings were used to give quicker bedding in.

The connecting rods now featured a strengthened section (again, bring the Speed Twin into line with the T100).

The balance factor was changed to 64%.

Carburettor A new float chamber, number 1ATM, was fitted. The complete carburettor number was 276 DK/1AT/M.

Speedometer cable	
Length	44in
Extras	
Prop stand	£1 11s 9d
Pillion seat	£1 11s 9d

Frontbrake To improve the effectiveness of the front brake, a Mehenite cast iron brake drum was fitted, replacing the pressed steel composite pattern previously used

Speedometer The speedometer dial was recalibrated to bring the 30-70mph section to the top of the instrument,

A new era dawns

1951 Speed Twin with optional twin seat.

A late 1951 advertisement showing painted handlebars. These also featured in 1952.

to allow easier reading. Coded 5467/99/L, it replaced the earlier S467/19 type. The speedometer cable length was amended to 45in.

Electrical A new tail lamp, with a tapering body that gave a larger reflective area, was fitted, Lucas number 53216A. A stop lamp could be incorporated, the switch controlled by the rear brake rod.

Price £185 8s 5d

Extras

Spring wheel	£20 6s 5d
Twinseat	£2 4s 6d
Prop stand	£1 11s 9d
Valanced mudguards	Available to special order
Pillion footrests	£1.0s 4d
Heel & toe f/change lever	Available to special order
Pillion seat	£1 11s 9d
Stop Lamp	No price quoted

1952 Model 5T 1954 Speed Twin

Engine prefix: 5T
Engine and frame numbers: 16000NA — 18.11.1951 to 22000 — 2.1.1952 then 26096 — 24.3.1952 to 31901 — 19.8.1952

The Triumph Speed Twin & Thunderbird Bible

The most obvious change for 1952 was the restyled nacelle. This was now larger in diameter, and gave the motorcycle a much bolder look. It also had a small pilot light slung under the main headlamp where, in 1951, there had been louvres or vents.

The fork springs were shortened slightly to lower the front end a little when the motorcycle was stationary. Always on the alert for what he called 'eyeability,' Edward Turner disapproved of the painted section of the fork being interrupted by the seal holder showing. The slightly shorter spring overcame this.

Apart from a slight change to the engine numbers (the NA-suffix was dropped) no changes were made to this unit.

The gearbox and transmission stayed as per 1951.

A new frame was introduced which had an 'eye' in the seat downtube to provide a straight entry from the air filter to the carburettor. There was also a new D-shaped Vokes air filter, mounted between the battery and the oil tank. The exit tube and the carburettor connecting rubber went directly through the frame tube eye.

The pommel on the back of the oil tank was deleted, and replaced by a welded-on strap fixed to the rear mudguard. This was aimed at reducing tank failure due to splitting at the pommel fixing.

The brake pedal footpad was reduced in size (and was now almost square in shape), and had a pinnacled finish.

The rear brake drum and sprocket were integrated, and made of cast iron, replacing the bolted-on type sprocket and separate brake drum.

The petrol tank now had a central weld running from front to rear. This was due to the new method of manufacture, where two deep drawn pressings were made and joined in the centre. This meant that there were no bottom seams on the outside base of the tank from which fuel could leak.

The bridge pipe connecting the left and right hand sides of the tank was dispensed with, being very bothersome when tank removal was required as the fuel had to be drained off first. Its place was taken by a blanking plug in the right hand threaded boss, and by a normal main and reserve tap on the left. The braided steel fuel pipe was replaced by a clear plastic one.

With the new air filter located more centrally, the battery carrier was replaced by the pre-1947 type, which had a straight back bracket instead of one of the cranked 'dog leg' pattern.

Triumph introduced positive earth electrics because the motor trade was of the opinion that less terminal corrosion took place when this arrangement was used.

A sealed beam 7in diameter light unit was fitted in the new nacelle and gave far better illumination than before (it had the added advantage that many car light units would fit the motorcycle). There was also a new pilot lamp.

The finish of the 1952 Speed Twin was compromised by the world nickel shortage. Parts that had always been chrome-plated (over a base nickel plating) had now to be painted. On the Speed Twin, this meant that handlebars were painted Amaranth Red, wheel rims were painted silver, with red centres lined in gold, and the kickstart lever, clutch operating arm, and exhaust pipe finned clips were cadmium-plated.

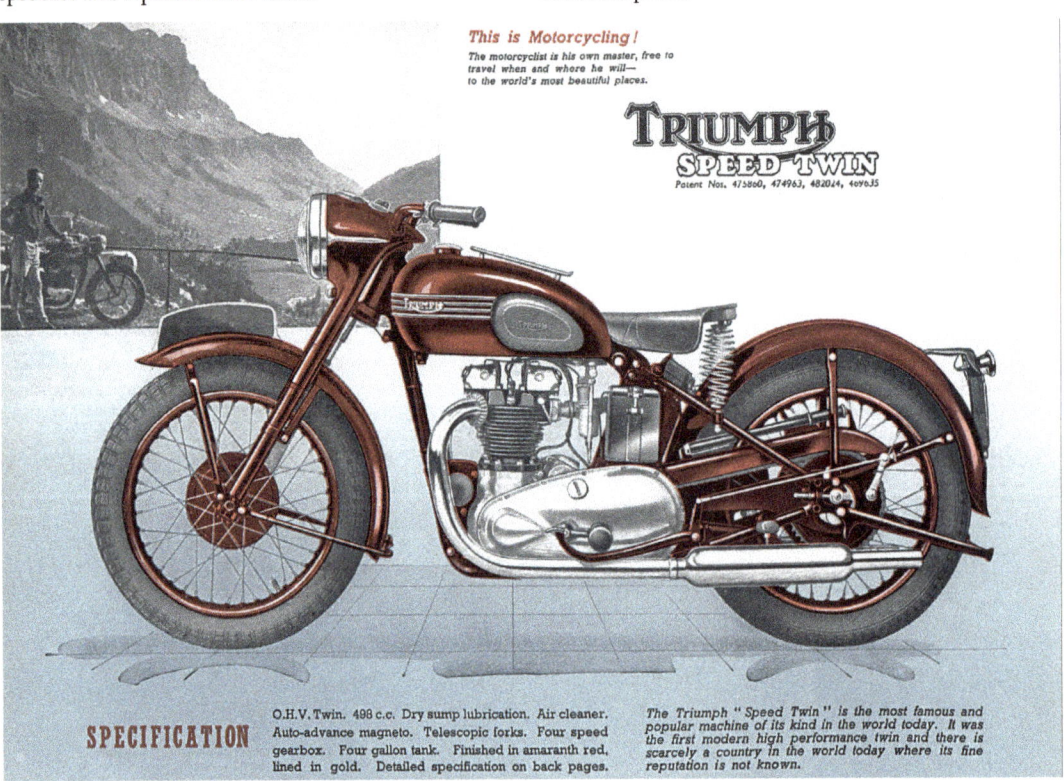

A drive-side view of the 1952 model.

A new era dawns

It's not possible to state with certainty which engine and frame numbers were affected, but it is certain that this policy was in effect in August 1951, just prior to the start of the 1952 season, and it could well have run into the start of the 1953 season. Most restored 1952 models one sees around today take no account of this utilitarian finish.

Engine The engine number system was changed. After 20306NA the suffix letters were deleted and only numbers were used on the frame and engine. The numbers remained identical on both engine and frame.

Frame The 'eye' type frame was introduced from 16000NA.

Air filter The new D-type Vokes air filter was introduced from 16000NA.

Oil tank A new oil tank with revised fixing was introduced from 16000NA. The vent pipe from the oil tank was now taken into the rear of the primary chaincase via two small flexible rubber connections joined by a steel pipe. Prior to this, the vent had been down the seat tube, with overflows becoming a trifle messy where they exited.

Front forks A new nacelle unit and shorter fork springs (¾in less) were introduced from 16000NA.

Brake pedal Now fitted with a smaller footpad, introduced from 16000NA.

Rear wheel An integral brake drum and rear wheel sprocket was introduced from 16000NA.

Petrol tank A new tank, with a visible central weld and a blanking plug, was fitted from 16000NA.

Petrol pipes Clear plastic pipes were fitted from 16000NA.

Battery carrier A straight-backed carrier was fitted from 16000NA.

Electrical A new 7in sealed beam headlight and underslung pilot lamp were introduced from 16000NA. Positive earth was introduced from 19706NA.

Price £206 11s 2d

Extras

Spring wheel	£20 8s 11d
Twinseat	£2 4s 9d
Pillion seat	£1 12s 0d
Pillion footrests	£1 0s 6d
Prop stand	£1 12s 0d

1953 Model 5T Speed Twin

Engine prefix: 5T
Engine and frame numbers: 33868 — 14.10.1952 to 45575 — 6.10.1953

The new air filter, shown with SU carburettor, passing through the 'eye' in the frame tube.

A major change for 1953 was the adoption of coil ignition, with an AC alternator charging system mounted on the left hand crankshaft and chaincase. These early alternator models had two switches mounted in the nacelle; one to control the lights, and the other the ignition. Provision was made for emergency start should the battery be discharged. Ignition on/off was controlled by a removable key which, when rotated anti-clockwise, brought in this emergency start. This had the effect of putting most of the alternator output through the ignition system to provide direct ignition. It would seem the theory was better than the practice for, unless the ignition timing and alternator/rotor timing were precisely matched (they rarely were) rough running and misfiring resulted. However, Triumph's faith in the system was eventually validated, for nearly all motorcycles and cars were subsequently equipped with alternator systems.

Engine Due to the change from dynamo to alternator, the dynamo drive became redundant and new crankcases without this provision were used. A new left hand crankshaft with a parallel section for the alternator rotor mounting was now required.

New camshafts with quietening ramps, but which gave the same valve timing, were specified. Where these were used, the crankcase was marked with the spoked wheel sign alongside the engine number. Tappet clearance with these camshafts was 0.010in inlet/exhaust with a cold engine. The first engine to be fitted with these camshafts was 37560, February 16, 1953.

Transmission New inner and outer primary chaincases were required to house the Lucas alternator.

A new clutch with a built-in shock absorber was fitted. This took the form of a four paddle vane working in eight rubber blocks, giving drive and rebound cushioning. This was first fitted on 33868, October 14, 1952.

The Triumph Speed Twin & Thunderbird Bible

Pioneering again, Triumph introduced the AC charging system for 1953.

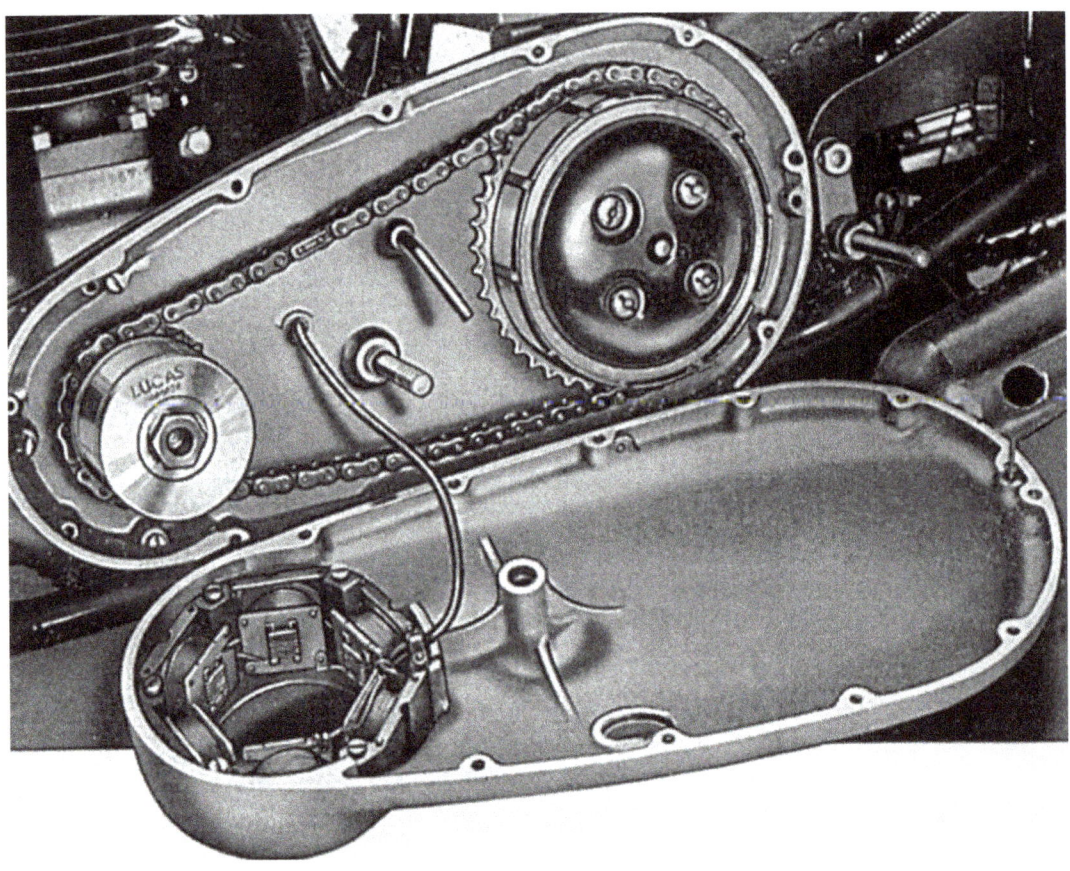

The charging unit.

A new era dawns

Exhaust system A new left hand exhaust pipe was required with a 'dog leg' bend to clear the new primary chainchase.

Frame The prop stand footpiece was extended around the exhaust pipe to provide easier application.

The front engine plates reverted to the 1938 pattern with no dynamo cutout.

Toolbox The toolbox lost its top P-clip fitting. As a tidying-up operation the toolbox was now bolted directly to the front half of the rear mudguard.

Rear number plate A new number plate was required to accommodate the oblong stop and tail lamp.

Electrical
Ignition
A Lucas DKX2A distributor replaced the magneto. A Lucas 6-volt Q6 coil was fitted above the distributor. Suppressors were now incorporated in the sparkplug caps.

Charging systems
The Lucas RM12 alternator had a 55-watt output. The original MkI system was fitted from 33868 to 35316.

From engine number 35317, on December 12, 1952, a modified MkII system was fitted. The modifications involved simplifying the wiring.

From 40294, May 6, 1953, a resistance unit was added. Fitted under the seat, its function was to absorb excess current and prevent wiring failures.

Tail lamp A new Lucas Diacon plastic stop and tail lamp, part number 53269A, was fitted. Operation of the stop light was via the rear brake rod, through a spring, with the Lucas stop switch fixed to a plate anchored to the pillion footrest bolt.

Rectifier A flat two-plate Westinghouse rectifier was housed under the seat, taking the place of the voltage control unit.

Price £208 3s 4d

Extras

Spring wheel	£20 8s 11d
Pillion footrests	£1 0s 6d
Pillion seat	£1 12s 0d
Prop stand	£1 12s 0d
Twinseat	£2 4s 9d

1953 Speed Twin road tests

The 1953 Speed Twin tested was equipped with coil ignition and alternator charging. The new system overcame one of the major drawbacks of coil ignition (reliance on battery condition) by incorporating an emergency start circuit whereby full generator output was fed directly to the coil when the battery was discharged.

The absence of dynamo and magneto drive resulted in an even quieter engine. All controls operated with an easy lightness, making the machine a delight to ride in town or on the open road.

The flexibility of the engine was such that, within the limits of available performance, cruising speed was dependent solely upon the mood of the rider. One could quite happily go through the gears without exceeding the speed limit in built up areas, for example, or whistle up to 70mph before engaging top gear. One could cruise at 40-70mph with the same unobtrusive hum from the silencers, and no more than a rustle from the engine.

Inside the shock absorber.

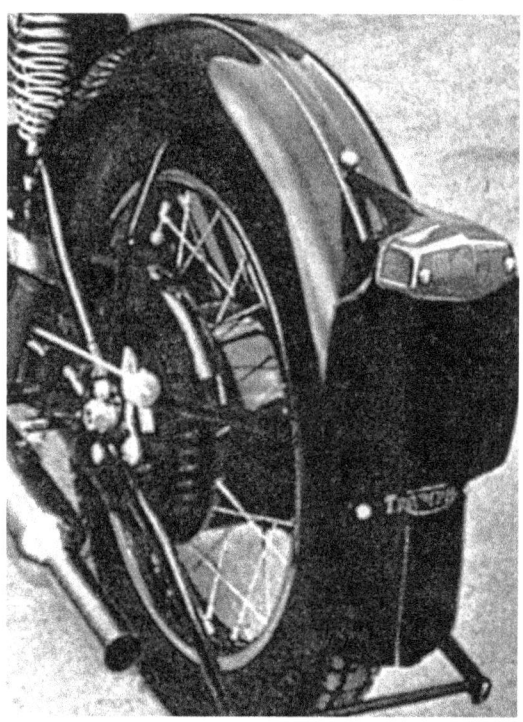

The new-look tail lamp.

Starting was exemplary, the first depression of the kickstarter invariably bringing the engine to life. The air lever mounted under the seat was only required when the engine was started from cold. Piston slap was noticeable when the engine was first started, but disappeared when normal running temperatures were reached. The new camshafts with quietening ramps contributed largely towards the quietness of the valve gear.

Transmission was above reproach, the new rubber in-compression clutch shock absorber smoothing out engine snatch. The gearbox was silent in the indirect ratios, and changes whether up or down were completely silent, provided a slight pause was made when changing between second and third. Gear pedal movement was silky smooth and light, and neutral could be engaged from first or second gear.

Comfort was enhanced by the adoption of the excellent Triumph Twinseat, although, with a heavily clad rider and passenger, a little more length to the seat would have been an advantage.

All controls were fully adjustable, and no problem was encountered in arranging these to suit the rider's tastes.

Further aids to comfort were provided by the front and rear wheel suspensions. The telescopic forks absorbed road shocks with a soft progressive action, damping was adequate, and bottoming could only be provoked by braking hard on a bumpy surface with a passenger on board. The spring wheel eliminated most shocks from the rear, though its short travel meant that severe bumps at high speeds were not completely absorbed.

Straightahead steering was positive and the steering damper was not required, and the Triumph could be leaned into bends and corners with every confidence. In keeping with the rest of the machine's performance, both brakes were smooth, progressive and powerful in action.

The large sealed beam light unit gave adequate lighting up to 70mph on straight roads, but the speedometer was found to be 10% fast at all speeds.

The four-gallon fuel tank was appreciated, with its offset filler cap allowing an easy visual check of the fuel level. The tank top parcel grid was commented upon favourably, and the new propstand was easy to operate. The Amaranth Red and chromium plate finish were excellent.

Maximum speeds
Top gear (5 to 1)   83mph 5400rpm
Third gear (5.95 to 1)   76mph 5860rpm
Second gear (8.45 to 1)   60mph 6570rpm

Measured quarter mile
Flying start   83.5mph
Standing start   54mph

Braking from 30mph
Front brake only   37ft
Rear brake only   48ft
Both brakes   30ft

Fuel consumption
Urban   64mpg
Overall   72mpg

1954 Model 5T Speed Twin

Engine prefix: 5T
Engine and frame numbers: 45578 — 7.10.1953 to 55493 — 8.7.1954

The electrical system introduced in 1953 was improved considerably, both in appearance and function. The previous two switches in the nacelle were changed to a single, double-banked, combined lighting and ignition switch (Lucas PRS8) and a circular, four-plate Sentercel rectifier of 4½in diameter was specified, replacing the square Westinghouse type. It was still located under the rider's seat.

The wiring was further simplified by the use of a Lucas RM 14 alternator.

The appearance of the machine was altered slightly by the use of the barrel-shaped silencers common to the swinging arm model.

1954 was effectively the last year of the rigid, or spring wheel, Speed Twin, though orders were still being fulfilled in 1955, and the last one of this type was built on June 6, 1955 (engine and frame number 68296). Most of these 1955 spring wheel models were the 5TR variant built for institutional use, usually the police.

Engine The right hand main bearing was increased in size to 1.125 x 2.812 x 0.812in and changed from a roller bearing to a ball journal (engine numbers 54946 to 54985 only).

The remaining 1954 engines up to 55493 reverted to the previous specification, i.e. a roller bearing 1.00 x 2.50 x 0.750in.

Gearbox No change.

Frame No change.

Silencers Barrel-shaped silencers as used on the swinging arm models.

Electrical A Lucas PRS8 combined ignition and lighting switch was used. A 4½in diameter round Sentercel rectifier was fitted under the seat. The alternator was updated by the use of a Lucas RM14 assembly.

The new combined ignition and lighting switch.

A new era dawns

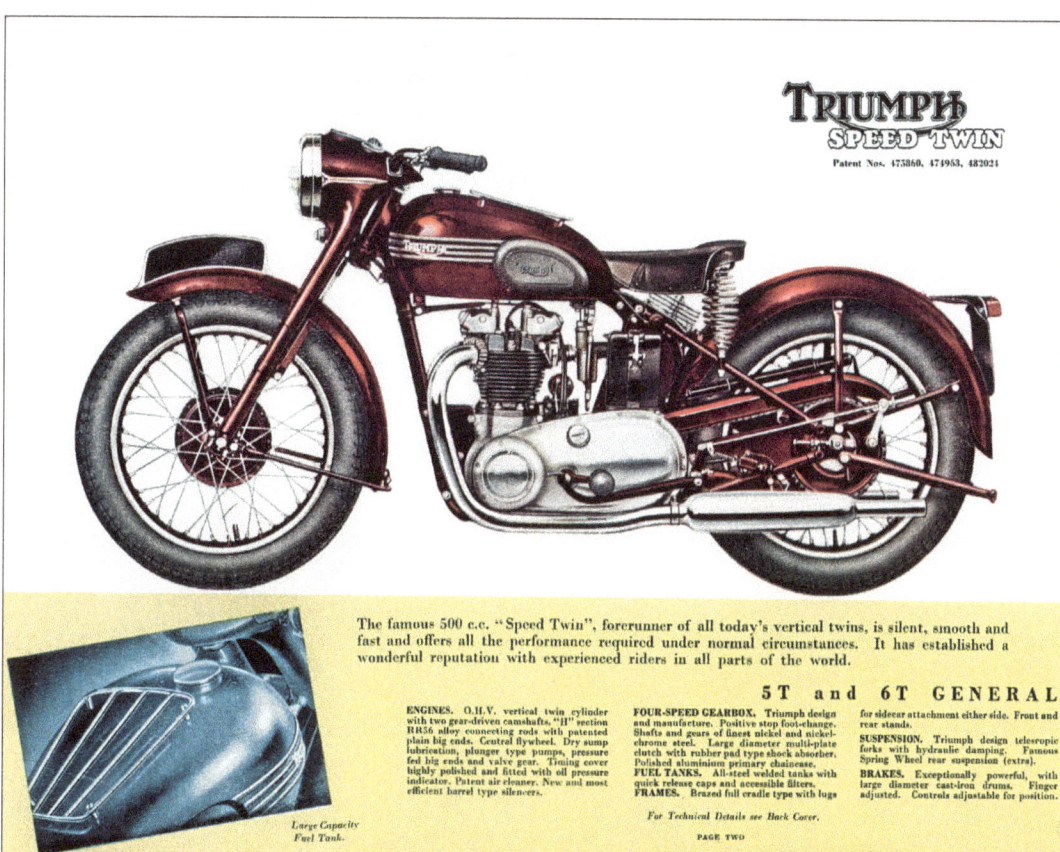

This 1954 view shows the circular rectifier and barrel-shaped silencers; both new items for the year.

Two Southend-on-Sea officers enjoy a run in the sun on 1954 Speed Twins. Legshields were a general fitment on police machines.

The Triumph Speed Twin & Thunderbird Bible

Price £190 16s 0d

Extras
    Spring wheel   £19 4s 0d
    Twinseat   £2 2s 0d
    Pillion footrests   £0 19s 3d
    Prop stand   £0 18s 8d
    Pillion Seat   £2 0s 0d

1955 Model 5T Speed Twin

Engine prefix: 5T
Engine and frame numbers: 55494 — 7.7.1954 to 70196 — 22.7.1955

The appearance of the 1955 Speed Twin was radically changed by the introduction of the swinging arm frame. This was the first major change in the bike's appearance since 1945, when the telescopic front fork was introduced. The new machine still resembled the 1945 model, but it had put on a few pounds in weight.

The Speed Twin gained swinging arm rear suspension in 1955.

The 1955 Speed Twin was the first Triumph model to specify the new Amal Monobloc carburettor.

A more robust crankshaft was introduced that year. It had a larger load capacity bearing on the right hand timing side, and larger big end journals.

As well as the new crankshaft, the 1955 Speed Twin had new, stronger connecting rods, with larger big end bearings.

Engine The timing side main bearing was increased in size to 1.125 x 2.812 x 0.812in and changed from a roller bearing to a ball journal. The crankpin size was increased to 1.6235/1.6240in. The connecting rod big end diameter was increased to 1.6250/1.6255in. Phillips cross head screws replaced the slotted cheese head type.

A sludge tube was fitted to the crankshaft, from engine number 56811, on August 24, 1954.

Engines with numbers 70076 to 70089, from July 20, 1955, were fitted with a 1956 type crankcase and cylinder barrel.

Police riders in Australia — all Triumph mounted.

A new era dawns

A 1955 Speed Twin in police trim for the London Metroplitan Police Force.

Carburettor

Amal Monobloc	376/25
Bore	15/16in
Main jet	200
Needle jet	0.1065
Throttle valve	3½in
Throttle needle	C
Needle position	3 (middle groove)
Pilot jet	130

Transmission

Primary chain	½ x 0.305in x 70 links
Secondary chain	⅝ x ⅜in x 100 links

Gearbox Phillips cross head screws replaced the slotted cheese head type.

The main gearbox casing now had a top pivot fixing to accommodate the swinging arm frame.

The gearbox inner cover was changed to provide an angled cable adjuster that would clear the gearbox mounting plates.

Primary chaincase Phillips cross head screws replaced the slotted cheese head type.

Shorter inner and outer primary cases were fitted to allow for the swinging arm frame. The inner cover now served as the mounting for the stator assembly, and provided more reliable concentricity between stator and rotor, and enabled the air gap between the two to be reduced to 0.008in. Prior to 1955 the stator assay was housed in the primary outer cover which because of the build up of tolerances gave less reliability.

Frame A completely new frame was used for the Speed Twin although it had been fitted to the 1954 Tiger 100 and 110 models. The swinging arm was controlled by Girling suspension units, with 12.9in between the fixing centres.

Front forks A slight modification to improve rigidity was the use of ⅜in diameter stanchion pinch bolts to replace the previous 5/16in ones.

The Triumph Speed Twin & Thunderbird Bible

Mudguards There was no change to the front mudguard, but the rear was completely new, having pressed steel valances spot welded to its sides. The main aim was to disguise the large gap between the wheel and the mudguard, and thereby improve the appearance, especially when the motorcycle was on the centre stand. The valances also provided better weather protection for the rider and passenger.

Wheels No change was made to the front wheel, but the rear dispensed with the old taper roller bearings in favour of ball journal bearings. The quickly detachable wheel used special thin taper bearings in the hub.

Twinseat The two level type was now standard fitment.

Electrical A smaller Sentercel rectifier, of 2¾in diameter (Lucas type FSX 150 1A) replaced the 4½in one. A new, oblong stop/tail lamp with a squared end was fitted. A reflector was built into the lens as a safety feature.

Dimensions
Wheelbase	56in
Seat Height	31in
Ground clearance	5in
Weight	395lb
Overall length	85½in

Price £210 12s 0d

Extras
Prop stand	£0 18s 8d
Pillion footrests	£0 19s 3d
QD wheel	£3 12s 0d

1956 Model 5T Speed Twin

Engine prefix: 5T
Engine and frame numbers: 71642 — 15.9.1955 to 82443 — 26.6.1956 then 0602 — 18.7.1956 to 0932 — 22.8.1956

Most of the changes for 1956 were relatively minor. The exception to this was the use of 650cc 6T crankcases and a cylinder barrel unique to the Speed Twin to accept those crankcases. This modification applied to all 1956, 1957 and 1958 models, right up to the introduction of the unit construction 5TA model.

The most noticeable visual change for 1956 was the relocation of the pilot light. This had always been located on the fork shrouds, just under the headlamp, but, for 1956, a chrome-plated grille occupied this position, so the pilot light was situated within the sealed beam light unit.

To combat petrol tank failures, usually associated with the T100 and T110 sports machines, a new, rubber-mounted rear bracket was standardised on all twin-cylinder models.

Engine From 72028, September 23, 1955, the inlet camshaft had only one hole, to reduce oil being vented through the breather pipe.

The 1956 Speed Twin featured the Amal Monobloc carburettor and a relocated pilot light.

A new era dawns

This is how the much travelled Speed Twin looked after the Triumph Service Department had worked its deft touches on it. Ridden overland from India, it was a very sorry sight when it arrived at the works main gate. The silencers and exhaust pipes were just about functioning, the wheels were far from round, with flattened rims, and the handlebars and controls were totally scrap. Many other parts had been welded and rewelded but, true to tradition, were still performing. The two travellers names are unknown, but second from the left is Export Manager A.J. Mathieu, and fourth from left is Advertising Manager I. Davies.

The conrods were redesigned to use Vandervell shell bearings on the big end journals.

650cc dimensions were employed on the cylinder flange and crankcase joint. As a result, the outer cylinder fixing holes were increased from 2in to 2¼in centres.

Carburettor The Monobloc carburettor sealing at the flange joint was improved by the addition of an O-ring.

Transmission A new friction material (Neo-Langite stick on pads) was used on the clutch friction plates.

Forks A chrome-plated grille replaced the underslung pilot light. The end plug of the hydraulic damper tube was redesigned to prevent bottoming during hard braking.

Frame Sidecar lugs were incorporated onto the main frame, and adjustable steering lock stops were fitted to the steering head lug. The top steering stem cup and cone were increased in size and made interchangeable with the bottom ones. As a result, the bearings were changed to 40 x ¼in ball. A fully rubber-mounted rear tank bracket was fitted.

The Triumph Speed Twin & Thunderbird Bible

Petrol tank A chrome-plated centre band was fitted to cover the centre weld. To miss the centre band on the tank, the middle bar of the tank grid was deleted, and a two bar grid introduced as a replacement.

Wheels The wheel rims were no longer painted but, instead, had a plain chrome finish.

Handlebars A new type of handlebar was fitted, with the threaded hole for the horn push deleted.

Electrical A new style wiring harness incorporated a 1mm thick plastic sheath. The pilot light was relocated in the sealed beam reflector. A combined horn and dip switch was mounted on the clutch lever clamp bracket to replace the two separate items used previously.

Price £217 4s 0d

Extras

Prop stand	£0 18s 8d
Pillion footrests	£0 19s 3d
QD rear wheel	£3 12s 0d

1957 Model 5T Speed Twin

Engine prefix: 5T
Engine and frame numbers: 01797 — 19.9.1956 to 010253 — 20.8.1957

The main visual changes for 1957 were the full-width front hub and the new 'basket weave' petrol tank badges.

The front brake, apart from the use of straight pull spokes, had little else to offer with the added disadvantage of increased weight.

Most of the other changes were of a minor, progressive nature, mainly aimed at eradicating customer complaints from the previous year. The changes mostly applied to other models in the programme, though the Speed Twin benefitted as these changes were applied across the board.

All Speed Twins built for police use have a W-suffix to the engine number.

Engine A garter-type oil seal was fitted to the drive side crankcase to prevent oil transference between the engine and the primary chaincase. The engine sprocket boss was machined to suit.

Gearbox The high gear sleeve bush was extended to protrude into the primary chaincase, and ensured that any oil leakage along the bush would be caught in the primary case. The bush could be fitted retrospectively, providing the sliding plate on the inner chaincase was modified to accept the bush.

Transmission More resilient and oil-proof drive and rebound rubbers were fitted to the shock absorber unit.

New tank motifs, full-width front brake, relocated coil, and extended chainguard identify this as a 1957 model.

A new era dawns

Front forks A more robust method of mounting the front wheel spindle, comprising split half clamps and ⁵⁄₁₆in bolts, was specified. The loose clips holding the front mudguard centre stay were dispensed with, and bottom members with welded-on lugs substituted.

Petrol tank Basket weave tank badges (chrome-plated with an amaranth red background) were fitted. Two horizontal chrome strips, one front and one rear, finished off the embellishment. A new tank with the appropriate screw pommels was required.

Wheels A 7in diameter, full-width, cast iron drum was introduced. This featured a steel pressed hub and double-butted, straight pull spokes. The brake shoes were retained by an alloy anchor plate, and a chrome styling plate was fitted on the opposite side.

Chainguard The chainguard remained basically the same as the previous years, but the rear end covering the sprocket was extended to prevent chain lubricant being thrown onto the machine.

Exhaust system Strengthened exhaust pipe brackets and added silencer brackets improved the method of mounting.

Controls A new front brake cable was fitted, with the cable adjuster and stop moved to the centre mudguard stay bracket position.

Electrical The ignition coil was repositioned and fitted above the distributor.

Weight 395lb

Price £251 14s 5d

Extras

Prop stand	£0 19s 3d
Pillion footrests	£0 19s 11d
QD rear wheel	£3 14s 5d

1958 Model 5T Speed Twin

Engine prefix: 5T
Engine and frame numbers: 011116 — 20.9.1957 to 0200074 — 28.8.1958

1958 saw the introduction of the controversial auto clutch, or, as Triumph designated it, the Slickshift. The idea behind this development was that gear changes could be achieved without the use of the hand-operated clutch lever (though, quite why anyone would want to was never determined). All one could say in its favour was that, should clutch cable failure occur, the machine could still be ridden until a repair was made. It seemed quite a penalty to offset such a rare occurrence.

When using the Slickshift it was rather unnerving to see the handlebar clutch lever move in and out each time the gearchange was operated.

The full-width front brake drum.

The new end cover on the gearbox houses the 'Slickshift' mechanism.

The Triumph Speed Twin & Thunderbird Bible

A typical Speed Twin power and torque graph.

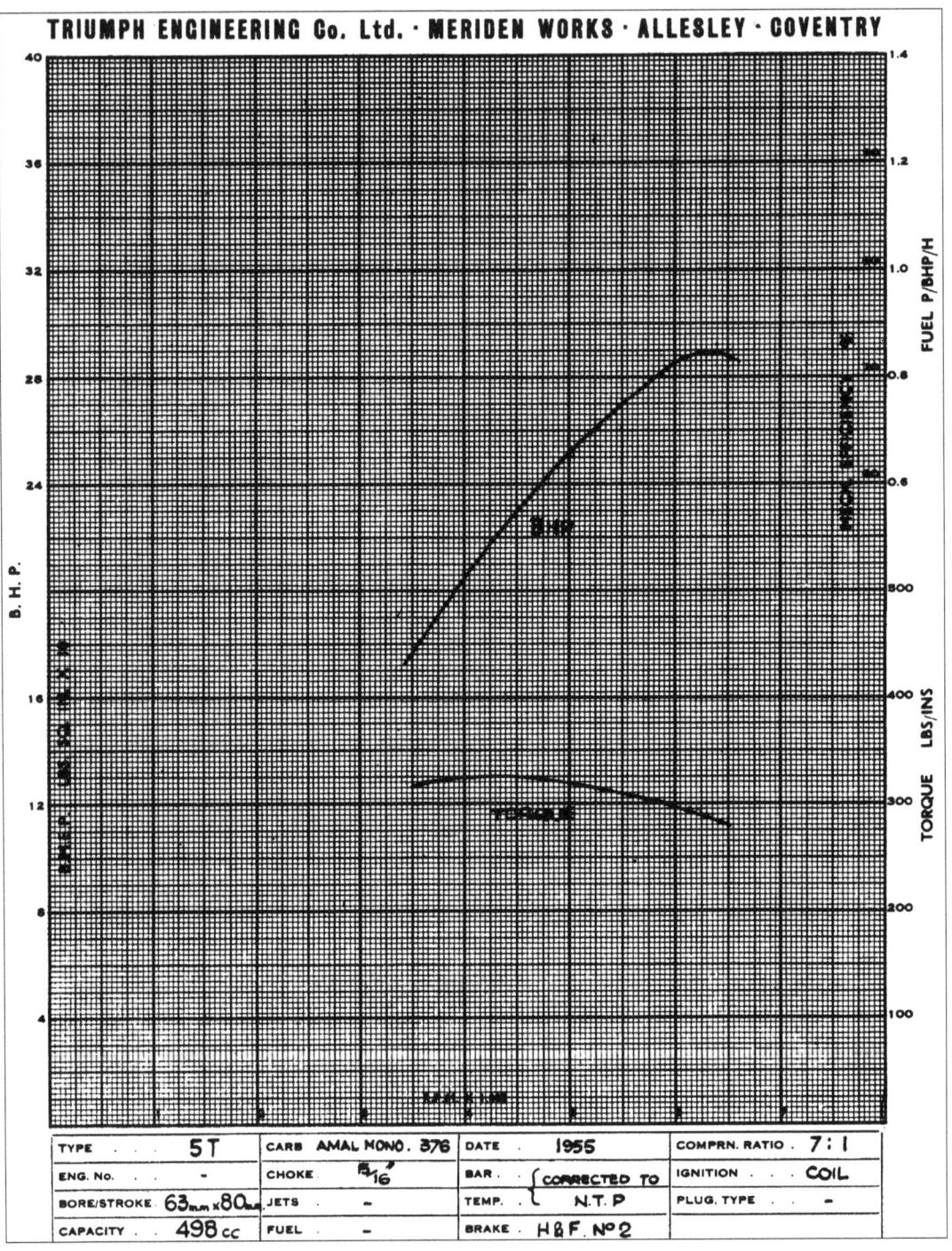

Press comments regarding the Slickshift were not very positive: *Motorcycling* reported "Unfortunately, the booted foot is less sensitive than the rider's hand" and said "The revs had to be about right, or there was noticeable evidence of strain on the transmission." A final word on this was provided by Bob Mcintyre after some miles testing Shell X 100 motor oil using a T110 "This thing will maim someone," was his comment to Frank Baker, Head of Triumph Experimental, upon returning the machine to the Works, although he actually used somewhat stronger words!

1958 also saw the introduction of an anti-theft lock. This took the form of a slot cut in the steering stem which, when the steering was turned to full-left lock, aligned with a tube in the head lug (the lock was inserted into this tube). Strangely, the lock and key were catalogued as an optional extra.

A new era dawns

Modifications for 1958 included valanced mudguards, a fluted front brake cover, and an easy-lift centre stand.

> The Triumph Speed Twin in its all amaranth red finish is possibly the best known motorcycle in the world today. It was the first of all the modern vertical twins and established the overwhelming popularity of this type of engine—designed, developed and proved entirely by Triumph. Chosen by over 150 police and similar bodies for its complete reliability and silent performance.
> *Full Specification on pages 10/11.*

Senior police officers were invited to inspect a fully-equipped Speed Twin. The legshields and the engine cowling are left and right hand one-piece mouldings. An Avon fairing completes the specification.

Safety bars and spot lamps have been added.

A very welcome modification concerned the oil tank filler cap. This was relocated towards the centre of the machine to obviate the painful contact that could occur with the rider's inside thigh when kickstarting.

The most obvious change was to the front and rear mudguards. These were now deep-drawn pressings with the side valances in one piece with the mudguard. Prior to this, the side valances had been spot welded to the mudguard, and rusting could occur at this joint.

Engine No change.

Gearbox The gearbox was modified to accept the auto clutch, or Slickshift as it was termed. This entailed new gearbox inner and outer covers, with the clutch cable stop being transferred from the top of the inner cover to the primary chain adjuster drawbolt. The cable adjuster at the gearbox end was dispensed with. A rubber sleeve on the kickstart spindle was introduced in the interests of better oil retention.

Frame An anti-theft steering lock was introduced.

Oil tank The oil tank filler cap was relocated to the centre of the machine to prevent fouling during kickstarting.

Front forks New mounting lugs for the centre mudguard stay were introduced on the inside of the fork member, giving a much neater and cleaner appearance.

The front brake cable stop was moved to the bottom of the right hand fork leg, with no adjuster at this point.

The top fork nacelle was modified by passing the brake and clutch cables through small grommets to provide easier routing and operation. The steering damper hole in the nacelle top was made larger.

Controls New clutch and brake cables were fitted, and had detachable barrel nipples at the lever ends. The front brake cable was extended to the bottom of the right hand lower fork leg, dispensing with the steel tube (which had been in use since 1945) over its lower run.

Mudguards Both mudguards were now manufactured from deep pressings. On the front mudguard, the two forward stays were dispensed with and a new centre stay was added.

The last pre-unit 1958 Speed Twin to be built as a production batch was 020074, August 29, 1958. However, there were a few were assembled in 1959 and these were:

Quantity		
1	020376	17.9.1958
24	022663-022687	10.12.1958
6	023699-023704	6.1.1959
9	023925-023933	2.2.1959

It's fairly safe to assume that these machines would closely follow the 1958 specification, but they may have had 1959 modifications added, such as:

Gearbox oil level indicator incorporated in the gearbox inner cover.

Induction–hardened gearbox camplate.

Front brake cam lever angle changed to give better brake operation.

Price £253 4s 11d

Extras

Prop stand	£0 19s 4d
Pillion footrests	£1 0s 0d
Steering lock	£0 13s 4d
QD rear wheel	£3 14s 11d

Chapter 4
Excitement & demise

The Model 5TA Speed Twin 1959-1966

A completely new design of Speed Twin was produced for 1959. With a capacity of 490cc, it closely followed the design of the existing 348cc model 21/3TA, but had an oversquare bore and stroke.

Based upon the 3TA, which had already been on sale for two years, the 5TA was expected to be relatively trouble-free: and so it proved.

Apart from the colour (the 5TA retained the Amaranth Red) there was very little in common with the earlier 5T. With its large valanced front mudguard and total rear enclosure, it had few sporting pretences. It was aimed more at the type of motorcyclist who wanted civilised, clean motorcycling, with the minimum of attention.

With its smaller frame and wheels (17in diameter) and its unit construction engine and gearbox, it weighed 35 pounds less than its predecessor.

The overhead valve gear was operated by high camshafts at the front and rear of the cylinder on the right hand side, these camshafts ran directly in the crankcase, with no bushes. On the left hand side, they ran in steel backed, thin-wall bronze bushes.

The completely redesigned Speed Twin for 1959.

The Triumph Speed Twin & Thunderbird Bible

The crankshaft assembly consisted of two parts. A one-piece forged steel crankshaft, over which was threaded a cast iron flywheel, was held to the crankshaft by three high-tensile bolts around its periphery. The crankshaft ran on a plain bush on the right hand side, and a large ball bearing on the left hand side. End float was determined by locking the crankshaft, via the alternator rotor and engine sprocket, to the left hand bearing.

The connecting rods were of H-section hiduminium alloy, bushed at the gudgeon pin end and with steel-backed shell bearings at the big end. Steel caps formed the bottom half of the big end/connecting rod.

The cylinder material was best grade cast iron with the cylinder bores machined directly into it. The cylinder head was of aluminium alloy, as were the rocker boxes. The rockers ran directly on steel spindles with no bushes, a method Triumph had used since the early Speed Twin in 1937.

Ignition was supplied by a Lucas distributor located behind the cylinder block, and driven by a pair of skew gears from the inlet camshaft.

An Amal 375/75 carburettor of $\frac{7}{8}$in bore supplied the mixture, the choke being of the spring-loaded plunger type, on top of the carburettor.

The Triumph manufactured gearbox had four speeds and was foot-controlled from the right side. The gearbox casting was integral with the engine crankcase. Primary drive waso way by duplex chain, with a slipper tensioner blade to provide adjustment.

The shock absorber was integrated with the clutch and comprised a four-paddle centre with rubber blocks in compression.

The frame was of the single down tube pattern, and had only a single lower tank rail (the petrol tank forming the upper member when bolted in position).

The telescopic front forks gave 6in of movement, and hydraulic damping was used to give an hydraulic lock on full depression and extension to prevent clashing.

The 3½-gallon steel petrol tank had a Ceandes turn-cam filler cap. A petrol tap was fitted on the left hand side, and provided a main and reserve position.

The oil tank was constructed of welded steel and was positioned under the side panels on the right hand side of the frame.

The Triumph brakes were 7in diameter; the front housed in a full-width cast iron hub with an alloy back plate, the rear (also of cast iron but having a steel back plate) integral with the rear sprocket. The front brake was cable-operated, while the rear was operated by a rod.

Both wheels were 17in diameter, with WM2 chrome steel rims. The front tyre was a 3.25in ribbed section, and the rear was a 3.50 Universal (both Dunlop).

The front mudguard was a deep valanced type, with a flared bottom end; the rear was a simple flat blade under the rear fairing.

A rubber tool tray with individually-moulded tool compartments was fitted above the rear mudguard under the Twinseat (hinged on the left hand side). The seat fixing plunger had a removable knob, which gave a degree of security.

The centre stand was fitted with an extension arm which provided a 'roll-on' facility when stood on. A prop stand was fitted to the left hand lower frame rail. The exhaust system had two, 1½in diameter pipes terminating into two barrel-shaped silencers with offset entry points.

The 6-volt electrical system was charged by a Lucas alternator via a rectifier. A single 6-volt coil was located on the rear mudguard and supplied the high tension voltage via a distributor.

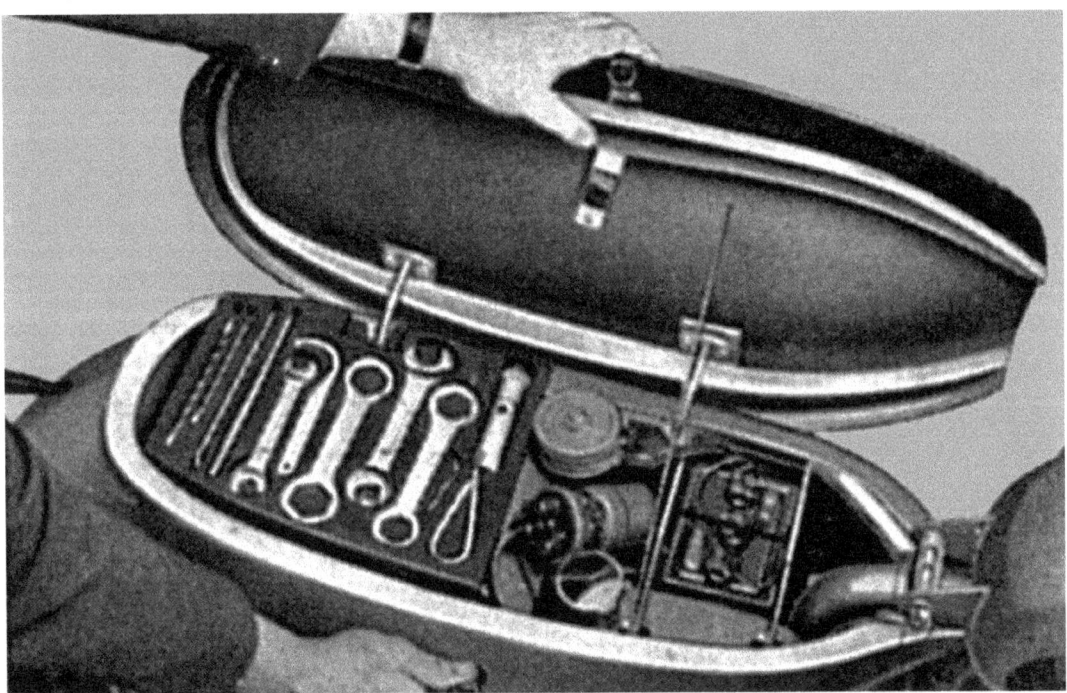

A tool tray with appropriately-shaped tool holders.

Excitement & demise

The 7in sealed beam headlamp and pilot light were controlled by a combined ignition and light switch (Lucas PRS8). An ammeter, like the ignition switch, was housed in the nacelle top. The horn was also located in the nacelle housing, and was operated by a combined push and light dip switch on the clutch lever.

The handlebars were 1in diameter, with a Triumph twistgrip, and both clutch and brake levers were fitted with knurled adjusters.

A plain dial 120mph Smiths speedometer was fitted, driven from the rear wheel via a speedometer gearbox.

The finish was Amaranth Red on all painted parts except the steering damper knob, pillion footrests, number plates, and front hub.

Technical details

Engine
Bore	69mm (2.716in)
Stroke	65.5mm (2.578in)
Capacity	490cc (30in³)
bhp	27 at 6500
Compression ratio	7.0:1

Cylinder head
Material	Aluminium alloy
Valve seat angle	45°
Valve seat width	
Inlet	0.050/0.060in
Exhaust	0.060/0.080in
Valve guide bore	0.4980/0.4985in

Valves
Stem diameter	
Inlet	0.3095/0.3100in
Exhaust	0.3090/0.3095in
Head diameter	
Inlet	1⁷⁄₁₆in
Exhaust	1⁵⁄₁₆in

Valve guides
Material	Chilled cast iron
Bore diameter	0.312/0.313in
Outside diameter	0.5005/0.5100in
Length	
Inlet	1.750in
Exhaust	1.750in

Valve springs
Inner	1½ ± ¹⁄₁₆in
Outer	1²¹⁄₃₂ ± ¹⁄₁₆in
Fitted load	63lb

Cam followers
Foot radius	0.750in
Stem diameter	0.311/0.3115in
Overall length nominal	2.775in

Valve clearances — cold
Inlet and exhaust	0.010in

Valve timing
IVO	26½°	BTDC
IVC	69½°	ABDC
EVO	61½°	BBDC
EVC	35½°	ATDC

0.020in clearance for checking the timing

Push rods
Material	Solid aluminium alloy with end caps at top only
Overall length	4.820/4.845in

Rockers
Bore diameter	0.4375/0.4380in
Spindle diameter	0.4355/0.4360in

Camshafts and bearings
Journal diameter	
Left hand	0.8100/0.8105in
Right hand	1.4355/1.436in
End float	0.013/0.020in
Lobe height	1.047/1.055in

Bush diameter
Left hand bore	0.8125/0.8135in
Left hand outer length	
LH inlet	1.094/1.0114in
LH exhaust	0.922/0.942in
RH housing diameter	1.437/1.4375in

Cylinder barrel
Material	Cast iron
Cylinder bore diameter	2.716/2.7165in
Maximum tolerable wear	0.007in
Tappet guide bore diameter	0.9985/0.9990in

Tappet block
Outer diameter	0.9995/1.000in
Tappet bore diameter	0.312/0.3125in

Piston rings
Ring gap in cylinder bore	
Compression ring	0.010/0.014in
Scraper ring	0.010/0.014in
Ring thickness	
Compression ring	0.0615/0.625in
Scraper ring	0.124/0.125in
Clearance in piston groove	
Compression ring	0.001/0.003in
Scraper ring	0.001/0.0025in

Pistons
Clearance in cylinder at maximum diameter (90° to gudgeon pin)	0.003/0.0045in
Gudgeon pin diameter	0.6882/0.6886in

Connecting rods
Small end bush outer diameter	0.782/0.783in
Small end bush length	0.890/0.910in
Small end diameter fitted	0.6905/0.6910in
Big end diameter	1.4385/1.4390in

Side clearance (fitted)	0.008/0.012in		Clutch rod length	9.562/9.567in
Length between centres	5.311/5.313in		Clutch plate segment	3/32in thickness
Bearing big end shell	Vandervell			

Crankshaft
Crankpin diameter　1.4375/1.4380in

Main bearing journals
Diameter	1.8135/1.8140in
Drive side	1.1805/1.1808in
Timing side	1.4375/1.4380in
Crankshaft end float	Nil with rotor nut tightened
Balance factor	52%

Crankshaft bearings
Drive side ball race	72 x 30 x 19mm
Timing side bush bore	1.4385/1.4390in
Time side bush outer	1.8115/1.8120in
Bearing type LH	Ball race
Bearing type RH	Vandervell VP3 bush

Oil pump
Feed plunger diameter	0.3744/0.3747in
Scavenge plunger diameter	0.4869/0.4872in
Feed bore	0.3748/0.3753in
Scavenge bore	0.4873/0.4878in

Carburettor
Type	375/3 Amal monobloc
Bore	7/8in
Main jet	160
Needle jet	0.105
Needle	B
Needle position	3
Throttle valve	375/3
Pilot jet	25

Ignition
Timing	1/64in BTC fully retarded
Distributor type	Lucas 18132 clockwise
Advance range (distributor)	15° (30° crankshaft)
Points gap	0.0012in

Spark plug　N5 Champion
Plug gap	0.020in
Thread size	14mm
Reach	3/4in

Clutch
Friction plates	4
Plain plates	5
Pressure springs	4
Spring free length	1.400/1.500in
Bearing rollers	20
Bearing size	
Diameter	0.2495/0.250in
Length	0.231/0.236in
Hub bearing diameter	1.3733/1.3743in
Sprocket bore diameter	1.8745/1.8755in
Clutch rod diameter	3/16in

Kickstart mechanism
Kickstart spindle diameter	1.060/1.0605in
Kickstart bore diameter	1.062/1.0625in

Gearchange mechanism
Quadrant plunger diameter	0.3402/0.3412in
Plunger bore diameter	0.3427/0.3437in
Plunger spring No. of coils	16
Plunger spring free length	1 1/16in

Footchange spindle
Diameter RH	0.621/0.6215in
Bush diameter RH	0.623/0.624in

Quadrant springs
Free length	1 7/8in
No. of coils	18

Camplate plunger
Plunger diameter	0.4360/0.4365in
Housing bore	0.4375/0.4380in
Spring length	2 1/2in
No. of coils	22

Mainshaft
Bearing LH	30 x 62 x 16mm ball
Bearing RH	17 x 47 x 14mm ball
Mainshaft diameter LH	0.7495/0.750in
Mainshaft sleeve bush	
Bore diameter	0.7520/0.7530in
Outside diameter	0.910/0.912in
Length overall	2 19/32in

Layshaft
Bearing diameter LH	0.6845/0.6850in
Bearing diameter RH	0.6870/0.6875in
Bush bore LH	0.6865/0.6885in
Bush outside diameter LH	0.8755/0.8760in
Bush bore RH	0.689/0.690in
Bush outside diameter RH	0.8125/0.8130in

Number of teeth on pinions

Layshaft		Mainshaft
18T	4th	26T
23T	3rd	28T
28T	2nd	23T
32T	1st	19T

Sprockets
Solo
Engine	26
Clutch	58
Gearbox	19
Rear wheel	43

Gear ratios internal
4th	1.00
3rd	1.19

Excitement & demise

2nd	1.76
1st	2.43

Overall ratios
4th	5.05
3rd	6.00
2nd	8.9
1st	12.3
rpm at 10mph top gear	720

Chains
Primary endless	⅜ x ¼in x 78 link duplex
Secondary	⅝ x ⅜in x 102 link

Frame — Steering head bearings
Top	24 x 3/16in diam ball
Bottom	24 x 3/16in diam ball

Swinging arm pivot
Bush bore	0.8745/0.8750in
Spindle diameter	0.8735/0.8740in
Spindle housing (frame)	0.8725/0.8730in
Maximum side play	0.015in

Frame head angle 67°

Rear suspension
Unit type	Girling SB4
Length between centres	11⅜in
Spring rate	145lb colour blue/yellow
Spring free length	8 3/16in

Front fork
Stanchion diameter	1.3025/1.3030in
Top bush inner diameter	1.3065/1.3075in
Top bush outer diameter	1.498/1.499in
Top bush overall length	0.995/1.005in
Bottom bush inner diameter	1.2485/1.2495in
Bottom bush outer diameter	1.4935/1.4945in
Bottom bush overall length	0.870/0.875in
Fork leg bore	1.498/1.500in
Spring free length	17¾in
Wire diameter	0.160in

Wheels
Rim size front and rear	WM2 x 17in

Tyres
Front	3.25 x 17in Dunlop ribbed
Rear	3.50 x 17in Dunlop Universal
Pressures front/rear	20psi

Wheel bearings
Front	20 x 47 x 14mm ball journal
Rear standard	20 x 47 x 14mm ball journal
Rear quickly detachable	¾ x 1 27/32 x 9/16in Timkin taper roller

Spokes
Front	40 x butted 80/10 gauge, overall length 5 1/16in straight
Rear	20 x butted 80/10 gauge, overall length 7⅛in 110°
	20 x butted 80/10 gauge, overall length 7⅛in 90°

Wheel offset

Front — Dimension from drum edge to centre of rim: 1½in

Rear — dimension from outer edge of sprocket to centre of rim: 3 5/32in

A 1959 sidecar-kitted frame.

The Triumph Speed Twin & Thunderbird Bible

Electrical
Alternator	Lucas RM 13/5
Voltage	6V
Earth	Positive
Battery	Lucas 6V PUZ7E-11
Horn	Lucas type HF 1441
Headlamp	Lucas 7in pre-focus
Tail lamp	Lucas 564
Bulb main	6V 30/24W
Bulb pilot	6V 3W
Bulb speed	6V 3W
Bulb tail/stop	6V 8W
Coil	Lucas 6V MA6
Distributor	Lucas 18132 clockwise
Rectifier	Lucas FSX 18498
Stop switch	Lucas 6SA (D-shape)

Dimensions
Wheelbase	52¾in
Overall length	81in
Overall width	26in
Seat height	29¼in
Weight	350lb
Ground clearance	5in

Lubrication
Engine	
Summer	SAE 40-50
Winter	SAE 20-30
Gearbox	EP 90
Primary case	SAE 20

Telescopic fork
Summer	SAE 30
Winter	SAE 20

Capacities
Fuel tank	3½gal (16L)
Oil tank	5 pt (2.8L)
Gearbox	⅔pt (375cc)
Primary case	½pt (300cc)
Telescopic fork	⅓pt (150cc)

Torque settings model 5TA
	lb/ft
Flywheel bolts	33
Connecting rod bolt nuts	26
Cylinder head bolts	18
Kickstart ratchet pinion nut	40
Clutch centre nut	50
Rotor fixing nut	50
Stator fixing nuts	10
Stanchion pinch bolt nuts	25
Gearbox sprocket nut	80
Fork top nuts	80
Camshaft pinion nuts	50
Crankshaft pinion nut	50

Left hand threads
Camshaft pinion nuts.

1959 Model 5TA Speed Twin

Engine prefix: 5TA
Engine and frame numbers: H5 785 — 25.9.1958 to H11032 — 21.8.1959

Engine Taper-faced compression rings were fitted to pistons from H7116, December 2, 1958.

Price £237 12s 0d

Extras
Prop stand	£0 18s 9d
Pillion footrests	£0 19s 4d
QD wheel	£3 12s 5d

1959 Speed Twin road test

The new, unit construction Speed Twin was, to all intents and purposes, identical to the already established 350cc model Twenty One. Typically Triumph, it had all the attributes one had come to expect from this manufacturer. It combined the weight of a lightish 350cc with true 500cc performance.

Its style may have been rather unorthodox, when compared with previous Speed Twins, but with its sleek lines and partial enclosure it could be thoroughly cleaned in 10-15 minutes, a point appreciated by the majority of riders.

With its square (69 x 65.5mm) bore and stroke giving a short engine, as well as the integral gearbox, no 500cc could be more compact. Compactness was a feature of the whole machine. Wheel diameter was 17in, saddle height 28½in, wheelbase 52in, and the total weight 350 pounds.

All the controls were fully adjustable, with knurled cable adjusters integrated into the front brake and clutch control levers. The combined horn button and dip switch was positioned conveniently close to the left handlebar grip.

On the open road at 60-65mph, only a muted drone with no mechanical noise was detectable. Acceleration was clean and impressive, yet the engine was perfectly happy in top gear at 25mph. At the other end of the scale, 85mph was comfortably clocked. The unit was leak free except for a slight seep at the oil pressure indicator button.

Starting was faultless. Full choke operated by a spring-loaded plunger on top of the carburettor was required when cold, but when warm the unit responded to a gentle prod from the kickstart. The ease of starting was, no doubt, aided by the coil ignition system used.

The transmission worked well, but if held in third gear one became conscious of gearbox whine. All indirect gears were noisy by Triumph standards but third was especially so. The gear pedal movement was light, with slightly more travel than previously, and, as before, really silent changes required a slight pause in pedal travel. Downward changes could be made just as fast as the controls could be operated. As was usual with Triumphs, the clutch needed to be freed before starting by depressing the kickstart pedal with the clutch disengaged to ensure quiet bottom gear engagement.

The Speed Twin's steering was characteristically light, to the point that, on greasy surfaces, it could be a shade too light to give a truly positive feeling. Straightahead steering, however, was true, and negotiating sharpish corners a delight. There appeared no limit to the angle to which the machine could be leaned over.

Long, sweeping bends could be treated as if they did not exist. On bumpy surfaces, though, the suspension gave the impression that the spring poundage could be reduced, both fore and aft.

Brakes worked well, the centre stand was exemplary, with its roll-on tread down lever requiring no effort on the part of the rider. The prop stand held the machine steady, even on cambers, and could easily be operated by the foot due to the extended lever.

Finally, mudguarding scored 99 out of 100 for its efficiency.

Maximum speeds
   Top gear (4.8 to 1)   87mph
   Third gear (5.62 to 1)   77mph
   Second gear (8.35 to 1)   54mph

Fuel consumption
   Urban   62mph
   Overall   75mph

Braking from 30mph
   Both brakes   29ft 6in

1960 Model 5TA Speed Twin

Engine prefix: 5TA
Engine and frame numbers: H11962 — 8.10.1959 to H18626 — 1.9.1960

Engine The main bearing bush housing on the right hand side was retained by a locking plate and screw to prevent lateral movement from H12014, October 10, 1959.

Gearbox No change.

Transmission A primary chain adjuster was introduced at H13115, on December 3, 1959. The rear sprocket size was reduced to 43 teeth from 46 and the gear ratios were changed accordingly (to 5.33, 6.32, 9.37 and 12.96) from H11962, October 8, 1959.

Finish The traditional Speed Twin Amaranth Red was abandoned, after 22 consecutive years, in favour of a brighter red from H11692, October 8, 1959.

Price £227 19s 8d

Extras
   Prop stand   £0 18s 9d
   Pillion footrests £0 19s 4d
   QD rear wheel   £3 12s 5d

1960 Speed Twin

The Triumph Speed Twin & Thunderbird Bible

Stylishly modern in every detail and with an exciting performance, the famous Triumph Speed Twin is a firm favourite with discerning riders in every part of the world. Light in weight, easy to handle and with first-class brakes and roadholding it typifies the modern trend to refinement in motorcycling.

All Speed Twins for 1961 were now finished in ruby red.

1961 Model 5TA Speed Twin

Engine prefix: 5TA
Engine and frame numbers: H19215 — 6.11.1960 to H24755 — 22.8.1961

Engine Crown shaved timing gears were fitted to give a quieter operation from H19215, November 11, 1960.

Gearbox A 20-tooth gearbox sprocket was fitted from H19215, November 6, 1960. The low gear bush was staked to prevent movement from H23348, June 2, 1961.

Frame The steering head angle was changed to 67° from H19215, November 6, 1960.

Brakes The front and rear brakes were modified to a fully floating brake shoe arrangement from H19215, November 6, 1960. These new type shoes can be fitted retrospectively.

Tool tray The nice, but not very waterproof sponge rubber toolholder was replaced by a steel fabrication, fitted between the battery and the oil tank.

Price £243 13s 3d

Extras
Prop stand   £0 19s 11d
Pillion footrests £0 19s 11d
QD rear wheel   £3 16s 0d

Policemen collect their new mounts from the factory — spring 1961.

Excitement & demise

The famous "Speed Twin" in its rich ruby red finish is similar in most details to the "Twenty-one" but enjoys the enhanced power output of a 500 c.c. engine. A smooth running model with many attractive features which will appeal to the discriminating and experienced rider.

Patent Nos. 475860, 723073, 684685

1962 Model 5TA Speed Twin

Engine prefix: 5TA
Engine and frame numbers: H25904 — 26.9.1961 to H29727 — 24.9.1962

There were only a few alterations to the 1962 models, and those that were made were aimed at eliminating customer complaints and reducing the cost to the company.

Engine Modified head bolts with extended hexagon portions for easier spanner application were fitted from H29151, June 30, 1962.

Gearbox The clutch cable could now be replaced without having to remove the gearbox outer cover. The cable was attached to a spoke and a threaded thimble housed in a sleeve screwed into the outer cover. The change was made from H25904, September 26, 1961.

Front fork The steering damper assembly was deleted as a cost reduction exercise, and the hole in the nacelle top was plugged by a rubber grommet from H25904, September 26, 1961.

Exhaust system A siamese, downswept right hand exhaust system, with a single barrel-shaped silencer with a concentric entry for the exhaust pipe was fitted from H25904, September 26, 1961.

Electrical The sheath covering the distributor and the high tension leads was deleted. A Lucas 8H electric horn was fitted, and the alternator was changed to a Lucas RM19 from H25904, on September 26, 1961.

Finish The red finish introduced for 1960 was changed slightly, and was described by Triumph as Ruby Red.

Price £253 19s 4d

The 1962 Speed Twin featured a grey top and trim band twin seat, along with a siamesed exhaust system.

A works photo of a 1962 show model. The siamesed exhaust system is just visible.

The Triumph Speed Twin & Thunderbird Bible

Extras
Prop stand £1 2s 9d
Pillion footrests £1 2s 1d
QD rear wheel £4 2s 10d

1963 Model 5TA Speed Twin

Engine prefix: 5TA
Engine and frame numbers: H30289 — 1.11.1962 to H32361 — 1.8.1963

Engine Due to the persistent loss of rocker box inspection caps, retaining spring clips were introduced. Fitting under the rocker box fixing nuts and bearing on the milled edge of the inspection cap, the clips were fitted from H32118, July 10, 1963.

Transmission A three-vane shock absorber unit in the clutch centre gave improved movement and a smoother cushioning effect. The clutch was redesigned with the object of reducing low speed rattle. The clutch load was taken directly on the sprocket face by a thrust washer located between the sprocket and clutch hub. The rear chain was lengthened to 102 links.

Front fork New oil seals with larger sealing areas were fitted from H30289 to give better oil retention.

Chainguard Two ³⁄₁₆in holes were pierced in the rear chainguard to provide a mounting for the repositioned stop lamp switch.

Wheels Grease retaining washers were fitted inboard of the hub bearings on both front and rear wheels. The rear brake drum/sprocket-to-hub nuts were changed to self locking types, and the lock tab washers were deleted. The rear wheel spokes received minor alterations and now comprised:

20 x left hand side 8/10G x 7⅛in x 90°
20 x right hand side 8/10G x 7⅜in x 90°

Exhaust system The exhaust system reverted to the 1961 type, with two separate left and right hand pipes and silencers.

Electrical A miniature Lucas 2DS 506 silicon rectifier was fitted from H30289. A pull-type Lucas 31383 stop switch was mounted on the rear chainguard, and was operated through a spring attached to the rear brake rod.

Finish Cherry Red was now the official colour.

Price £274 4s 0d

Extras
Prop stand £1 4s 8d
Pillion footrests £1 4s 0d
QD rear wheel £4 9s 5d

1964 Model 5TA Speed Twin

Engine prefix: 5TA
Engine and frame numbers: H32918 — 14.10.1963 to H35986 — 6.7.1964

The 1964 Speed Twin looked very different from the 1963 model. Not only had it lost its red finish, but it had also lost the full rear enclosure. 1964 also saw the introduction of coil ignition, activated by twin contact breakers which were driven by the exhaust camshaft and housed in the timing cover. Less obvious, were the new front forks with external springs, and the smaller diameter handlebars with new control levers and twistgrip. These changes were a first for the Speed Twin, as all telescopic forks since 1943 had featured internal springs, and the Triumph-manufactured twistgrip had been a well-recognised trademark dating back to 1937.

Little change for the 1963 Speed Twin.

Excitement & demise

Engine New crankcases with the provision for the contact breaker lead to pass through them were fitted. A threaded plug filled the hole left by the, now obsolete, distributor, until unchained crankcases became available.

A new exhaust camshaft with an internal taper on the drive end was fitted to accommodate the 4CA Lucas auto advance unit.

A new timing cover was specified with a housing adjacent to the end of the exhaust camshaft to carry the 4CA twin contact breaker and condenser assemblies.

Pushrod cover tube sealing was improved by the use of square section sealing rings top and bottom. This necessitated the use of new cover tubes and tappet blocks.

Gearbox The selector camplate was induction hardened to give better wearing properties adjacent to the plunger track. Additionally, a bridging strap was incorporated, spanning the selector slots, to prevent these widening in use.

The clutch operation was improved by the use of a lift mechanism, similar to that fitted on the larger Triumph twins. It comprised two steel pressings with three indents in each, and three steel ⅜in ball bearings interposed between them. Rotation of the plate caused the bearings to ride up the indents and move the push rod. Advantages included a lighter clutch action and better wearing properties.

Front fork The fork was completely redesigned, and featured external springs of 8¾in length x 0.192in wire diameter. Larger seal holders were fitted, with a seal of 1.875 x 0.435 x 1.235in. The fork sliders contained a short taper oil restrictor to provide damping, and a hydraulic stop on full bump position. New separate spring and headlamp nacelle covers completed the changes.

Handlebars These were shaped as before, but the diameter was reduced from 1 to ⅞ in. The U-bolt fixings and the top fork yoke were left at 1in diameter and four packing pieces were added to take up the difference.

Controls The reduced handlebar diameter meant fitting new clutch and brake lever assemblies. As well as being different in diameter, to aid cable removal, the actual clamp bracket was slotted, as was the adjuster and lock ring. Fixed-barrel cable nipples were reintroduced, replacing the loose barrel nipples required with the previous non-slotted clamp brackets. A standard Amal twistgrip, and shorter Amal handlebar grips replaced the Triumph ones.

Petrol tank A revised petrol tank was fitted, with recesses either side of the centre tunnel to accommodate the two ignition coils.

Oil tank This was now rubber-mounted to prevent fatigue failure at the mounting brackets. This modification brought the Speed Twin into line with the other twin cylinder models.

A separate oil drain plug was incorporated to assist servicing. Prior to this, the feed pipe and filter had to be removed to allow drainage, resulting in a messy operation.

Side panels Small quarter panels replaced the full enclosure previously fitted.

Rear mudguard With the above small panels, a full rear mudguard was reintroduced. This was fitted with a wrap round rear stay and a new rear number plate compatible with the mudguard.

Air filter A small round air filter with a perforated chrome plated band was fitted directly onto the carburettor, the side panels being shaped to accommodate it.

Abbreviated rear panels were a feature of the 1964 model.

The Triumph Speed Twin & Thunderbird Bible

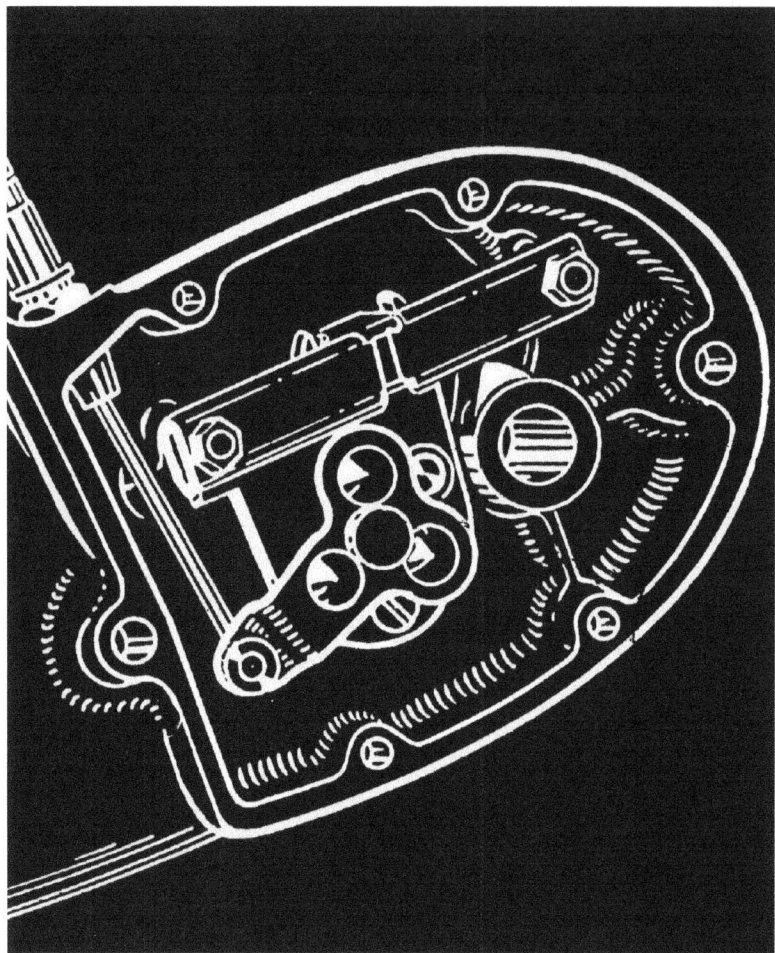

The new clutch operating system.

Finish Silver and Black.

Petrol tank Gloss Black top half and around the knee grips with a Silver Sheen lower half. A Gold line separated the two colours. The badge background was Gold, as was the Triumph lettering. The background of the Triumph lettering was Black.

Mudguards Silver Sheen.

Rear panels Silver Sheen.

Front forks Nacelle top, lower nacelle covers and spring covers were Gloss Black, with the lower fork sliders Silver Sheen.

All other painted parts were finished in Gloss Black.

Price £283 1s 5d

Extras
Prop stand	£1 6s 0d
Pillion footrests	£1 5s 0d
QD rear wheel	£4 14s 1d

Tool tray The tool tray was redesigned and relocated to fit onto the rear mudguard, just to the rear of the battery.

Speedometer A Smiths magnetic SSM5002/00 speedometer was fitted, replacing the Smiths Chronometric SC 3304/11 instrument used previously.

Electrical The ignition system was greatly improved by the use of a Lucas 4CA twin contact breaker and automatic advance assembly. Twin Lucas MA6 6-volt coils were fitted on the bottom frame rail, and they were housed in recesses in the petrol tank.

The single Lucas PRS8 combined ignition and light switch gave way for the use of separate Lucas 88SA light and ignition switches. These were of the plug and socket type, and were prone to unplug until a small steel pressing and an elastic band were fitted as retainers.

A smaller diameter Lucas type 2AR ammeter was fitted, as was a Lucas 8H horn.

A Lucas MLZ8E battery was used for this season, bringing the Speed Twin into line with the other models. This replaced the previous Lucas PUZ7E-11 battery.

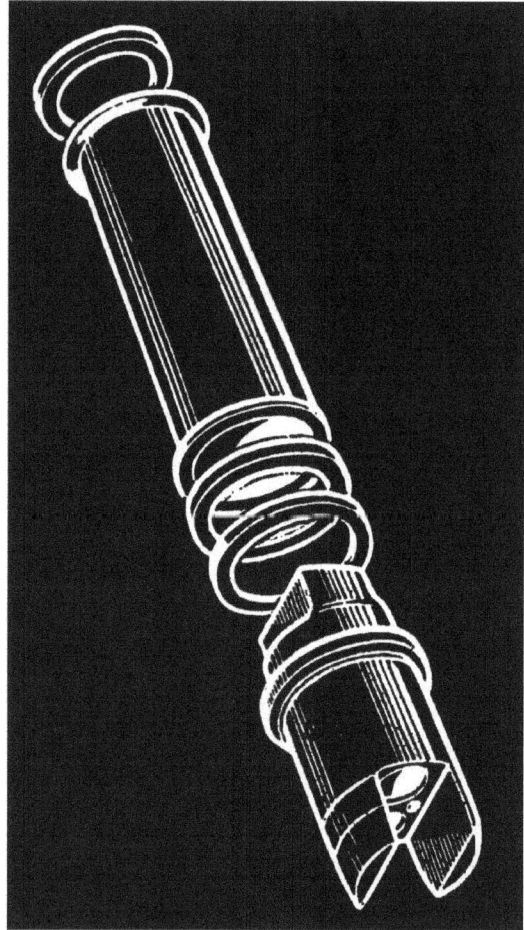

Redesigned oil sealing on the push rod cover tubes.

Excitement & demise

1965 Model 5TA Speed Twin

Engine prefix: 5TA
Engine and frame numbers: H36615 — 29.91964 to H39838 — 1.6.1965

Engine The flywheel periphery was drilled to accept a service tool to locate TDC and the 38° BTDC firing point. The oil pressure release valve tell-tale button was deleted and replaced by a plain dome nut.

Frame/petrol tank A new petrol tank was fitted, rubber mounted at its four corners. The frame now had a bolt-in top rail to replace the former fuel tank that had doubled up as a stressed member. If used as a kit, it could be fitted retrospectively.

Front fork A revised design was fitted with shorter bottom sliders and longer 9¾in springs to give greater rider comfort. The bottom sliders were made from one-piece extrusions. Previously, they were comprised of tubes brazed onto forgings. The new replacements gave a neater appearance and were cheaper to produce.

Front mudguard A semi-sports blade with bolt-on front stays replaced the large valanced pattern used previously.

Rear number plate The rear number plate was extended to accommodate the seven-digit registration figures.

Front number plate The front number plate lost its chrome-plated surround, and reverted to the plain steel blade last used on the Speed Twin in 1938.

Price £283 1s 9d

1965 models featured a sportier front mudguard.

A WD Speed Twin (known at the factory as a T50WD). Only seventeen were built. The most obvious departures from standard were a petrol tank with snorkel tube to provide clean air, full rear chain enclosure, and a 1950s front brake assembly.

The Triumph Speed Twin & Thunderbird Bible

Extras
Prop stand   £1 6s 0d
Pillion footrests   £1 5s 0d
QD rear wheel   £4 14s 1d

1966 Model 5TA Speed Twin

Engine prefix: 5TA
Engine and frame numbers: H42227 — 8.9.1965 to H46431 — 25.5.1966

1966 was the final year of the Speed Twin, the very last one was built on May 25, 1966.

Engine A sports camshaft was fitted (inlet 3134 form and exhaust 3325 form). The 3134 camshaft height from base circle was 1.120/1.128in and the 3325 camshaft height from base circle 1.102/1.110in.

Camshaft timing
IYO	34°	BTDC
IVC	55°	ABDC
EVO	48°	BBDC
EVC	27°	ATDC

0.020in clearance for timing

Tappet clearance — cold engine
Inlet   0.002in
Exhaust   0.004in

Gearbox The gearbox sprocket was reduced by one-tooth to 19.

Transmission The clutch push rod adjuster was increased in diameter from ¼ to ⅜ in. This change necessitated a new pressure plate with a larger inserted nut.

Frame The previously bolted-on top tube was now welded in from H42227.

Oil tank The oil tank was increased in capacity to six pints, and was fitted with an adjustable rear chain oiler. This took the form of a spring-retained screw positioned just inside the oil tank filler neck. A pipe was then routed down the left side terminating at the brake torque stay. A small extension pipe directed oil onto the rear chain.

Petrol tank New 'bird wing' style tank motifs were used from H42227 replacing the basket weave pattern.

Side panels Only one side panel was used, a reverse copy of the oil tank pressing, and fitted on the left hand side covering the battery.

Handlebars White rubber fluted grips were fitted from H42227.

Front wheel A change in wheel size to WM2 x 18in required a new tyre. A Dunlop 3.25 x 18in ribbed was chosen. New spokes were also required, 40 x 8/10G x 5⅝in.

Rear wheel A change in wheel size to WM2 x 18in required a new tyre, a Dunlop Universal 3.50 x 18in was chosen. New spokes were also required:
20 x 8/10G x 7⁷⁄₁₆in x 90°, 20 x 8/10G x 7⅞in x 90° for the standard and quickly detachable wheels respectively.

The standard wheel sprocket reverted to the pre-1952 type, comprising a 46-tooth steel sprocket ring bolted to the cast iron brake drum by eight bolts. The sprocket and brake drum remained integral, and of cast iron in the case of the quickly detachable wheel.

A 1966 model Speed Twin.

Excitement & demise

Electrical The charging system was now 12-volt, diode controlled. The battery was a single Lucas PUZ5A. The diode was mounted on an aluminium plate bolted to the battery carrier.

The stop lamp switch remained as before, but its operation differed insofar as the spring connection was dropped in favour of a fixed metal bracket fitted to the brake rod, with the switch lever abutting it.

Bulbs — 12V
Headlamp	50/40W LH dip pre-focus
Pilot	4W MCC
Tail lamp/stop	6/21W offset pin
Speedometer	3W MES

Coils
Lucas MA12	12V

Horn
Lucas 8H	12V
Fuse	35A

Price £283 1s 5d

Extras
Prop stand	£1 6s 0d
Pillion footrest	£1 5s 0d
D rear wheel	£4 14s 1d

The end of the line

Unfortunately, 1966 was not a good year for the Speed Twin. One look at what was offered as a Speed Twin will be sufficient for most to agree that the model was little more than a collection of parts, borrowed from other models in the range.

It would seem, on the one hand, that the company didn't want to continue production of the Speed Twin, but, on the other hand, because of its long pedigree and illustrious past, it didn't want to kill it off, either.

Looking back at its history, one sees the Speed Twin emerging as a motorcycle with huge potential in 1938, carrying the firm through in the late forties (along with its sister model, the Tiger 100), then losing ground a little when the Thunderbird was released in the early 1950s, and most definitely being relegated to the back row in the mid-1950s when the Tiger 110 was the most sporty motorcycle one could possess.

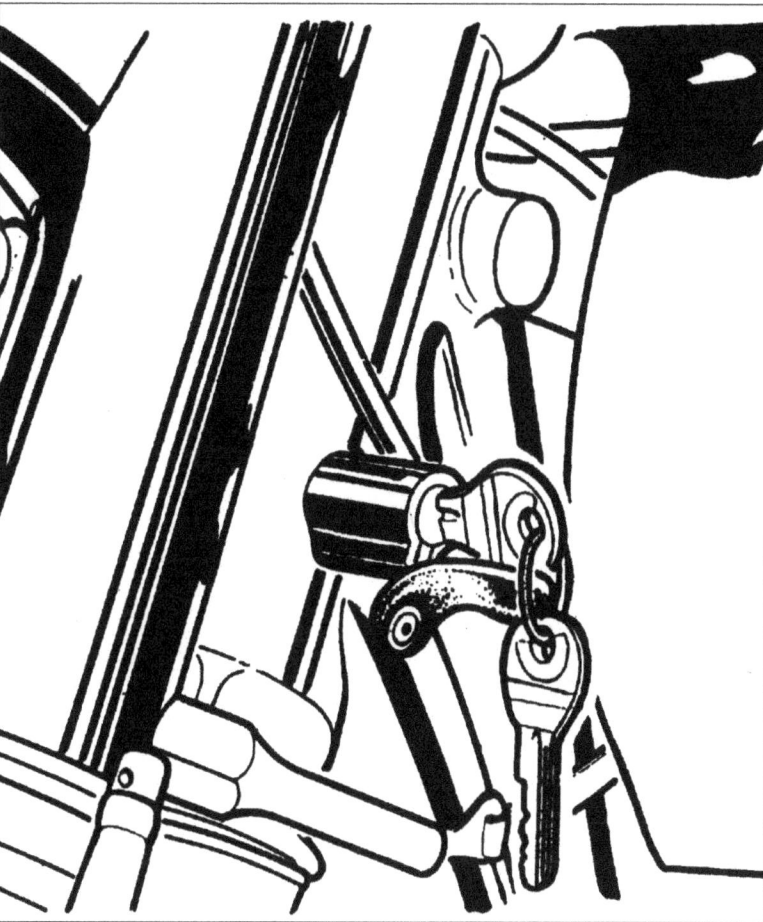

The built-in steering lock.

In the late 1950s, the Speed Twin, with its full-skirted rear panels, was once again in the limelight, but fashions had changed and Triumph's markets were now in the United States where sports motorcycles were in demand. I am led to believe that Edward Turner was very disappointed at the turn of events (although not with the sales) as he would have liked to have seen a more civilised two-wheeled form of transport, perhaps a 650cc scooter, but it was not to be.

With fashion changing, the Speed Twin found itself with a rapidly diminishing market. The 500cc was hardly the model to buy for riding to work — this function was admirably filled by the 200cc Triumph Cub and, as the Speed Twin had no sporting pretensions, it had really come to the end of the line.

Performance figures: 500cc

Make	Model	Flying ⅓-mile (mph)	Flying ¼ mile (mph)	Year
Norton	ES2	81.8	49.4	1938
Rudge	Special	75.0	45.68	"
Rudge	Ulster	89.1	51.72	"
Triumph	5T	91.8	51.70	"
Matchless		84.0	-	"
HRD	Comet	90.0	48.9	"
BSA	Gold Star	89.0	51.4	"
AJS	Model 18	81.8	50.5	"
Norton	ES2	81.81	50.56	1939
Norton	18	81.08	50.56	"
OEC		80.6	47.40	"
Rudge	Ulster	89.0	50.50	"
Triumph	T100	95.74	56.96	"
Triumph	5T	89.19	52.63	"
Velocette	MSS	83.72	48.65	"
Norton	International	94.71	56.01	1947
Ariel	Red Hunter	86.53	52.32	"
Moto Guzzi		85.7	51.7	1950

It must have given Triumph quite a lift to see, when tested in 1938, that the Speed Twin was the fastest 500cc motorcycle over the flying quarter-mile, and second fastest over the standing quarter-mile, losing out by only 0.2mph to a Rudge Ulster.

In 1939, the road tests showed it was bettered only by its sister machine, the Tiger 100, in the 500cc class. This time it beat the Rudge Ulster by 0.19mph over the flying quarter mile, and by 2.13mph over the standing quarter. When one considers that the tests included the Rudge, Norton, BSA, and Velocette sports models of the day, the Speed Twin results can be even more appreciated.

Speed Twin notable registration numbers

CKV 59	Factory registered *Motor Cycling* road test machine, October 1937
CVC 750	Factory registered *Motor Cycle* road test machine, October 1937
EDU 224	Maudes Trophy award machine, March 1939
EXR 3	Sir Malcolm Campbell's Speed Twin, 1939
ERW 36	Factory registered *Motor Cycle* road test machine, November 1939
ENX 673	Factory registered *Motor Cycling* road test machine, January 1946
FUE 870	Factory registered *Motor Cycle* road test machine, August 1947
HHP 90	International Six Day Trial machine, September 1948 rider A. Jefferies
HHP 91	International Six Day Trial machine, September 1948 rider P. Alves
HHP 92	International Six Day Trial machine, September 1948 rider B. Gaymer
HUE 552	Factory registered *Motor Cycling* road test machine, March 1949
KWD 457	Factory demonstrator/loan machine, 1949
LYV 222	Automobile Association combination, 1950
NAC 288	Factory registered *Motor Cycle* road test machine, March 1953
RNX 592	Factory registered *Motor Cycle* road test machine, May 1955
698 AAC	Factory registered *Motor Cycle* road test machine, January 1959
239 BUE	Factory registered Speed Twin, 1959

Excitement & demise

Speed Twin colours 1938-1966

	1938-49	**1950**	**1951-58**	**1959**	**1960-62**	**1963**	**1964-66**
Petrol Tank	Chrome with Amaranth red top & side panels twin gold lining	Amaranth red	Amaranth red chrome styling bands with amaranth red background.	Amaranth red	Ruby red	Cherry red	Black & silver sheen & gold lining
	1938-1959	**1960-62**	**1963**	**1964-66**			
Frame	Amaranth red	Ruby red	Cherry red	Black			
	1938-59	**1960-62**	**1963**	**1964-66**			
Mudguards	Amaranth red. Gold lining	Ruby red	Cherry red	Silver sheen			
	1959	**1960-62**	**1963**	**1964-66**			
Rear panels	Amaranth red	Ruby red	Cherry red	Silver sheen			
	1959	**1960-62**	**1963**	**1964-66**			
Front forks	Amaranth red	Ruby red	Cherry red	Black nacelle upper & lower. Silver sheen btm members			
	1938-51	**1952**	**1953-55**	**1956-66**			
Wheel rims	Chrome with amaranth red. Centres gold lined	Silver sheen amaranth red. Centres gold lined.	As 1938-51	All chrome rims			
	1938-47	**1948-61**	**1962-66**				
Steering damper knob	Black Bakelite self colour	Gloss black	Non fitted				
	1938-66						
Pillion footrests	Gloss black						
	1939-66						
Stand springs	Gloss black						
	1955-58	**1960-62**	**1963**	**1964-1966**			
Rear suspension units	Amaranth red and chrome	Ruby red and chrome	Cherry red and chrome	Black and chrome			

	1938-59	**1960-62**	**1963**	**1964-66**
Front brake drum and hub	Amaranth red	Ruby red	Cherry red	Black
Rear brake drum and hub	Amaranth red	Ruby red	Cherry red	Black

	1938-51	**1952**	**1953-66**
Handlebars	Chrome red	Amaranth	Chrome

	1938-1952
Voltage control unit	Black

	1952	**1953-62**	**1963-66**
Rectifier	Black	Light grey	Self colour

	1938-48	**1949-61**	**1962-66**
Electric horn	Black with chrome rim	Black	Silver cadmium plated

Amal carburettor settings

Year	Type	Bore	Main Jet	Needle	Needle Jet	Position	Throttle valve	Float chamber	Pilot Jet
1938-1946	276 LH	15/16in	140	6	.107	3	6/3	LH	-
1947-1948	276 RH BN/1AT	15/16in	140	6	.107	3	6/3	RH	-
1949-1954	276 RH DK/1AT	15/16in	140	6	.107	3	6/3½	6/3½	-
1955-1958	376/25 Mono bloc	15/16in	200	C	.1065	3	3½	-	30
1959-1966	375/35 Mono bloc	7/8in	160	B	.1065	3	3	-	25

Excitement & demise

Overall gear ratios

1938-1949 Gearbox

Gears	Standard				Wide ratio				Close ratio			
	4th	3rd	2nd	1st	4th	3rd	2nd	1st	4th	3rd	2nd	1st
Engine Sprocket												
17	6.46	7.75	11.35	16.40	6.46	9.36	14.83	19.82	6.46	7.08	9.32	11.20
18	6.10	7.33	10.50	15.50	6.10	8.84	14.00	18.70	6.10	6.68	8.78	10.58
19	5.80	6.95	10.00	14.70	5.80	8.40	13.30	17.80	5.80	6.35	8.35	10.08
20	5.50	6.60	9.50	14.00	5.50	7.96	12.62	16.88	5.50	6.02	7.92	9.54
21	5.24	6.28	9.05	13.30	5.24	7.60	12.02	16.08	5.24	5.74	7.55	9.08
22	5.00	6.00	8.65	12.70	5.00	7.25	11.48	15.34	5.00	5.48	7.20	8.67
23	4.78	5.75	8.26	12.10	4.78	6.93	11.00	14.70	4.78	5.24	6.88	8.36
24	4.57	5.49	8.03	11.60	4.57	6.63	10.49	14.03	4.57	5.01	6.58	7.93
Gearbox Reduction	1.00	1.20	1.73	2.54	1.00	1.45	2.30	3.07	1.00	1.095	1.44	1.733

1950-1958 Gearbox

Gears	Standard				Wide ratio				Close ratio			
	4th	3rd	2nd	1st	4th	3rd	2nd	1st	4th	3rd	2nd	1st
Engine Sprocket												
17	6.46	7.70	10.94	15.80	6.46	9.22	14.30	18.85	6.46	7.06	8.42	11.00
18	6.10	7.28	10.32	14.90	6.10	8.70	13.50	17.80	6.10	6.66	7.65	10.40
19	5.80	6.90	9.80	14.15	5.80	8.25	12.80	16.85	5.80	6.32	7.54	9.84
20	5.50	6.55	9.30	13.40	5.50	7.84	12.18	16.00	5.50	6.00	7.15	9.35
21	5.24	6.24	8.85	12.80	5.24	7.46	11.58	15.25	5.24	5.72	6.81	8.90
22	5.00	5.95	8.45	12.20	5.00	7.13	11.05	14.55	5.00	5.45	6.50	8.50
23	4.78	5.69	8.09	11.69	4.78	6.82	10.60	13.90	4.78	5.23	6.23	8.12
24	4.57	5.45	7.75	11.20	4.57	6.54	10.14	13.35	4.57	5.00	5.96	7.78
Gearbox Reduction	1.00	1.19	1.69	2.44	1.00	1.42	2.21	2.91	1.00	1.09	1.30	1.695

1959-1966 Gearbox

Gears	Standard			
	4th	3rd	2nd	1st
Engine Sprocket				
18	5.31	6.30	9.32	13.00
19	5.05	6.00	8.90	12.30
20	4.80	5.62	8.35	11.56
Gearbox Reduction	1.00	1.17	1.74	2.41

The Triumph Speed Twin & Thunderbird Bible

Chains

Primary

Year	Size	Number of links	
		Solo	Sidecar
1938-1954	⁵⁄₁₆ x ½in	78	77
1955-1958	⁵⁄₁₆ x ½in	70	68
1959-1966	¼ x ⅜in duplex	78	

Secondary

Year	Size	Number of links
1938-1954	⅜ x ⅝in	92
1955-1958	⅜ x ⅝in	100
1959-1964	⅜ x ⅝in	101
1964-1965	⅜ x ⅝in	104
1966	⅜ x ⅝in	103

5T Show Models

Listed below are the engine/frame numbers of Speed Twin models built for various shows that the company supported throughout the years.

TF 15216/88793
TF 15217/88865
    Built 11.9.1947 for Paris Show as 1948 model. All fitted with a spring wheel.

TF 23951/101198
    Built 16.9.1948 for Paris Show as 1949 model. All fitted with a spring wheel.

TF 25372/101935
TF 25373/102460
TF 25374/102162
TF 25375/102163
TF 25376/102521
TF 25377/101933
TF 25378/102161
TF 25379/101220
TF 25380/101934
    Built 12.11.1948 for Earls Court London Show as 1949 model. Only the first three were fitted with a spring wheel.

TF 29510/102522
    Built 13.4.1949 for works showroom. All fitted with a spring wheel.

1009N
1010N
1011N
1012N
1013N
1014N
1015N
1016N
    Built 18.10.1949 for Earls Court London Show as 1950 model. All fitted with a spring wheel.

1066N
    Built 10.10.1949 for Paris Show as a 1950 model. All fitted with a spring wheel.

14872N
    Built 06.10.1950 for Earls Court London Show as 1951 a model.

13725NA
13726NA
    Built 19.9.1951 for Frankfurt Show as a 1952 model. All fitted with a spring wheel.

Excitement & demise

14663 NA	
14664 NA	
14665 NA	Built 5.10.1951 for Earls Court London Show as a 1952 model. All fitted with a spring wheel.
14666 NA	
14667 NA	
15764 NA	Built 31.10.1951 for Earls Court London Show as a 1952 model. All fitted with a spring wheel.
29280	Built 11.6.1952 for Canadian Show as a 1952 model. All fitted with a spring wheel.
29292	
33223	Built 23.9.1952 for Paris Show as a 053 model. All fitted with a spring wheel.
33224	
34059	
34060	
34061	Built 20.10.1952 for Earls Court London Show as 1953 model. Only the first two were fitted with a spring wheel.
34062	
34063	
34406 s/w	
34407 s/w	
34408	
34410	
34412	
34413	Built 5.11.1952 for Earls Court London Show as 1953 model. Only those indicated by s/w were fitted with a spring wheel.
34414	
34416 s/w	
34417	
34418	
34419	
34420	
34421	
34430	
34447	Built 7.11.1952 for Earls Court London Show as 1953 model. All fitted with a spring wheel.
34448	
34451	
35361	
35362	Built 8.12.1952 for Philippine Islands Show as 1953 model. All fitted with a spring wheel.
35363	
45578	
45579	
45580	Built 6.10.1953 for Earls Court London Show as 1954 model. All fitted with a spring wheel.
45581	
45582	
45583	
58990	Built 6.11.1954 for Earls Court London Show as 1955 model. All fitted with a spring wheel.
58991	
58992	
58994	Built 9.12.1954 for works showroom as a 1955 model.
58993	

60693 60694	Built 24.11.1954 for Brussels Show as 1955 model.
62089 62090	Built 5.1.1955 for Amsterdam Show as 1955 model.
71642 71643 71644 71645	Built 15.9.1955 for Earls Court London Show as 1956 model.
71827	Built 20.9.1955 for Paris Show as a 1956 model.
73883 73884	Built 10.11.1955 for Brussels Show as 1956 model.
02064 02065 02066	Built 25.9.1956 for Earls Court London Show as 1957 model.
02911 02912	Built 24.10.1956 for Milan Show as 1957 model.
011072 011073	Built 6.9.1957 for Paris Show with magneto and dynamo as police specification.
011858	Built 21.10.1957 for Milan Show as a 1958 model.
011961	Built 24.10.1957 for Venezuela Show with magneto and dynamo as police specification.
013267	Built 9.12.1957 for works showroom as a 1958 model.
H5483 H5484	Built 17.9.1958 for Earls Court London Show as 1959 model.
H6187	Built 3.10.1958 for Earls Court London Show as a 1959 model.
H12614	Built 22.10.1959 for USA Show as a 1960 model.
H18611	Built 22.8.1960 for Paris Show as a 1961 model.
H18627 H18628	Built 1.9.1960 for Earls Court London Show as 1961 model.
H18638 H18639	Built 24.10.1960 for Earls Court London Show as 1961 model. These two were not built to show finish.
H30289	Built 1.11.1962 for Earls Court London Show as a 1963 model.

H35134 H35135	Built 11.5.1964 for Tel Aviv Show as standard 1964 model.
H36072	Built 12.91964 for Earls Court London Show as 1965 model.
H36716	Built 28.10.1964 for Earls Court London Show as 1965model.
H42227	Built 8.9.1965 for Earls Court London Show as 1966 model.

Parts serviceability

As a result of running a 1947 Speed Twin for 83,221 miles the Triumph Experimental Department recorded the following failures:

Engine	**Miles**
Main bearing RH	36214, 48300
Main bearing LH	48236
Piston rings	12032, 48300, 72000
Head gasket	12032, 48300, 72000
Cylinder head	72000 valve seats sunk
Valves	48300, 72000
Valve springs	12032, 48300, 72000
Valve guide	48300, 72000
Magneto	3630, 54420, 75260
Auto advance unit	47575 seized
Dynamo	52717, 64805, 75260
Gearbox	
High gear bush	53307
Layshaft 2nd gear	75043 broken tooth
Chains	
Primary	14138, 18472, 23357, 34996, 52599
Secondary	12832, 18472, 41894, 51552
Clutch	
Corked plates	11168, 26774
Wheels	
Bearings front	32907
Brake linings front	48326, 67525
Brake linings rear	58743
Tyre front	22839, 32906, 43720, 66400, 79646
Tyre rear	16112, 22840, 44485, 54597, 64790, 76570
Frame	
Rear	12353 saddle spring lug fractured
Petrol tank	42898 fractured
Clutch cable	44185, 71306
Throttle cable	21021, 43780
Electrical	
Ammeter	26326, 79246, 79400
Battery	23636, 83321
Speedometer	11933, 12832, 14100, 49999, 50884, 52301, 71921
Speedometer drive gearbox	13875

From this summary it will be seen that some components, generally not of Triumph manufacture, have a higher incidence of failure, and, as this was a company mileage machine, its usage would have been fairly hard. It is not suggested that a privately-owned Speed Twin would show the same regularity of failures, but it still gives an indication of what long-term ownership may represent.

Chapter 5
The launch of the Thunderbird

Although the T100 and the 5T 500cc twins were well regarded in the USA, and were selling quite well, many American riders considered them too small, in terms of cubic inches, especially when compared to the Harley-Davidson and Indian V-Twins. In addition, American distributors often told Edward Turner that they could increase sales if larger capacity machines were available. Under Turner's direction, therefore, Triumph designers investigated the possibility of boring and stroking the engine of the 498cc Speed Twin. Adding 2mm to the stroke and 9mm to the bore meant that the crankshaft of the Speed Twin could be used, but a new cylinder barrel would be required. Thus it was that the 649cc Thunderbird was conceived, with a bore and stroke of 71 x 82mm, respectively.

With a compression ratio of 7 to 1, the engine produced 34bhp at 600rpm (7¼bhp more than the Speed Twin at a similar engine speed). More importantly, however, it developed the same bhp at 4000rpm as the Speed Twin did at 6000rpm. The increase in torque allowed the use of higher gearing which, in turn, allowed higher cruising speeds with less engine stress. This went a good way towards addressing the requirement in America for sustained, high-speed highway motoring.

The new engine slotted directly into the Speed Twin frame, and gave the company another model in the range (with very little development outlay, typical of Turner's approach).

It's doubtful that Turner foresaw how popular the 649cc machine would become in the guise of the T120 Bonneville and TR6 Trophy. In fact, it's on record that he considered 500cc the optimum capacity for a parallel twin, and only reluctantly assented to the production of the 650. However, knowing that the larger engine capacity would cost very little more to manufacture, but would yield a greater profit margin, this probably influenced his decision.

As the Thunderbird was originally made for the American market, Turner knew that a spectacular launch of the new model was required.

3 x 90 x 500 Montlhéry demonstration

Whilst being tested in secret, the prototypes had demonstrated that they were capable of sustained high speeds. Tyrell Smith and Ernie Nott of the Triumph Experimental department had logged considerable mileages between them. Both ex-racing men, they assured Edward Turner that his idea for the launch of the new model (a demonstration covering 500 miles at an average speed of 90mph) was feasible.

The only venue thought to be suitable for the high speed demonstration was Montlhéry, a banked racetrack near Paris. In July 1949, Turner, accompanied by Smith and Nott, with tester Alex Scobie following on one of the prototypes, made the journey to the circuit. Scobie soon got into lapping swiftly, but the demo came to an untimely halt when a connecting rod broke, wrecking the engine, with only 3912 miles covered.

Undeterred, Scobie and Nott returned a month later with two machines. The first day's riding went quite well until one of the machines developed clutch slip, which ultimately resulted in a burnt-out clutch. The friction material was cork, however, so a few wine bottle corks were substituted and testing continued the next day. The test was halted on the advice of the Dunlop representative after 375 miles, however, because the canvas was beginning to show through the left hand side of the rear tyres.

Back at Triumph, and with time rapidly running out, Turner decided to go ahead with the demonstration, taking three of the new models straight from the production line.

So that no accusations of 'special parts' or prior tuning could be made, he asked that the whole process be supervised by an observer from the *Auto Cycle*. The gentleman nominated was Harold Taylor, a very experienced rider in sidecar events (having only one leg didn't seem to impair him much), and manager of Britain's Motocross Team.

The Triumph Speed Twin & Thunderbird Bible

This advertisement was placed in the weekly motorcycle magazines immediately after the Montlhéry demonstration. However, it was soon withdrawn after comments to Edward Turner that it bore resemblance to the Riders of the Apocalypse. Turner did not like the comparison, reasoning that his Thunderbird represented joy and life, not doom and gloom.

The three production machines were joined by one other (mainly to act as a spares back-up and transport), and all four were fitted with panniers carrying the spares most likely to be needed, including tyres.

Two days before the demonstration, the four machines were ridden from the Meriden factory, through London, and on to Folkestone and the ferry. Upon landing in France, they were ridden to the race track at Montlhéry.

When they arrived, the panniers were removed, the machines were checked over, and then ridden around the track in preparation for the main event.

In the interests of safety and rider comfort, some departures from the standard specification had been made. To enable the riders to adopt a crouched position, easing the strain on arms and back, smaller Trophy saddles and rearward fixed footrests were fitted. Stronger clutch springs were fitted, and the gearing was raised by

The launch of the Thunderbird

fitting a 25-tooth engine sprocket. 210 carburettor jets replaced the 190s, and KLG racing plugs were fitted. Following advice from Dunlop, racing tyres were used to cope better with the sustained high speed. Because one of the electric horn brackets had fractured in practice, they were all removed for safety reasons.

The six riders nominated were: Alex Scobie, the company's test development rider; Len Bayliss, ace grass track star and works tester; Bob Manns, competition rider and works tester; HG Tyrell-Smith, ex-works road racer for the Rudge Factory and manager of Triumph's Experimental Department; Allan Jefferies and Jim Alves, both works riders in trials and ISDT (although, to be accurate Allan was ex-works as he had recently announced his retirement from competition riding).

After a couple of warm-up laps of the 1.583 mile concrete oval, with its steeply-banked curves, the demonstration began at 9.15am, with Alex Scobie first out on No 1 machine. His first flying lap was clocked at 67 seconds — 85mph; his second at 61 seconds, and his next at 60 seconds — 95mph, at which point he was given the signal to slow down slightly. At 9.21am, Bob Manns set off on No 2 machine and soon started turning in laps of 93mph. Jim Alves went out at 9.40am on the No 3 machine and lapped consistently at 91mph. The three machines were now lapping reliably, with the timekeepers juggling the fast and slow lap boards to keep the riders on schedule.

When Scobie came in after 66 laps at an average speed of 91.95mph, the only problem he reported was keeping the speed down. Petrol and oils were replenished, and Len Bayliss took over the machine. The No 2 machine came in after the first hour, having completed 63 laps at an average speed of over 92mph, and, like the No 1 machine, there were no problems to report. Once the machine was refuelled, Manns handed over to Allan Jefferies who, after some very spirited riding, was soon instructed to slow down. Jim Alves' 91mph was actually considered too slow, on the other hand, and he was instructed to speed up, before eventually handing over to Tyrell-Smith.

There was a lull in the proceedings for a while, as the machines lapped the track hour after hour. The monotony was broken at 1pm, however, when Len Bayliss pulled into the pit area to report a leaking petrol tank on the No 3 machine. The petrol tank was replaced by the one from the spare No 4 machine, and Bayliss was on his way again in slightly under 15 minutes. Again the monotonous routine resumed, only broken when the riders were changed and the machines refuelled. There was a moment of panic, though, when Allan Jefferies came in to report a high pitched screaming noise coming from the rear chain area. This was diagnosed as a loose lower chainguard, however, but this was quickly removed and Allan was on his way again in under three minutes.

When the 500 miles had been completed, the machines were checked over and, other than the

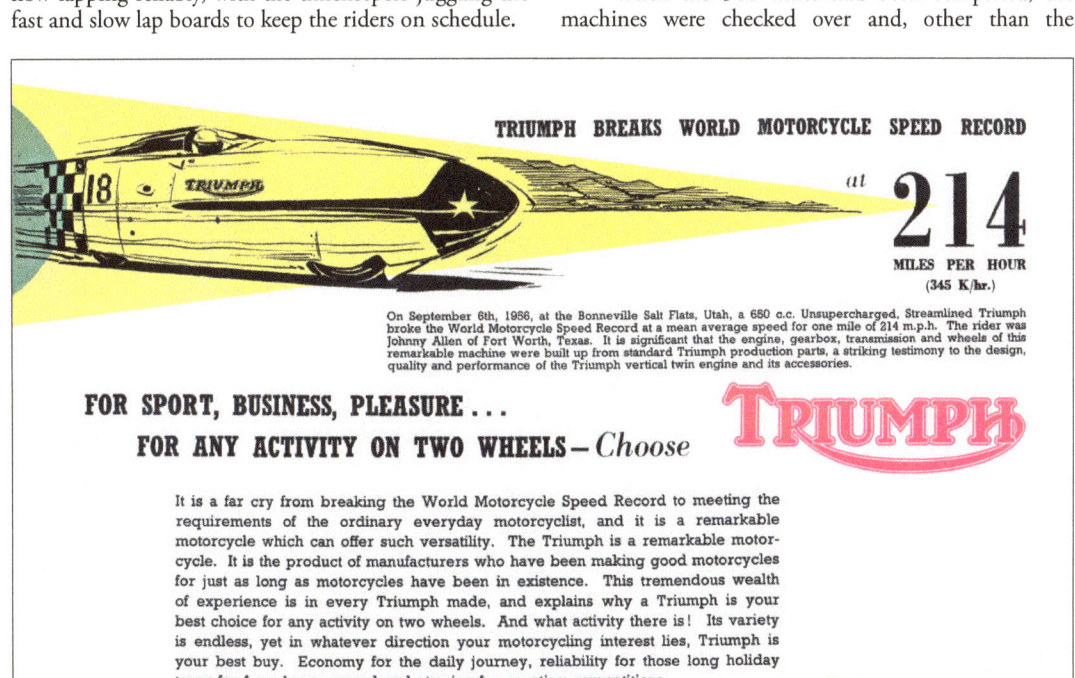

On September 6, 1956, at the Bonneville Salt Flats in Utah, Johnny Allen, riding a 650cc supercharged, streamlined Triumph, broke the World Motorcycle Speed Record at a mean average speed of 214mph. The engine, gearbox, transmission, and wheels of this remarkable machine were built up from standard Triumph production parts.

89

rear chains being badly out of adjustment, nothing required attention. With the chains adjusted, each machine did a flying lap (with Manns, Bayliss and Scobie in the saddles). Respective speeds were 100.71, 100.71 and 101.78mph.

The three bikes had covered the 500 miles at an average of 92.23, 92.33 and 92.48mph. Taking into consideration stops for rider change, refuelling, and even the petrol tank replacement, the averages were 90.93, 90.30 and 86.07mph. To say that the riders and pit crews were delighted with the result is, perhaps, an understatement, and even Edward Turner had a huge grin on his face.

With the main event concluded, the machines were ridden back to the Meriden factory where, with Harold Taylor from the ACU in attendance, they were stripped for examination. The ACU representative reported that, apart from one machine suffering a worn primary chain due to lack of lubrication, all were considered capable of a repeat performance.

A great deal of publicity was generated by the demonstration. *Motor Cycling* and *The Motorcycle* both did an article on the event, and statements such as "great achievement," "wonderful reliability," and "outstanding performance" were used. Even the BBC got involved, and Edward Turner and the riders were interviewed by David Martin.

No 1 machine was registered JAC 769
No 2 machine was registered JAC 770
No 3 machine was registered JAC 771

The economy run

In July 1952, Edward Turner devised a scheme to demonstrate how economical the 650 Thunderbird was and, at the same time, the suitability of fitting an SU carburettor to a motorcycle. A standard model was chosen for the test, and the following modifications were made: the gearing was raised by fitting a 25-tooth engine sprocket, the standard M9 needle in the SU was replaced with an EB to give a leaner mixture at low throttle openings, and the tyres were inflated to 35psi. A ten-mile circuit around the leafy lanes of Warwickshire was then mapped out, choosing the flattest area possible, and the riders were chosen.

So that the test would be judged to be unbiased, Turner contacted journalists from the well-known weekly magazines - Dennis Hardwick from *Motor Cycling*, and Kevin Gover from *The Motorcycle* — knowing that if the test went well, an article would appear in both the magazines, giving even greater free publicity.

The other three riders were Edward Turner, HG Tyrell-Smith, Experimental Department manager, and Ginger Wood, ex-TT rider and SU company representative.

On a rather breezy day (which may have adversely affected the test) the riders were assembled and 300cc of petrol was put in a small container fixed to the parcel grid. Riding at 30mph on a constant throttle opening, keeping the machine in top gear as much as possible, and braking as little as possible, 155 miles per gallon was achieved. Average speed throughout the test was 30mph.

Edward Turner was very pleased with this demonstration and, of course, with the subsequent publicity it accorded him and the company.

Sporting achievements

Although originally designed as a touring motorcycle, the Thunderbird acquitted itself quite well in straight-line speed events, and it didn't take long for the Americans to realise its potential as a record breaker.

Johnny Allen about to do a run for the BBC *Sportsview* cameras at the Wellesbourne Airfield in November 1956.

The launch of the Thunderbird

In 1950, for example, Bobby Turner set a new AMA record for unstreamlined machines of 135.84mph at the Rosamund dry lake in the Mojave desert. Then, in 1951, he set a new record for the 40-cubic inch class with a two-way run of 129.24mph, and a best one-way run of 136mph. Later, at the Bonneville salt flats, Turner set a class C record of 132.26mph. This was the fastest class C record for any engine size on pump fuel, and his record stood for seven years!

In 1951, the 80-cubic inch class in the Peoria TT was won by Jimmy Phillips on a Thunderbird and, at the Catalina Grand Prix in 1951, Walt Fulton won the inaugural 100-mile race. Of the eight times this event was held, Triumphs won the Open class five times, though not all on Thunderbirds.

In September 1955, Johnny Allen set a two-way average of 193.30mph on a Thunderbird Streamliner at the Bonneville salt flats in Utah. This speed broke the pending World Record set by Burns and Wright on a Vincent twin by 8mph.

Unfortunately for Allen, his achievement wasn't recognised as a World Record by the Federation Internationale Motocyclisme (FIM) claiming that no FIM-approved observers were present at the event.

Allen was back at Bonneville in 1956 aiming at even higher speeds as the German NSU factory had upped the record to 210mph. This time Allen put in a best two-way run of 214.17mph. However, the FIM again refused to ratify Allen's attempt, stating that the timing clock certificates were in error. Edward Turner recognised the attempt for what it was, however, and decreed that every Triumph leaving the factory would bear a transfer stating World Motorcycle Speed Record Holder. Although threatened many times by the FIM over this, Turner took no notice, and eventually Triumph had its FIM licence suspended for two years.

In 1963, Rich Richards set a new AMA record of 149.56mph in the 40-cubic inch class, beating the previous record of 144.33mph held by Blackie Bullock (both used Thunderbird 6Ts).

Chapter 6
Technical development

1950 Model 6T Thunderbird

Engine prefix: 6T
Engine and frame numbers: 1017N to 15000N
Build dates: 07.10.1949 — 11.10.1950

Engine The crankshaft assembly consisted of a left and right crankshaft bolted to a central flywheel by six high-tensile bolts. This assembly was supported in the aluminium alloy crankcase by large ball journal bearings.

Plain bearings were used for the big end of the connecting rods. White metal was fused to the lower steel end caps, whilst the upper half of the bearing was machined directly from the hiduminium alloy connecting rod. Bronze bushes were fitted to the small ends to provide a bearing for the gudgeon pin.

The cylinder and cylinder head were of best grade cast iron. Separate aluminium alloy rocker boxes were bolted to the cylinder head, housing the rockers and giving full enclosure and lubrication to all the moving parts. The oil feed to the rocker assembly was from a

The original 1950 6T Thunderbird, along with the motif that was carried on the nacelle top.

Technical development

T-junction on the oil tank return pipe, and drainage from the rocker boxes was by external pipes into the pushrod cover tubes.

The overhead valve gear was operated by high camshafts working in phosphor bronze bushes inside the alloy crankcase. Separate steel cam followers connected the tubular steel pushrods to the ball-ended rocker levers.

The main lubrication was of the dry sump, pressure and scavenge being maintained by a twin piston plunger pump driven by an eccentric peg on the inlet camshaft pinion retaining nut. Pressure was controlled by a piston-operated release valve housed in the timing cover.

Ignition A flange-mounted BTH (British Thompson & Houston) magneto was situated to the rear of the cylinder barrel and driven from the inlet camshaft pinion. A BTH automatic advance and retard unit controlled the ignition.

Carburation A 1in Amal 276 carburettor (changed mid-season to 1 1/16in for improved performance) with a left hand-mounted float chamber. A Triumph twistgrip with an adjustable knurled knob for friction control controlled the throttle. The choke was operated by a cable from a control lever mounted on the left hand chain stay under the seat.

Gearbox The four-speed Triumph was operated by a positive stop, right-side foot lever. The nickel chrome steel shafts and gears were housed in an aluminium alloy casing. The mainshaft and high gear ran on ball journal bearings, and the layshaft used phosphor bronze bushes. The gearbox inner cover carried the speedometer drive gears and the speedometer drive cable attachments. Pivoting the gearbox from the lower fixing bolt allowed primary chain adjustment.

Transmission A 1/2 x 0.305in single row, Perry or Reynolds chain connected the engine sprocket to the clutch chainwheel. An engine shaft shock absorber was incorporated in the engine sprocket, and comprised a two-lobe cam and a spring. The clutch was a multi-plate affair, with alternate steel and cork plates. Four springs, retained in cups set in the outer pressure plate, transmitted the drive. The clutch was operated by a rod passing through the centre of the mainshaft to a lever pivoting in the gearbox outer cover, and then by cable to the left hand-mounted handlebar control.

Frame The full cradle-frame used forged steel lugs, pinned and brazed to the frame tubes. The front frame had a tapered, single front down tube, and the bolt-on rear frame had twin tubes under the engine and gearbox which joined two tubes from the saddle nose at the rear wheel spindle lugs.

A rear propstand pivoted just below the rear wheel spindle, and was retained in the up position by a large spring anchored to the right hand pillion footrest pivot.

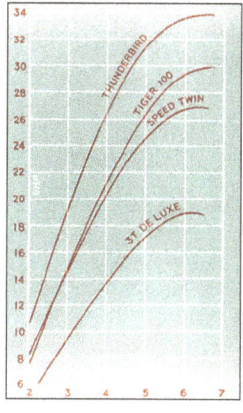

This graph shows the comparative brake horse power developed by the four Triumph engines. High output at reasonable rpm is a feature of the 650cc Thunderbird.

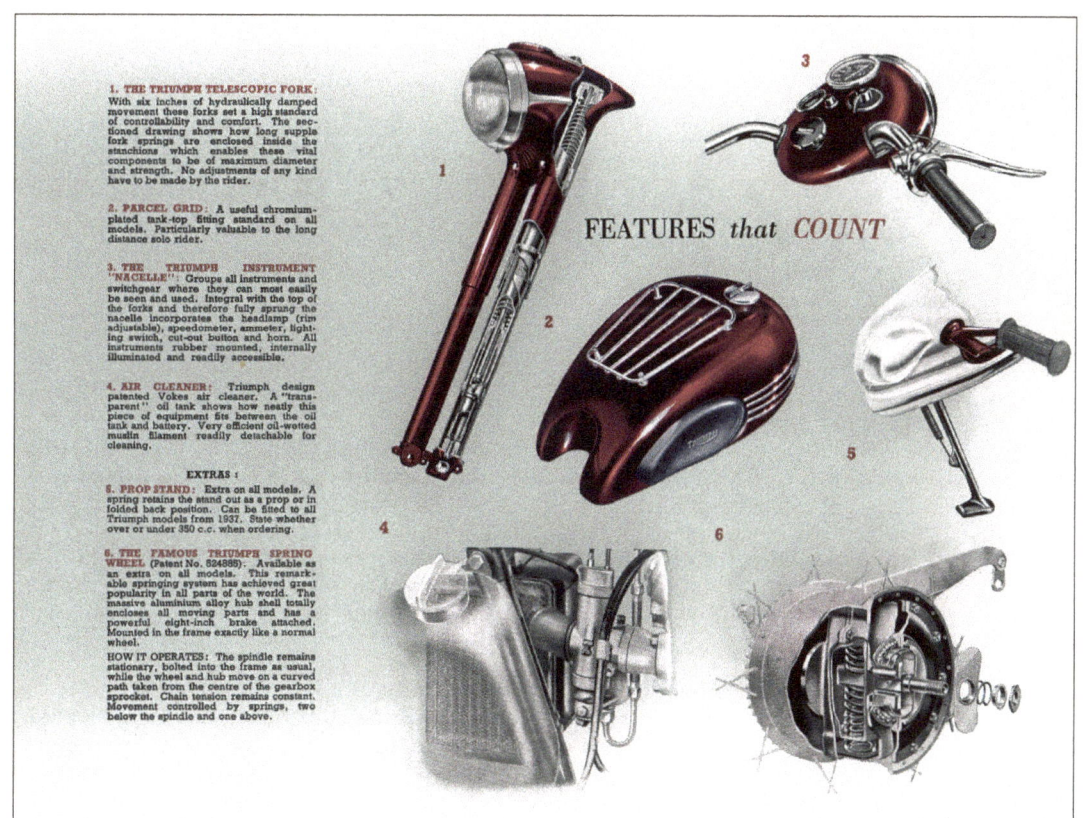

A few of the features that appeared on the Thunderbird.

It's 1950 and nice to be by the seaside.

Suspension The Triumph-designed, telescopic, hydraulically-damped front fork gave 6.5in of movement. The upper part of the fork assembly incorporated the nacelle which housed the headlight, the speedo, and the switches. A manually-operated, friction disc steering damper was fitted.

Rear suspension (an optional extra) took the form of a spring wheel or spring hub. Needing no frame modifications, it could be fitted retrospectively. Because of a number of bearing failures, the MkI spring wheel was replaced by the MkII from 7439N, April 7, 1950.

Petrol tank The all-welded tank had a capacity of four gallons, and originally featured a quick-release hinged filler cap (superseded at 13856N on September 14, 1950, by a Ceandes, bayonet-fitting chrome cap which required a redesign of the tank neck). A push-pull, two-way tap, with provision for reserve, was fitted on the left hand side, with a connecting pipe across the rear of the tank. The knee pad area of the tank was recessed to reduce overall width and the rubber knee pads were retained by two screws either side. Chrome plated styling bands with raised flutes carried the Triumph badge, and a three-bar parcel grid graced the top.

Oil tank All steel, welded at the seams, the oil tank had a capacity of six pints. Up to 13959N, September 18, 1950, an aluminium filler cap was threaded into the neck of the tank. This was replaced by a Ceandes, chrome-plated bayonet fitting cap, and the tank filler neck was modified to suit.

Exhaust system Two 1¾in diameter down pipes, one on each side, terminated into parallel tubular silencers mounted directly onto the pillion footrest frame lugs.

Handlebars/controls The 1in diameter chrome-plated handlebars were reduced at the right hand end to carry the Triumph twistgrip. The clutch and brake levers were chrome-plated steel pressings. A ⅜in x 26tpi threaded hole was provided on the left side to accept the push button for the Lucas horn.

Mudguards Both steel mudguards featured a raised central band. The front mudguard had a centre stay, attached by rivets, and a welded-in bridge piece was provided for the bolt-on front stays. The bottom mudguard stay was attached to the mudguard by a single fixing nut which, when released, enabled the stay to be swung down to act as a stand aiding removal of the front wheel. The front number plate had a chromium-plated beading, and was fixed to the front mudguard by two studs. The front of the mudguard was flared and given a slight upward tilt.

The rear mudguard consisted of two parts, joined together just beneath the saddle. The rear portion, along with the mudguard stays, could be detached to allow rear wheel removal. The rear number plate, which incorporated a lifting handle for operating the rear stand, was bolted to the mudguard. The tail end of the rear mudguard was finished with a slight outward flare.

Technical development

Toolbox A triangular-shaped toolbox was fitted between the rear chain stays on the right hand side. The lid hinged from the lower edge, and was secured in the closed by a slotted push-and-twist Dzus fastener. Two P-clips around the frame tubes, and one bracket to the pillion footrest fixing bolt, retained the toolbox to the frame.

Wheels The front wheel had a WM2 x 19in rim, with a 3.25 x 19in Dunlop ribbed tyre. The 7in diameter, single leading shoe drum brake was a steel pressing with a spoke flange welded on, and the brake shoes were retained on a polished alloy anchor plate. The rear wheel had a WM2 x 19in rim with a 3.5 x 19in Dunlop Universal tyre. The standard rear wheel was fitted with a 7in, single leading shoe brake with a cast iron drum with a bolt-on steel sprocket. The optional spring wheel carried the same size rim and tyre, but an 5in diameter brake with cast iron drum and integral sprocket were fitted. The sprocket size was the same on both wheels (46 teeth).

Front and rear wheels had chromium-plated rims with gold-lined Thunder Blue centres.

Seat A deluxe Lycett or Terry seat was fitted, and featured long, barrel-shaped, chrome-plated springs, adjustable for height. A black, sponge-filled pillion seat was offered as an extra.

Electrical A 60W E3L-Ll-0 Lucas dynamo supplied current to a 6V Lucas PUW7E/4 12Ah battery via a Lucas regulator MCR-2-L. The Lucas horn (HF 1441 Altette) was housed within the nacelle, which also contained the light switch, ammeter and ignition cut-out button.

Ignition was supplied by a BTH magneto, gear-driven from the inlet camshaft pinion. Advance and retard was automatically controlled by a BTH centrifugal unit.

A 6in headlamp with a fluted domed lens was fitted, and the reflector housed the main and pilot bulbs. The headlamp dipper switch was housed in a chrome cover, mounted on the front brake lever clamp.

Speedometer The Smiths 5467/43 1600rpm speedometer showed miles per hour and engine revolutions in each gear, but the 5467/47 1000rpm kph model only had a plain kph dial.

1950 Model 6T Thunderbird technical data

Engine
Bore	71mm (2.795in)
Stroke	82mm (3.228in)
Capacity	649cc (40in³)
bhp	34 @ 6300rpm
Compression ratio	7.0:1

Cylinder head
Material	Cast iron
Valve seat angle	45°
Valve seat width	
Inlet	0.050/0.060in
Exhaust	0.060/0.080in
Valve guide bore	0.498/04985in

Valves
Stem diameter	
Inlet	0.3095/0.3100in
Exhaust	0.3090/0.3095in
Head diameter	
Inlet	1½in
Exhaust	1⁷⁄₁₆in
Length overall inlet	3¹³⁄₁₆in
Exhaust	3²⁵⁄₃₂in

Valve guides
Material	Chilled cast iron
Bore diameter	0.3120/0.3130in
Outer diameter	0.5005/0.5010in
Length	
Inlet	1³¹⁄₃₂in
Exhaust	2¹¹⁄₆₄in

Valve springs
Free length	
Inner	1⅝ ± ¹⁄₁₆in
Outer	2¹⁄₃₂ ± ¹⁄₁₆in
Fitted length	
Inner	1.187in
Outer	1.281in

Cam follower
Foot radius	0.750in
Stem diameter	0.3110/0.3115in

Valve clearance — cold
Inlet	0.002in
Exhaust	0.004in

Valve timing — ± 2½°
IVO	26½°	BTC
IVC	69½°	ABC
EVO	61½°	BBC
EVC	35½°	ATC

set tappets at 0.020in for timing.

Valve lift   0.294in

Push rods
Material	Tubular steel with end caps
Overall length	6.300/6.325in

Rockers
Bore diameter	0.5002/0.5012in
Spindle diameter	0.4990/0.4995in

Camshafts
Journal diameter	
Left hand	0.8100/0.8105in
Right hand	0.8730/0.8735in
Fitted end float	0.013/0.020in
Lobe height	1.047/1.055in

Camshaft bush
Bore diameter (left)	0.8125/0.8135in
Bore diameter (right)	0.874/0.875in

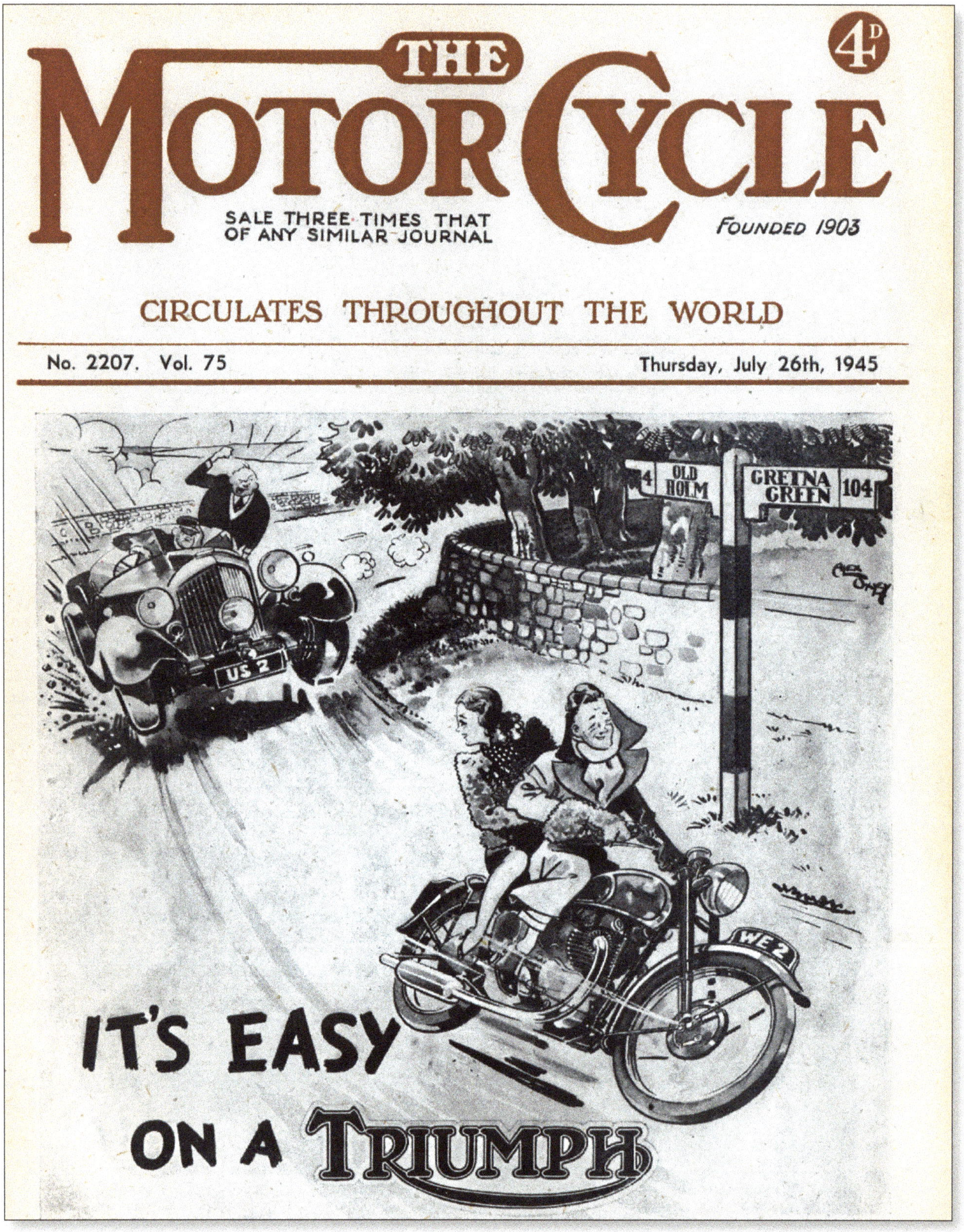

Triumph placed Alex Oxley's amusing adverts in both *The Motorcycle* and *Motorcycling Weekly*.

Technical development

Overall length
    Inlet (left)   1.000/1.010in
    Exhaust (left)   0.932/0.942in
    Inlet/Exhaust (right)   1.010/1.020in

Cylinder barrel
  Material   Cast iron
  Cylinder bore   2.7948/2.7953in
  Tappet block bore   0.9985/0.9990in

Tappet block
  Material   Cast iron
  Outer diameter   0.9995/1.000in
  Tappet stem bore   0.3120/0.3125in

Piston rings
  Ring gap fitted
    Compression ring   0.010/0.014in
    Oil control ring   0.010/0.012in
  Ring thickness
    Compression ring   0.0615/0.0625in
    Oil control ring   0.214/0.125in
  Clearance in groove
    Compression ring   0.001/0.003in
    Oil control ring   0.0005/0.0025in

Piston to bore
  Clearance at top of skirt   0.0088/0.0098in
  Clearance at bottom of skirt   0.0033/0.0043in
  Gudgeon pin bore   0.6882/0.6885in

Connecting rod
  Big end bearing bap   White metal
  Big end diameter   1.4375/1.4385in
  Length between centres   6.499/6.501in
  Side clearance fitted   0.012/0.016in

Small end bush
  Material   Phosphor bronze
  Outer diameter   0.8140/0.8145in
  Length   1.030/1.031in
  Finished bore diameter   0.6890/0.6894in

Gudgeon pin
  Diameter   0.6882/0.6885in
  Length   2.250/2.260in

Crankshaft
  Crank pin diameter   1.4360/1.4365in
  Main bearing journal diameter (left)   1.1247/1.1250in
  Main bearing journal diameter (right)   0.9997/1.000in
  Oil feed journal diameter   0.622/0.623in
  Crankshaft end float fitted   0.003/0.017in
  Balance factor   52%
  Main bearing (left)   1.125 x 2.812 x 0.812in ball journal
  Main bearing (right)   1.00 x 2.50 x 0.750in ball journal
  Oil feed bush bore   0.6245/0.6255in

Oil pump
  Body material   Brass
  Bore diameter
    Feed   0.31270/0.31290in
    Scavenge   0.4375/0.4377in
  Plunger diameter
    Feed   0.3121/0.3125in
    Scavenge   0.4371/0.4374in
  Spring length   ½in
  ball valve diameter   7/32in
  Pressure release valve
    Pressure release   60/75lb/in²
    Indicator spring length   9/32in
  Release spring length   31/32in
  Piston diameter   0.5605/0.5610in

Carburettor
  Type   Amal 276
  Bore   1in mid-season change to 1 1/16in
  Main jet   170
  Needle jet   107
  Needle   6
  Needle position   3
  Throttle valve   6/3½in

Ignition
  Magneto   BTH KC2 with automatic ignition control
  Timing   37° or 3/8in BTDC fully advanced
  Points gap   0.012in
  Sparkplugs   Champion L10S
  Plug gap   0.018in
  Thread size   14mm
  Reach   ½in

Clutch
  Corked plates   5
  Plain plates   6
  Pressure springs   4
  Spring free length   1½in
  Bearing rollers   20
    Diameter   0.2495/0.250in
    Length   0.231/0.236in
  Hub bearing diameter   1.3733/1.3743in
  Sprocket bore diameter   1.8745/1.8755in
  Clutch rod diameter   7/32in
  Clutch rod length   11¾in nominal

Kick start mechanism
  Case bore diameter (left)   0.6245/0.6255in
  Bush bore diameter (right)   0.751/0.752in
  KIS spindle diameter (left)   0.6215/0.6225in
  KIS spindle diameter (right)   0.748/0.749in
  Ratchet sleeve outer diameter   0.8747/0.8752in
  Ratchet spring free length   ½in

Gearchange mechanism
  Plunger outer diameter   0.4315/0.4320in

The Triumph Speed Twin & Thunderbird Bible

Plunger bore diameter	0.4320/0.4330in
Plunger spring number of coils	12
Plunger spring free length	1¼in

Footchange spindle

Diameter (left)	0.6215/0.6235in
Diameter (right)	0.747/0.749in
Bush bore (left)	0.6245/0.6255in
Bush outer diameter (left)	0.8755/0.8765in
Bush bore (right)	0.7495/0.7505in
Bush outer diameter (right)	0.8755/0.8765in

Quadrant springs

Free length	1¾in
Number of coils	9½

Camplate plunger

Plunger diameter	0.436/0.4365in
Housing bore	0.4375/0.438in
Spring length	2½in
Number of coils	20

Gearbox mainshaft

Bearing (left)	1¼ x 2½ x ⅝in ball journal
Bearing (right)	¾ x 1⅞ x ⁹⁄₁₆in ball journal
Diameter (left)	0.8098/0.8103in
Bush bore fitted	0.8135/0.8145in
Bush outer diameter	0.909/0.910in
Bush overall length	2¼in

Gearbox layshaft

Diameter (left)	0.6845/0.6850in
Diameter (right)	0.6845/0.6850in
Bush bore (left/right)	0.6855/0.6865in

Number of teeth on pinions

Layshaft		Mainshaft	
20	4th	26	
22	3rd	24	
26	2nd	20	
30	1st	16	
Sprockets	Solo	Sidecar	
Engine	24	21	
Clutch	43	43	
Gearbox	18	18	
Rear wheel	46	46	

Gear ratios

	Internal	Solo	Sidecar
4th	1.0	4.57	5.24
3rd	1.19	5.45	6.24
2nd	1.69	7.75	8.85
1st	2.44	11.20	12.8

Chains

Primary	⁵⁄₁₆ x ½in x 80 link
Secondary	⅜ x ⅝in x 92 link

Wheels

Rim size (front/rear)	WM2 x 19in

Tyres		
Front		3.25 x 19in Dunlop Ribbed
Rear		3.50 x 19in Dunlop Universal
Tyre pressure		
Front		18psi
Rear		16psi
Bearings		
Front		20 x 47 x 14mm ball journal
Rear K1163 x K1120NI		⁹⁄₁₆ x 1¾ x 1³⁄₁₆ x ⁹⁄₁₆in taper roller
MkII rear spring hub		3½ x 5 x ¾in ball journal

Spokes

Front		
Left inner	10 x 8¹¹⁄₃₂in x 10G 88° head	
Left outer	10 x 8¹¹⁄₃₂in x 10G 90° head	
Right inner	10 x 6⅜in x 10G 83° head	
Right outer	10 x 6⅜in x 10G 96° head	
Rear		
Left inner	10 x 8¾in x 9G 76° head	
Left outer	10 x 8¾in x 9G 100° head	
Right inner	10 x 9in x 9G 76° head	
Right outer	10 x 9in x 9G 100° head	

Spring hub

Left/right	40 x 5⁵⁄₁₆in x 10/8G butted straight

Wheel offset

Front	From drum edge to centre of rim 2³⁄₁₆in
Rear	From outer edge of sproket to centre of rim 3⁵⁄₃₂in
Rear spring hub	Hub faces central to rim

Brakes

Front	7 x 1⅛in
Rear	7 x 1⅛in
Rear spring hub	8 x 1⅛in

Frames

Steering head bearings	Cup and cone
Bearing top	22 x ³⁄₁₆in ball
Bearing bottom	20 x ¼in ball

Front fork

Stanchion length	22in

Technical development

Oxley showing the swift acceleration of the Triumph.

Stanchion diameter	1.3025/1.303in
Top bush internal diameter	1.3065/1.3075in
Bottom bush outer diameter	1.4935/1.4945in
Top bush overall length	0.995/1.005in
Bottom bush overall length	0.870/0.875in
Fork leg bore	1.498/1.500in
Spring free length	20in ± 3/16in
Spring wire diameter	0.160in Solo/0.168in Sidecar

Electrical

Dynamo	Lucas E3L-LI-0 60W
Voltage regulator	Lucas MCR-2-L
Voltage	6V
Earth	Negative
Battery	Lucas PUW 7E/4 12Ah
Horn	Lucas HF 1441 Alette
Headlamp	Lucas
Tail lamp	Lucas MT10
Bulb main	6V 24/24W bayonet
Bulb pilot	6V 3W bayonet
Bulb speedo	6V 3W bayonet
Bulb tail	6V 3W bayonet

Speedometer

Type	Smiths 5467/43L 120mph rpm dial
Cable length	44in

Dimensions

Wheel base	55in
Overall length	84in
Overall width	28½in
Seat height	29½in
Ground clearance	6in
Weight (dry)	370lb
	385lb with optional spring hub

Capacities

Petrol tank	4gal (18L)
Oil tank	6pt (3.5L)
Gearbox	¾pt (450cc)
Primary case	½pt (300cc)
Front forks	⅙pt (100cc)

Lubrication

Engine	
Summer	SAE 40-50
Winter	SAE 20-30
Gearbox	EP 90
Primary case	SAE 20
Front fork	SAE 20
Grease	LM

Torque settings

Flywheel nuts	12lb/ft (1.65kg)
Camshaft pinion nuts	50lb/ft (7kg)
Big end nuts	28lb/ft (3.9kg)
Crankshaft pinion nut	50lb/ft (7kg)
Cylinder head bolts	18lb/ft (2.49kg)
Kick start ratchet nut	45lb/ft (6.3kg)
Gearbox sprocket nut	80lb/ft (11.1kg)
Clutch centre nut	50lb/ft (7kg)
Rotor fixing nut	30lb/ft (4.1kg)
Fork cap nut	80lb/ft (11.1kg)
Stanchion pinch bolt nut	25lb/ft (3.5kg)
Zener diode nut	1.5lb/ft (.21kg)

General settings

¼in diameter	12lb/ft
5/16in diameter	15lb/ft
⅜in diameter	18lb/ft

1951 Model 6T Thunderbird

Engine prefix: 6T
Engine numbers: 136 NA to 15808 NA
Build dates: 03.11.1950 to 01.11.1951
New NA suffix to engine and frame numbers

Engine The timing side main bearing was changed from a ball journal bearing to a twin-lipped roller bearing of the previous dimensions. Three keyway camshaft pinions replaced the single keyway ones. Stronger connecting rods were fitted from 915 NA to cope with the increased power of the 6T, and, at the same time, the balance factor was increased from 52% to 64%.

To combat camshaft and tappet wear, stalite-tipped tappets were fitted from 10345 NA, June 26, 1951.

Taper-faced piston rings were fitted to aid the bedding in process from 3918 NA, February 6, 1951.

Gearbox A hexagon-headed filler cap replaced the knurled edge as before, giving better accessibility.

Petrol tank Taper lever taps, left and right, with petrol pipes to match.

Exhaust system As 1950, but with added right-angle brackets from the lower front engine plate stud to welded tags on the exhaust pipes.

Wheels The 7in diameter front brake drum was changed to a Mehanite casting replacing the steel pressing. The aim was to give a more effective front brake with no distortion.

Speedometer The speedometer dial was recalibrated to bring the 30-70mph section to the top of the instrument so it was easier to read. New numbers were issued 5467I1 07/L 120mph dial, 5467/47/L 180kph.

Saddle The Triumph Twinseat was offered as an optional extra to the single saddle and pillion seat.

Electrical A Lucas K2F magneto with a Lucas automatic advance and retard control was added to the specification, allowing the use of a BTH or Lucas component.

Technical development

Carefree motorcycling in the days before helmets became compulsory.

1952 Model 6T Thunderbird

Engine prefix: 6T
Engine and frame numbers: 15809 NA — 01.11.1951 to 21999 NA — 02.01.1952
And then 25001 — 26.02.1952 to 32300 — 28.08.1952

Engine The suffix NA was deleted from the engine number at 25001, June 26, 1952. The Amal carburettor was replaced by an SU MC2 vacuum instrument. The oil pump check valve plugs were castellated to give better support to the ball valves.

Frame A new front frame featured an 'eye' in the seat downtube to provide a straight entry from the carburettor to the air filter. The lower oil tank fixing clip was deleted from the seat tube. The rear brake pedal was fitted with a smaller pinnacled footpad to give a neater appearance.

Suspension The front forks were fitted with a larger diameter nacelle. The earlier, louvered area under the headlight was replaced by a small oblong pilot light. The mechanical parts of the forks remained as before, except for the springs, which were shortened to 19¼in so that the cadmium seal holder would not show when the machine was static (this was a result of Edward Turner fussing over the bike's appearance).

1950 Thunderbird with one of the riders at Montlhéry taking the chequered flag.

The Triumph Speed Twin & Thunderbird Bible

GENERAL SPECIFICATION
(All Models)

ENGINES. O.H.V. vertical twin cylinder with twin gear-driven camshafts. Totally enclosed valve gear with positive lubrication. Rigid crankcase of high tensile aluminium. "H" section connecting rods with patented plain big-ends. Crankshaft mounted on massive ball and roller bearings (3T, ball only) with central flywheel. Dry sump lubrication with high capacity plunger type pumps giving positive feeds to big-ends and valve gear. Pressure indicator on timing cover. Gear driven magneto and separate dynamo. Amal carburetter with patent air cleaner and Triumph adjustable quick action twist grip.

TRANSMISSION. Primary chain in polished cast aluminium oil-bath case. Rear chain positively lubricated and protected on both runs.

FOUR SPEED GEARBOX. Triumph design and manufacture. Large diameter shafts and gears of hardened nickel and nickel-chrome steel. Special dogs for easy changing. Positive stop footchange fully enclosed. Integral speedometer drive. Large diameter multiplate clutch.

PETROL TANK. All-steel welded streamline design. Quick opening plated filler cap. Two-way tap with reserve. Exclusive plated parcel grid on tank top.

OIL TANK. All-steel welded design with accessible filters, drain plug and separate vent. Leak-proof filler cap.

FRAME. Brazed full cradle type (except on TR5) with large diameter front down tube.

FRONT FORKS. Triumph design telescopic type with six inches of hydraulically damped movement.

BRAKES. Triumph design of exceptional power. Finest quality linings, finger adjustment back and front. Polished front brake anchor plate. New cast iron front drum.

HANDLEBAR. Triumph design. Quick-action twist grip with finger adjustment friction control. Integral horn push. Adjustable plated clutch and brake levers.

MUDGUARDS. Wide "D" section with streamline stays. On 5T, 6T and T100 rear guard detaches completely for rear wheel accessibility. Narrow alloy competition type guards on TR5.

WHEELS AND TYRES. Triumph design wheels with heavy-duty dull plated spokes. Dunlop tyres.

TOOLBOX. All-steel large capacity with quick release fastener. Complete set good quality tools and greasegun.

NACELLE. (Patent No. 647670). Integral with top of forks and groups all instruments and switchgear in most convenient position. Incorporates speedometer, ammeter, lighting switch, cut-out button, horn and headlamp. All instruments rubber mounted.

EQUIPMENT. Lucas 6 volt 60 watt dynamo with full ball-bearing armature. Powerful built-in headlamp with adjustable chromium rim. Electric horn. Triumph design rubber kneegrips. Adjustable de Luxe saddle (Twin-Seat on T100). Smiths 120 m.p.h. (or 180 k.p.h.) chronometric speedometer with r.p.m. scale and internal illumination. Tyre inflator.

AIR CLEANER. Triumph design patented Vokes air cleaner, mounted behind the battery, neat and efficient.

EXTRAS

SPRING WHEEL. (Patent No. 524885). Available as an extra on all models. This remarkable springing system has achieved great popularity in all parts of the world. The massive aluminium alloy hub shell totally encloses all moving parts and has a powerful 8in. brake attached. Mounted in the frame exactly like a normal wheel.

HOW IT OPERATES. The spindle remains stationary, bolted into the frame as usual, while the wheel and hub move on a curved path taken from the centre of the gearbox sprocket. Chain tension remains constant. Movement controlled by springs, two below the spindle and one above.

PROP STAND. Extra on all models. A spring retains the stand out as a prop or in folded back position.

TWIN SEAT. Triumph design. Provides an attractive alternative to the normal saddle and pillion seat. All over Latex foam cushion covered in long wearing black "VYNIDE" completely waterproof. Mounted on specially shaped steel base pan. (Fitted standard on T100, extra on 5T and 6T.)

ILLUSTRATED AT SIDES

LEFT
TR5 and T100 die-cast alloy Cylinder Head.
Thunderbird Connecting Rods.
Thunderbird Pistons.
Thunderbird Crankshaft.
Triumph 4-Speed Gearbox.

RIGHT
Tank-top Parcel Grid
Air Cleaner.
Triumph Instrument Nacelle. (Patent No. 647670).
Triumph Front Brake with new cast iron drum.
Triumph Spring Wheel.

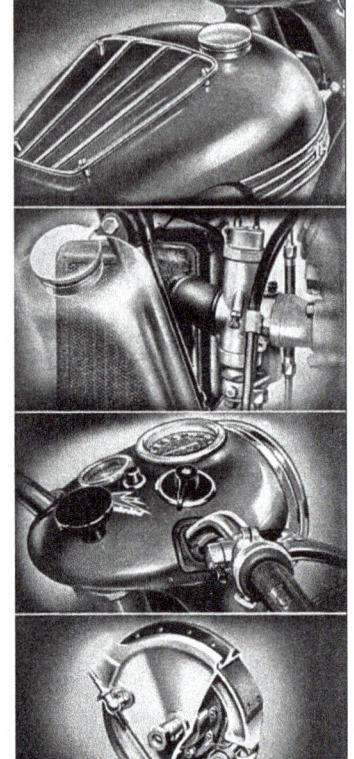

Thunderbird specification.

Petrol Tank A new method of construction eliminated the bottom outside edge seams, but left a visible central weld on top of the tank. The left hand tap was deleted and replaced by a threaded plug. Clear PVC petrol pipes were specified.

Oil tank The rear fixing pommel was deleted in favour of a plain welded-on strap, which was then bolted to the rear mudguard.

The oil vent pipe from the tank was re-routed into the rear of the primary chaincase via a steel bundy tube with rubber connections either end.

Handlebars/controls The handlebars were stove-enamelled blue.

Wheels Both front and rear wheel rims were stove-enamelled blue. The rear sprocket was now integral with the brake drum, replacing the bolt-on. The spring wheel remained as before.

Air filter A new D-type Vokes air filter was fitted, a detachable lid enabling the filter element to be cleaned or renewed.

Electrical The electrical system was changed to positive earth, to conform with the motorcar industry. To provide a more visible light, the tail lamp was cone-shaped, increasing the lit area.

A new 'pre-focus' 7in headlamp assembly was fitted, and a separate Lucas 517 pilot light was attached to the upper nacelle cover beneath the headlamp. The headlamp bulb was a Lucas 373 30/24W flange fitting bulb, the pilot bulb was a Lucas 988 6W.

Note. Due to the shortage of nickel, some items normally chrome-plated were now cadmium-plated, the following were affected:

Pushrod cover tubes
Rocker feed spindle dome nuts
Exhaust pipe pin clips
Kickstart pedal
Footchange lever
Clutch pushrod lever

Technical development

A 1950 Thunderbird at the Earls Court Motorcycle Show.

DETAILS...

Whenever you look on a Triumph you will find small exclusive items designed to give the superior service and satisfaction for which the Triumph is famed. For instance:

(1) Highly polished front brake anchor plate, primary chain case, timing cover and gearbox end-cover for better appearance and ease of cleaning.

(2) Plated streamline beading on front number plate banishes dangerous and rust collecting sharp edges.

(3) Twist grip friction can be adjusted instantly—while you are riding if necessary.

(4) Brake adjustment is a minute's work, without tools.

(5) A drain plug in the oil tank makes oil changing a simple job.

(6) Easily seen, trouble-free oil pressure indicator on the timing cover.

(7) Chainguards to **both** runs of rear chain.

(8) Footrests, handlebars, brake pedal and gear change pedal easily adjustable to suit all riding positions.

(9) Battery conveniently located for easy topping up.

(10) Attractive design rear number plate with lifting handle combined.

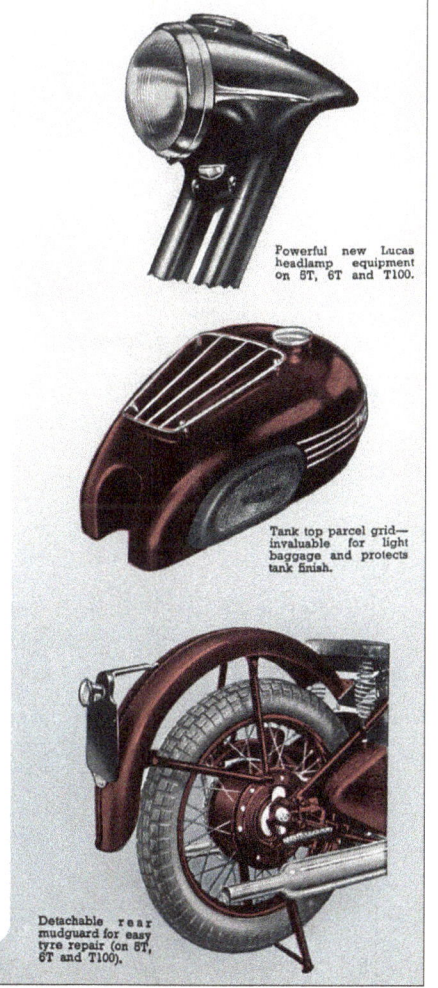

1952 features showing the redesigned MkII spring wheel, and the new location of the pilot lamp.

103

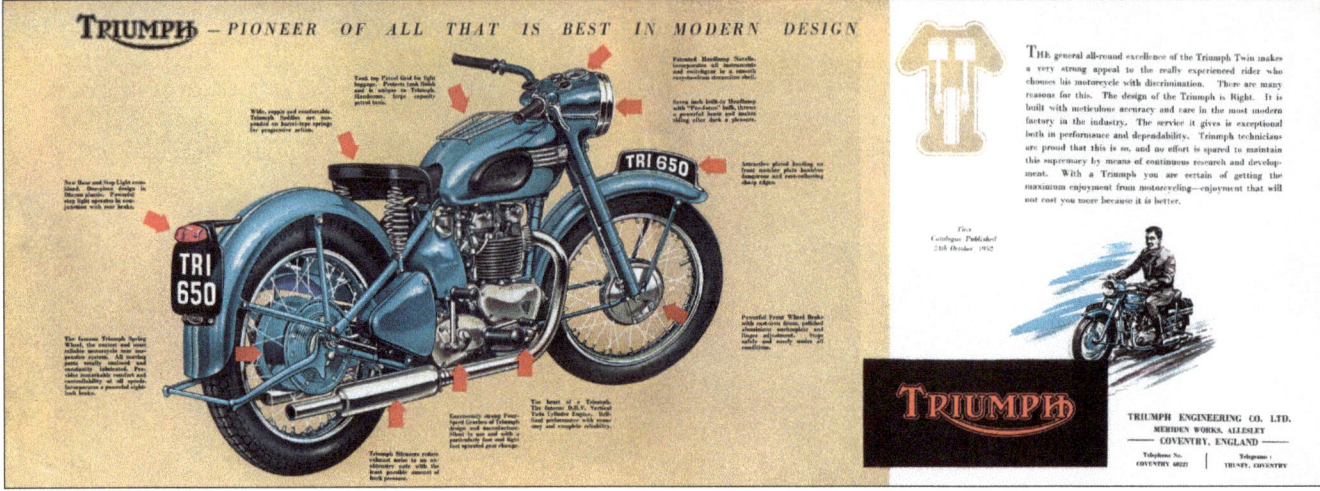

1952 catalogue picture.

1953 Model 6T Thunderbird

Engine prefix: 6T
Engine and frame numbers: 32304 to 44821
Build dates: 29.08.1952 to 15.09.1953

Engine From 37630, February 18, 1953, new E3275 camshafts were introduced with ramps on the opening and closings. They required 0.010in tappet clearance and, for identification purposes, the crankcase was stamped with a cartwheel mark.

Note. Ginger Wood, the SU representative, averred that a better all-round performance would be obtained if the tappet setting was increased to 0.013in when the SU was fitted.

Gearbox A steel gear selection camplate replaced the wear-prone alloy one at 42654, May 6, 1953.

Transmission The cam and spring engine shaft shock absorber was deleted, and a splined sprocket, retained by a plain nut and lockwasher, was fitted. The shock absorber now took the form of a four-paddle centre, with rubber inserts set in a cast iron housing within the clutch assembly.

Frame The propstand footpiece was extended around the exhaust pipe for easier operation.

Toolbox The loose P-clip which fixed the top of the toolbox to the frame was deleted. The rear of the toolbox was bolted directly onto the lower section of the rear mudguard, creating a tidier fixing.

Rear number plate A redesigned rear numberplate was required to accept the rectangular rear lamp.

Electrical The new Lucas 525 'Diacon' plastic lens stop and tail lamp was fitted. Stop lamp operation was via the brake rod connected by a spring to the Lucas stop switch. The stop switch was fixed to a small plate anchored to the left hand pillion footrest bolt.

Ignition was by a BTH magneto or a Lucas K2F magneto, both featuring automatic advance control.

Suppressors were incorporated in the KLG or Champion sparkplug covers.

Note. The restriction on the use of chrome-plate may have extended into the early 1953 season models. Unfortunately, no positive identification is available.

1954 Model 6T Thunderbird

Engine prefix: 6T
Engine and frame numbers: 44235 to 55593
Build dates: 31.08.1953 to 09.07.1954

The major change for the 1954 Thunderbird was the adoption of coil ignition and a crankshaft driven AC alternator. This system was not entirely new to Triumph, as it had been fitted successfully to the Speed Twin a earlier.

Engine A new crankshaft with larger diameter big end journals (1.6235/1.6240in) and a larger diameter timing side main journal (1.1247/1.1250in) was specified. To carry the AC rotor, the drive side crankshaft was provided with a parallel section outboard of the engine sprocket splines. The crankshaft was now supported on two $1\tfrac{1}{8}$ x $2\tfrac{13}{16}$ x $\tfrac{13}{16}$in MSII ball journal bearings. To compliment the new crankshaft, connecting rods with larger diameter big ends (1.6250/1.6255in) were required. A balance factor of 52% was now specified.

The new timing side crankcase had a main bearing housing diameter of 2.8095/2.8100in and, with the deletion of the DC dynamo, no provision for the drive was required on the crankcase or timing cover.

Gearbox The clutch cable adjuster lug was repositioned from the vertical to a slight forward angle, bringing the 6T into line with the T100 and T110 swinging arm models.

Transmission Internally as 1953, but new inner and outer primary chaincases were required to house the Lucas RM14 alternator.

Technical development

The SU carburettor and Diacon tail lamp were specified for 1953 on the Thunderbird.

For tough riding conditions where sustained high performance is called for the Thunderbird is without equal. Its 650 c.c. 34 b.h.p. engine has a tremendous reserve of power for all occasions, which it delivers in a smooth and effortless manner. Equally at home solo or with a heavily laden sidecar. Beautifully finished in polychromatic blue with gold lining.

GENERAL SPECIFICATION
ALL MODELS

ENGINES. O.H.V. vertical twin-cylinder type with two gear-driven camshafts. All valve gear totally enclosed and positively lubricated. "H" section connecting rods in RR56 hiduminium alloy with patented plain big-ends. Crankshaft mounted on massive ball and roller bearings, with central flywheel. Die-cast alloy head and barrel on T100, T100c and TR5; cast-iron on 5T and 6T. Dry sump lubrication with full capacity plunger type pumps pressure feeding to big-ends and valve gear. Timing cover highly polished and fitted with oil pressure indicator. Patent air cleaner. Amal carburetter on T100, T100c (2), 5T and TR5; S.U. carburetter on 6T. Twin large diameter plated exhaust pipes with efficient cylindrical silencers. Small diameter two-in-one pipe and single silencer on TR5.

TRANSMISSION. Primary chain totally enclosed in polished aluminium case with accessible oil filler. Rear chain protected on both runs and positively lubricated.

FOUR-SPEED GEARBOX. Triumph foot-change specially dogged for fast and easy use. Positive stop foot-change specially dogged for fast and easy use. Pedal adjustable for position. Robust shafts and gears of finest nickel and nickel-chrome steel. Integral speedometer drive. Large diameter multi-plate clutch with built-in rubber pad type shock absorber.

FUEL TANKS. All-steel welded petrol and oil tanks with quick-release plated filler caps, accessible filters, drain plug and separate vent to oil tank.

FRAMES. T100, T100c, 6T and 5T brazed full cradle type with large diameter tapered front down tube. Lugs for side-car attachment either side. Front and rear stands. TR5 has special competition type short wheelbase frame.

FRONT FORKS. Triumph design telescopic pattern with hydraulic damping and long supple springs with six inches of movement.

BRAKES. Exceptionally powerful and smooth acting, with large diameter cast-iron drums front and rear, finest quality linings, finger adjustment. Pedal adjustable for position.

HANDLEBAR. Designed for comfort and complete control. Triumph patented quick-action twist-grip throttle with adjustable friction control. Integral horn push. Adjustable plated front brake and clutch levers. Handlebars adjustable for position.

WHEELS AND TYRES. Triumph design wheels with heavy-duty dull-plated spokes. Dunlop tyres.

TOOLBOX. All steel, large capacity, with quick-release fastener. Complete set of good quality tools and grease gun in container.

MUDGUARDS. Efficient "D" shaped guards with central rib. Rear guard detachable for rear wheel accessibility. Aluminium competition type on TR5.

NACELLE. Triumph Patent No. 647670. Neat streamline shell integral with top of forks, encloses headlamp, instruments and switchgear. All instruments rubber mounted and internally illuminated.

ELECTRICAL EQUIPMENT. Powerful Lucas 7 in. built-in headlamp on T100, T100c, 6T and 5T, with combined reflector/front lens assembly. "pre-focus" bulb and adjustable rim. Separate parking light below. TR5 has 6 in. headlamp with quick detachable harness. T100, T100c, 6T and TR5 fitted with Lucas 6 volt 60 watt dynamo with full ball bearing armature. Automatic voltage control. Lucas gear-driven magneto. Lucas 12 a.h. battery. Powerful wide angle rear/stop light. 5T fitted with Lucas A.C. Lighting-Ignition set in place of separate dynamo and magneto. Other details as 6T. (See page 2 for full description).

SPEEDOMETER. Smiths 120 m.p.h. (or 180 k.p.h.) chronometric speedometer with r.p.m. scale, internal illumination and trip recorder.

OTHER EQUIPMENT. Well sprung adjustable saddles on 5T, 6T and TR5. Twinseat on T100 and T100c. Comfortable rubber knee-grips on T100, T100c, 5T and 6T. Tyre inflator, rubber handlebar grips, footrest and kick-start pedal rubbers. Unique plated parcel grid on petrol tank top. Attractively shaped rear number plate with lifting handle combined.

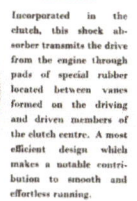

CLUTCH SHAFT SHOCK ABSORBER
Incorporated in the clutch, this shock absorber transmits the drive from the engine through pads of special rubber located between vanes formed on the driving and driven members of the clutch centre. A most efficient design which makes a notable contribution to smooth and effortless running.

EXTRAS

SPRING WHEEL (Triumph Patent No. 524885). This famous rear suspension system is unique because it requires no maintenance or greasing except at very long intervals. There are no external moving parts to wear, everything is totally enclosed in a massive aluminium alloy hub shell. On the road it gives a comfortable ride at all speeds, solo or sidecar, and exceptional controllability. The wheel is mounted normally in the frame, which is quite unchanged, enabling a sidecar to be fitted without any complication. Operation is simple, the spindle bolting into the frame as usual, while the wheel and hub move on a curved path taken from the centre of the gearbox sprocket, which ensures constant chain tension. Movement is controlled by springs—two below the spindle and one above. Available as an extra on all models.
PROP STAND. Retained by spring in both positions, out as a prop or folded back. An extra on all models.
TWINSEAT. Triumph design, of supple Latex foam covered with black waterproof VYNIDE. Steel base pan (Standard on T100 and T100c, extra on 5T and 6T.)
PILLION FOOTRESTS. Folding type for all models, fit to special lugs on frame. Rubber covered.

AIR CLEANER (Top)
Triumph design patented Vokes cleaner mounted behind saddle tube with straight line air intake through a special "eye" in the frame. Oil-wetted felt element quickly detachable for cleaning.

REAR/STOP LIGHT (Centre)
New wide-angle lamp of Diacon plastic with no external metal parts. Incorporates a stop light operated through a switch connected to the rear brake pedal.

TRIUMPH SPRING WHEEL (Patent No. 524885) (Bottom)
The neatest and most reliable rear suspension system available on a motorcycle. The massive alloy hub shell encloses all moving parts, keeping them free from dirt and wear.

Items fitted to the 1953 Thunderbird.

Triumph brochure featuring the Thunderbird.

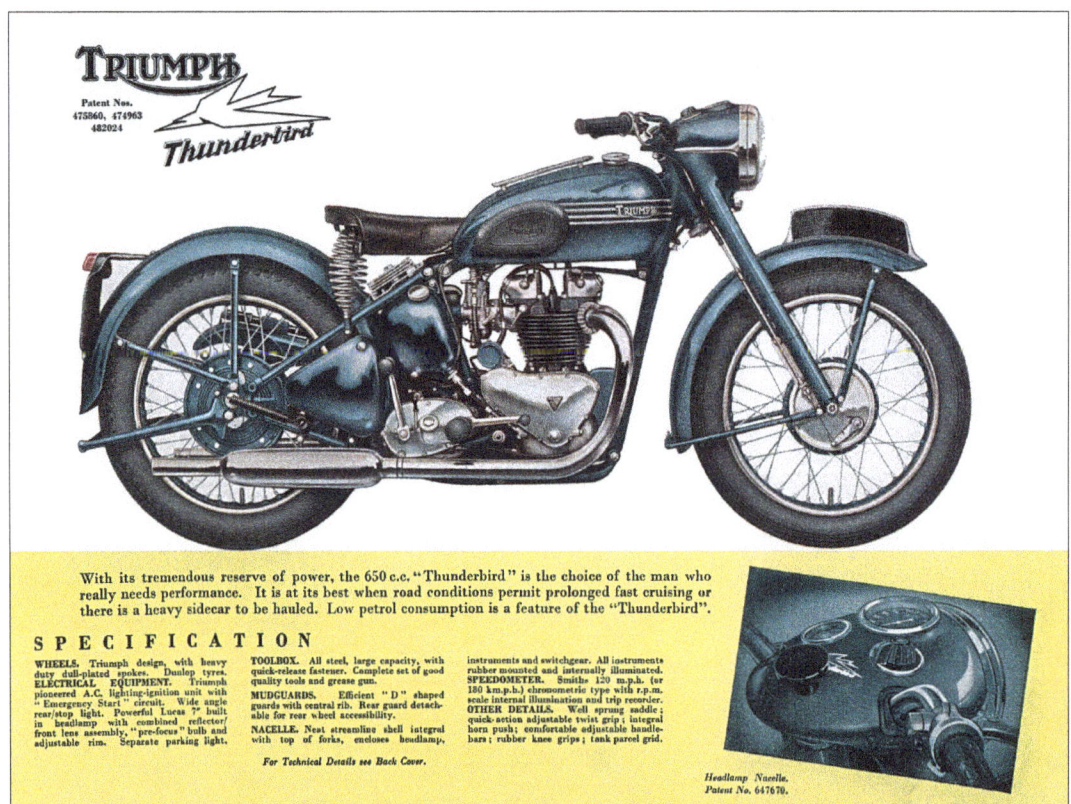

1954 model. The inset picture shows the position of the Lucas PRS8 ignition/light switch, ammeter, and Thunderbird logo.

Technical development

Petrol tank A push-pull petrol tap with reserve facility was fitted on the right hand side, with a blanking plug on the left.

Frame The front engine fixing plates were left blank as the dynamo apertures were no longer required.

Suspension The fork springs were lengthened to 20in of free length.

Exhaust system A new left hand exhaust pipe was required needing a 'dog leg' bend to clear the bulkier primary chaincases.

Taper-bodied silencers, bringing the 6T into line with the swinging arm models, replaced the parallel tubular ones.

Electrical A Lucas PRS8 combined ignition and lighting switch was fitted in the nacelle top cover along with a 2in diameter Lucas ammeter. The ignition coil was a Lucas 6V Q6, fitted above the Lucas DKX2A distributor. The alternating current from the generator was fed to a 4½in diameter Sentercel rectifier fitted under the seat. At 55494, July 7, 1954, a 2¾in diameter rectifier replaced the 4½in one.

The last rigid frame 6T Thunderbird built was 55593 on September 7, 1954.

1955 Model 6T Thunderbird

Model prefix: 6T
Engine and frame numbers: 56700 to 70874
Build dates: 20.08.1954 to 25.08.1955

The major change for the 1955 season was the introduction of the swinging arm rear suspension frame. This frame, although new to the 6T, had already been featured on the 1954 T100 and T110 models.

Engine Phillips crosshead screws replaced slotted cheesehead, the gudgeon pin bore was reduced and internally tapered at both ends, the crankshaft was fitted with a sludge tube between the two crank webs, and an Amal Monobloc carburettor was specified for the USA.

Gearbox Apart from a new main casing, with fixing lugs top and bottom, and the use of Phillips crosshead screws, the gearbox remained unchanged.

Transmission The primary chain remained at ½ x 0.305in but the length changed to 79 links. Similarly, the rear chain was changed to 101 links. New primary chaincases were required to fit the swinging arm frame, and an opportunity was taken to mount the alternator stator independently of the primary outer cover. The alternator stator was now bolted to the primary inner giving more accurate concentricity. Phillips crosshead screws joined the two cases together.

Frame The swinging arm frame followed the traditional Triumph method of construction (tubes and brazed-on lugs). A bolt-on rear section, which provided support for the Girling suspension units, continued under the gearbox and engine and bolted to the front frame.

Suspension Girling units with adjustable spring-loading were fitted. Adjustment was via a three-cam ring at the lower end. Normally, 110-pound rate springs of 8.4in free length were fitted to the units which had a length of 12.9in between centres.

Oil tank A new six-pint oil tank was styled as a one-piece unit with the battery case and toolbox. The filler cap was a chrome-plated Ceandes push and twist cap, 2½in diameter, and was very similar to the petrol cap except that it lacked the breather hole. The tank vent pipe was still connected to the rear of the primary inner case, and consisted of an oil-proof rubber tube.

Mudguards The front mudguard remained as before, but the rear was entirely new. Valances, spot welded to the sides of the mudguard, disguised the gap between mudguard and rear wheel.

Toolbox This was a compartment within the battery container on the left side of the machine. A styled lid was retained by a long slotted screw.

Wheels There was no change to the front wheel, but the standard rear dispensed with the taper roller bearing in favour of two 20 x 47 x 14mm ball journal bearings. The cast iron brake drum and integral 46-tooth sprocket was retained.

A quickly-detachable rear wheel, whereby removal of a threaded spindle. enabled the wheel to be removed whilst leaving the splined brake drum, chain and sprocket in situ, was offered as an option.

The wheel hub was fitted with .750 x 1.8504 x .566in taper roller bearings, while the brake drum and sprocket bearing was a ⅞ x 2 x 9/16 ball journal. Both conditions of wheel had WM2 x 19in rims.

Twinseat The split level twinseat was a standard fitting. It was retained by a nut and bolt at the nose, and at the rear by the top fixing bolts of the suspension units.

Air filter The Vokes air filter was sandwiched between the oil tank and the battery case. Similar to the 1954 item, it had the mounting brackets and connecting tube modified to suit its new location. A rubber hose connected the filter to the carburettor.

Electrical A new Lucas stop/tail lamp (564) incorporating integral reflectors and a rubber-mounted bulb holder was specified. A Lucas stop switch (22B 31383) operated directly from the brake lever. A 6V/12Ah Lucas PU7E-9 battery with positive earth was specified. The Lucas ignition coil was relocated from above the distributor and fitted under the twinseat.

The Triumph Speed Twin & Thunderbird Bible

The first modern "over 500 c.c." vertical twin, the Thunderbird's vast capacity for hard work coupled with a modest petrol consumption has earned it an unequalled reputation among discriminating owners. Fast, smooth and powerful it is a joy to ride at all times.

5T and 6T GENERAL

ENGINES. 5T 500 c.c. : 6T 650 c.c. : Vertical twin cylinder O.H.V. with two gear-driven camshafts. Central flywheel. "H" section RR56 alloy connecting rods with patented plain big ends. Dry sump lubrication, high capacity plunger type pumps, pressure-fed big ends and valve gear. Highly polished timing cover fitted with oil pressure indicator. Patent air cleaner. Efficient barrel type silencers.

FOUR-SPEED GEARBOX. Triumph design and manufacture. Positive stop footchange. Shafts and gears of finest nickel and nickel-chrome steel. Large diameter multi-plate clutch with rubber pad type shock absorber. Polished aluminium primary chaincase.

FUEL TANKS. All-steel welded tanks with quick-release caps and accessible filters.

FRAME. Brazed cradle type frame with swinging arm rear suspension with hydraulic damping instantly adjustable to varying loads. Also available to rigid frame specification.
FORKS. Triumph telescopic forks with hydraulic damping. Provide accurate steering with comfort at all speeds.
BRAKES. Exceptionally powerful with large diameter cast-iron drums. Finger adjustment.

The toughest conditions are easy on a Triumph! ("The Motor Cycle" Photo.)

1955 model.

1956 Model 6T Thunderbird

Engine prefix: 6T
Engine and frame numbers: 70970 — 26.08.1955 to 82222 — 25.06.1956, 0654 — 19.07.1956 to 0943 — 29.08.1956.

To prevent the frame and engine numbers going into six digits, the numbering sequence went back to 0101 on July 5, 1956, though this was a T110 model. The Thunderbird started at 0654. The SU carburettor was still used, but was renumbered 590.

Engine Steel-backed, Vandervell shell bearing inserts were fitted to the connecting rod big ends from 75103, December 12, 1955.

The number inlet camshaft breather holes was reduced to one, to prevent oil splatter from the breather tube exit. An alternative carburettor was specified for the USA.

Gearbox The phosphor bronze layshaft bushes were replaced by sintered bronze bushes as a cost saving measure.

Transmission The cork clutch plates were replaced by plain steel plates with bonded-on neo-Langite pads.

Frame A sidecar fixing lug was incorporated at the lower end of the seat tube. The steering head lug gained a new forging, increasing its size and so harmonising top and bottom bearing cups. As a result, the ball bearing quantity was revised to 40 x ¼in diameter.

The new steering head forging was provided with adjustable steering lock stops in the form of bolts screwed into the threaded forging. The rear tank mounting bracket was rubber-mounted to the frame to reduce tank fractures in that area.

Technical development

IN the Speed Twin and Thunderbird models, the discriminating rider has the choice of two motorcycles with world-wide reputations for zestful performance and easy handling. The Speed Twin, used by eighty police forces, is fast, smooth, and tractable while the 650 c.c. engine of the Thunderbird provides that *extra* power demanded by some riders and is of course ideal for heavy sidecar work.

TRIUMPH Thunderbird
Patent Nos. 475860, 474963, 482024

Living in an Australian nature sanctuary these kangaroos readily feed from the hands of visitors.

Suspension The hydraulic damper tube end plug was now tapered to prevent the fork bottoming during hard braking. A chrome grille replaced the underslung pilot light.

Petrol tank A chrome-plated centre styling band covered the petrol tank central weld. To provide clearance for the styling band, the three bars in the parcel grid were reduced to two.

Handlebars and controls A new handlebar bend obviated the threaded hole that had been used to retain the horn push button. A new clutch lever clamp bracket was used to mount the combined horn push and dipper switch.

Wheels The painted and lined wheel rim centres were replaced by plain chrome-plated rims.

Electrical A new style wiring harness, wherein a thick plastic sheath was used to encase all the wires, was fitted. The horn push and dipper combined switch was mounted on the clutch lever clamp bracket, replacing the two separate items. The ignition coil was relocated to the 1954, above the distributor. The pilot light was relocated in the sealed beam headlight reflector, making the separate pilot light unit obsolete.

1957 Model 6T Thunderbird

Engine prefix: 6T
Engine and frame numbers: 01406 to 011110
Build dates: 10.09.1956 to 18.09.1957

Engine Single keyway camshaft pinions were reintroduced. A garter oil seal was fitted to the drive side crankcase to prevent oil transfer between the engine and the primary chaincase. The SU carburettor was renumbered to 603. An Amal Monobloc carburettor was specified for the USA.

For 1956, the Thunderbird finish was Polychromatic Crystal Grey.

The Triumph Speed Twin & Thunderbird Bible

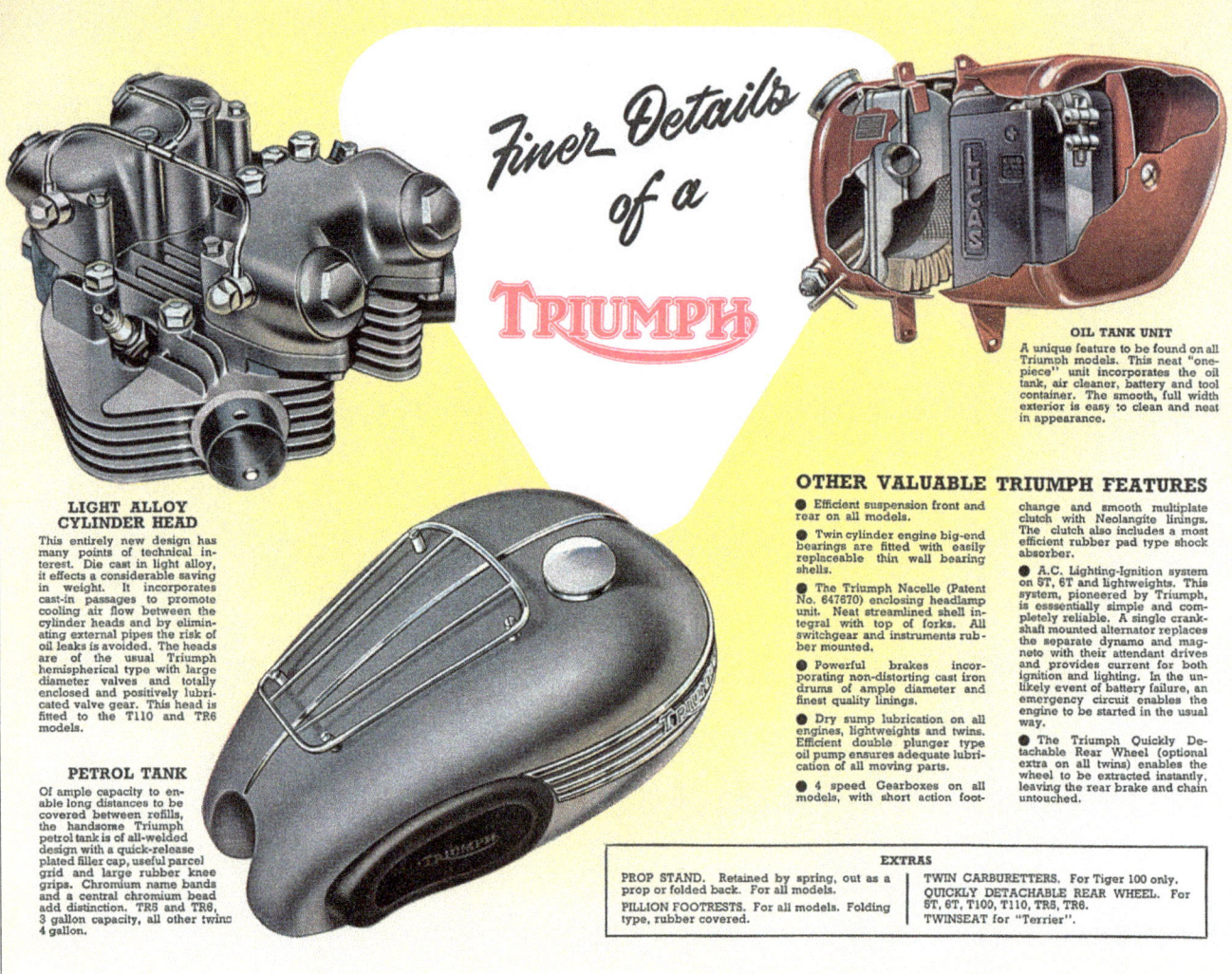

Some of the features available for the 1957 Thunderbird.

Gearbox The high gear sleeve bush was extended to protrude into the primary chaincase, thus ensuring that any seepage between the gearbox mainshaft and the sleeve bush was deposited into the chaincase.

Transmission The inner boss of the engine sprocket was ground to suit the oil seal in the crankcase.

Frame The left hand swinging arm fork end was modified to provide an independent fixing for the rear chainguard (previously, the lower suspension bolt was used). The front end of the chainguard pivoted on a spring-loaded bolt and right angle bracket. This new chainguard was extended to cover more of the rear sprocket.

From 08374, June 3, 1957, the Easy-Lift centre stand was fitted as standard.

Suspension The front fork bottom sliders were fitted with caps and bolts to retain the front wheel spindle, and gave increased rigidity to the fork assembly. Brazed-on lugs replaced the wraparound dips mounting the front mudguard centre stay. Metalastic bonded bushes were fitted to the Girling suspension units

Petrol tank The new tank featured redesigned fittings for the 'Basket Weave' tank badges with front and rear chrome styling stripes.

Controls The front brake cable adjuster and abutment was relocated to the brazed lug on the right hand fork slider. The sliding tube casing was retained but was shortened.

Wheels A full-width, 7in diameter cast iron drum was fitted to the front wheel and laced with 40 8/10G butted, 6in, UH, straight-pull spokes. The aluminium alloy anchor plate retained the brake shoes whilst, on the opposite side, a chrome-plated styling disc was fitted, and featured concentric radial ribs. The wheel spindle was redesigned to accept the new front fork fixing. Both the standard and quickly-detachable rear wheels were laced with 8/10G butted spokes to overcome failures suffered by the previous 9G spokes.

Technical development

THUNDERBIRD

First in the field with the 500 c.c. vertical twin, Triumph took the lead again in the "over 500 c.c." class when the celebrated 650 c.c. "Thunderbird" was announced. With its 34 B.H.P. engine, it provides effortlessly the extra power demanded by the fast solo man, and is at its best dealing with the varied requirements of the sidecar driver. One of the most popular Triumph models ever, the Thunderbird has an enthusiastic following by riders of real experience.

Triumph Patent Nos. 475860, 474963, 482024

1958 Model 6T Thunderbird

Engine prefix: 6T
Engine and frame numbers: 011284 to 019824
Build dates: 26.09.1957 to 26.08.1958

Engine No change.
An Amal Monobloc carburettor was specified for the USA.

Gearbox The 1958 season saw the introduction of the auto-clutch (the Slickshift) which allowed the rider to change gear without using the clutch lever. This sounded fine in theory, but, in practice, it left a lot to be desired.

One of the drawbacks was that many riders, when changing gear, kept the gear lever depressed until they felt the drive taken up in the selected gear. With the Slickshift, this meant a disconnected drive giving a freewheel effect.

A rubber sleeve was fitted to the kickstart axle, between the kickstart lever and the clutch case, to aid oil retention.

Frame An anti-theft steering lock was fitted to the right hand side of the head lug casting. A keyed lock body held the steering on full left hand lock.

The primary chain adjuster now incorporated the clutch cable abutment, replacing the threaded cast lug on the gearbox inner cover.

Front forks A vertical groove was machined in the steering stem to accept the steering lock body. In the interests of appearance, new mounting lugs for the centre mudguard stay were located on the inner side of the bottom members. The front mudguard stay fixing lugs were deleted from the bottom members, as the new, valanced mudguard was self-supporting. The right hand bottom member was modified to accept the front brake cable stop.

The top nacelle cover was provided with two extra holes which, fitted with small rubber grommets, allowed the front brake and clutch cables to pass through. This provided better cable routing once the handlebar levers were fitted with cable adjusters.

Only the fuel tank and mudguards were coloured items for 1957; the frame, forks and ancillaries were black.

The Triumph Speed Twin & Thunderbird Bible

The 1958 UK market Thunderbird retained the SU vacuum carburettor, and this was the first year of the Slickshift gearbox.

Petrol tank No change.

Oil tank The oil filler neck and filler cap were relocated further inboard so as not to interfere with the rider's leg, especially whilst kickstarting.

Wheels The front hub styling cover was changed from radial rings to radial flutes.

Controls New brake and clutch levers with inbuilt cable adjusters were fitted. The cables had detachable barrel nipples at the lever ends, and the front brake cable dispensed with the steel tube at its lower end.

Mudguards Both front and rear mudguards were now deep pressings. The front mudguard was fitted with a new integral centre stay, and the two front stays were dispensed with. The rear mudguard had a much neater appearance now that the welded-in valances had been replaced by the deep drawn pressing.

Technical development

A 1958 Thunderbird with Amal Monobloc carburettor and raised handlebars. The small three-gallon petrol tank was usually fitted for the US market, as shown in this picture.

Valanced front mudguard and the one-piece valanced rear, new tank badges, and the Slickshift gearbox are shown on this 1958 model.

1959 Model 6T Thunderbird

Engine prefix: 6T
Engine and frame numbers: 020581 to 029362
Build dates: 10.09.1958 to 02.09.1959

A forged, one-piece crankshaft with a bolt-on, central cast iron flywheel replaced the three-piece. A mid season change was to increase the interference fit of the flywheel to crankshaft by 0.0025in to overcome flywheel retaining bolt failure.

Carburettor The vacuum SU carburettor was replaced by an Amal Monobloc (376/210) for all models.

A fully-fitted police Thunderbird built to Australian specification, circa 1958.

Bore	1¹⁄₁₆in
Needle jet	0.106
Needle type	C
Needle position	3
Main jet	270
Throttle valve	3½
Pilot jet	25

Gearbox An oil level indicator was built into the gearbox inner cover. Removal of the threaded plug allowed the oil level to be checked.

The gear control camplate was induction hardened to improve long term reliability from 023941, February 3, 1959. The clutch sprocket bore received the same treatment from 024029.

Technical development

Here we have an aristocrat of the Triumph range and one of the most famous of all – the Thunderbird. A fast, powerful and handsome motorcycle it has been a firm favourite with hard riders for many years – and particularly with the sidecar man. It will haul a heavy sidecar anywhere, and keep on doing it, with a minimum of attention and a maximum of economy.

Triumph is the world's most popular police motorcycle. Here we see Triumph mounted members of the Civil Aviation Constabulary at London Airport. Behind is one of the famous Viscount turboprop airliners.

Wheels The front brake cam lever angle was altered to improve braking. The reworked lever could be identified by a letter X stamping.

Twinseat A safety strap was specified on some US models.

Electrical A Lucas RM15 alternator assembly was specified, and gave a higher output than the previous RM14.

1959 was the last of the single downtube-framed, pre-unit 6T. The last one produced was 6T 029362, September 2, 1959.

1960 Model 6T Thunderbird

Engine prefix: 6T
Engine and frame numbers: D 507 to D 7711
Build dates: 30.10.1959 to 21.07.1960

Engine The engine number was prefixed with a letter D. The brass oil pump body was replaced by an aluminium casting from D 1564, December 29, 1959.

Transmission A 23-tooth engine sprocket replaced the previous 24-tooth sprocket. The rear chain now had 99 links.

Frame The frame was entirely new, with twin front downtubes and a bolted-on rear section. The new frame featured only one tank rail, though, which would cause problems later.

The primary chain - gearbox adjuster draw bolt was redesigned to provide a clutch cable abutment at the rear of the gearbox clamping stud. This was made necessary due to the full rear enclosure panels.

Suspension A redesigned front fork based on the unit 350 model was fitted. Internal tubular spring guides, top and bottom yokes, fork springs of 18$\frac{3}{16}$in free length were all new for the 1960 6T. The nacelle was shortened, and required new top and lower covers.

The 1959 Thunderbird looks rather sombre in its charcoal-grey finish. The Amal Monobloc carburettor was now standard for all markets.

SPECIFICAT[IONS]

TIGER CUB (T20-T20/C)

ENGINE High performance single cylinder o.h.v. with die-cast alloy cylinder head. Inclined large diameter valves. "H" section connecting rod with plain big-end. Dry sump lubrication with double plunger pump. Efficient barrel type silencer. Air cleaner.

FOUR-SPEED GEARBOX Built in unit with the engine in a highly finished streamlined casing. Multiplate clutch with Neolangite linings and rubber pad shock absorber. Positive stop footchange. Silent duplex primary chain.

FRAME Light, but very robust loop type main frame. Swinging arm rear suspension with hydraulic damping. Provision for anti-theft lock to steering head.

FORKS Triumph telescopic type with long, soft springs giving a comfortable ride and accurate steering.

BRAKES Very efficient smooth acting brakes with large diameter cast-iron drums.

WHEELS Triumph design with plated spokes and rims. Efficient mudguards front and rear. New and stylish rear enclosure panels.

FUEL TANKS New and attractively shaped all-steel welded petrol tank, chrome motif. Ample capacity oil tank. Quick release caps and accessible filters.

ELECTRICAL EQUIPMENT A.C./D.C. lighting-ignition system with crankshaft mounted alternator and emergency start circuit. Powerful head and rear lamps. Reflex reflector.

TOOLBOX All-steel with complete kit of good quality tools and tyre inflator.

NACELLE (Patent No. 647670). Neat streamlined shell encloses headlamp, instruments and switchgear and includes a gear-position indicator.

SPEEDOMETER Smiths 80 m.p.h. (140 Km.p.h.) speedometer mounted in nacelle.

OTHER DETAILS Finish: Silver grey and black. Quick-action twistgrip, rubber knee grips.

T20C A popular model for the sporting rider with general specification as above, but with larger diameter wheels and increased mudguard clearances. Upswept exhaust pipe and silencer. Modified gear ratios – for full details see Technical Data table, p. 11.

EXTRAS (T20/T20C) Pillion footrests. Prop stand. Steering lock.

TIGER 100 (T100) THUNDERBIRD (6T)

TIGER 100 ENGINE 500 c.c. o.h.v. vertical twin with two gear-driven camshafts. High compression pistons, die-cast alloy cylinder head and barrel with fine pitch finning. New one-piece forged crankshaft with bolt on central flywheel. "H" section RR56 alloy connecting rods with plain big-ends. Dry sump lubrication, plunger type pump, pressure indicator. Gear-driven dynamo and magneto with manual control. Polished aluminium oil bath primary chaincase. Air cleaner. Racing conversion parts available, also two carburetter head (optional extra).

GEARBOX Triumph design and manufacture. Shafts and gears of hardened nickel and nickel-chrome steel. Positive stop footchange with "Slickshift" auto clutch operation. Multiplate clutch with indestructible Neolangite linings and rubber pad shock absorber. Accessible filler and level plugs and simple primary chain adjustment.

FRAME Brazed cradle type frame with swinging arm suspension, hydraulically damped and adjustable for varying loads. "Easylift" centre and prop stands (latter optional extra). Provision for anti-theft lock to steering head. Front wheel stand.

FORKS Triumph design telescopic pattern with hydraulic damping and steering damper.

THUNDERBIRD ENGINE 650 c.c. vertical twin with two gear-driven camshafts. Cast-iron cylinder head and barrel. New one-piece forged crankshaft with bolt on central flywheel. "H" section RR56 alloy connecting rods with plain big-ends. Dry sump lubrication, plunger type pump. A.C./D.C. lighting-ignition system with emergency start circuit. Oil pressure indicator. Efficient air cleaner.

FUEL TANKS Handsome large capacity all-steel welded tanks. Quick release fillers. Parcel grid on petrol tank. Oil tank in "one-piece" unit with air cleaner, battery and tool container. 7-inch diameter with cast-iron drum integral with rear chain sprocket.

NACELLE (Patent No. 647670). Triumph design integral with top of forks enclosing headlamp instruments and switchgear. Instruments internally illuminated.

BRAKES Front: Full width hub, heavily finned, incorporating efficient large diameter brake. Rear: 7-inch diameter with cast-iron drum integral with rear chain sprocket.

WHEELS AND MUDGUARDS Triumph design wheels with plated spokes and rims. Fully valanced rear guard

TIGER 110 (T110) TROPHY (TR6)

TIGER 110/TROPHY ENGINE 650 c.c. o.h.v. vertical twin with two gear-driven camshafts. Alloy cylinder head, cast-iron barrel, high compression pistons, large bore carburetter. New one-piece forged crankshaft with bolt on central flywheel. "H" section RR56 alloy connecting rods with plain big-ends. Dry sump lubrication with plunger type pump and pressure indicator. Gear-driven dynamo and magneto with manual control. Polished aluminium oil bath primary chaincase. Air cleaner.

(except TR6) and side lifting handles. Aluminium front guard on TR6.

LIGHTING EQUIPMENT 6T: New Lucas RM15 alternator, crankshaft mounted. T100/T110/TR6: Lucas 6 volt 60 watt dynamo with ball-bearing armature.

All Models: 12 a.h. battery, powerful headlamp with combined reflector/front lens assembly, "pre-focus" bulb and adjustable rim. Wide angle rear/stop light with combined reflector.

SPEEDOMETER Smiths 120 m.p.h. (180 Km.p.h.) chronometric type with r.p.m. scale, internal illumination and trip recorder.

HANDLEBAR Comfortable shape with quick-action twistgrip and adjustable friction control. Integral horn push. Adjustable plated clutch and

brake lever with built-in cable adjusters.

TWINSEAT Triumph design. Latex foam cushion covered in black water-proof "Vynide."

TOOLS Kit of good quality tools and tyre inflator. 180-page Instruction Manual.

FINISHES 6T: Charcoal grey with black frame. T100/T110: Silver grey, black frame and forks. TR6: Aztec red/ivory, black frame and forks.

EXTRAS Prop stand all models. Pillion footrests all models. Quickly detachable rear wheel. (Wheel can be removed leaving brake, chain, etc., undisturbed.) Two-carburetter head all alloy with splayed inlet ports, T100 only. Dunlop Sports tyres, TR6 only. Two-tone finish, ivory/black – T100/T110 only. Steering lock all models.

Silent duplex chain primary drive on models T20 and T20C. Note also the robust clutch and crankshaft mounted alternator.

"Slickshift" gearchange on T100, T110, 6T and TR6. Moving the gearchange pedal automatically withdraws the clutch. An overriding normal hand lever is also fitted.

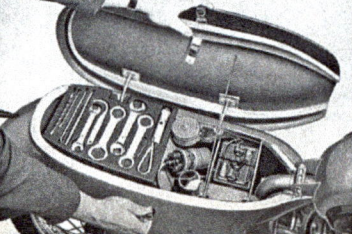

The unique grouping of tools, electrical components and oil tank under the seat of the 3TA and 5TA.

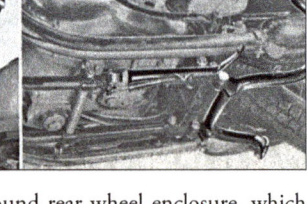

The Triumph "Easylift" centre stand which raises the machine on to its legs almost without effort.

Thunderbird specifications.

Petrol tank The petrol tank was completely new. Supported by three rubber buffers, with mounting lugs being part of the frame, it was retained to the frame by a central, stainless steel rubber-lined strap, which was tensioned by a threaded eye bolt at the head lug. The capacity remained at four gallons, and the chrome-plated parcel grid was fitted as before.

Oil tank A newly-designed oil tank with the filler neck inside the frame tubes was specified. A push and twist filler cap was still specified, but now of much smaller diameter.

Mudguards The front mudguard was a very deep valanced, with a flared-out bottom edge. Apart from the integral central stay, only one other was fitted (doubling as a front stand). At the rear, a simple pressing was fitted under the full wraparound rear wheel enclosure, which in turn was embellished with chrome-plated, scripted Thunderbird motifs.

Toolbox A tooltray was situated on the rear subframe under the seat.

Wheels The front wheel was now a WM2 x 18in rim, and was fitted with a 3.25 x 18in Dunlop ribbed tyre. The front hub chrome styling plate reverted to the radial concentric rings design. 40 x $5^{17}/_{32}$in 8/10G spokes were specified. The rear wheel was a WM2 x 18in rim fitted with a 3.50 x 18in Dunlop Universal tyre. The rear wheel sprocket was reduced to 43 teeth on both the standard and quickly detachable wheels. 20 x $7^{9}/_{16}$in UH 8/10G and 20 x $7^{7}/_{8}$in UH 8/10G butted spokes were used on both rear wheels.

Technical development

The 1960 Thunderbird featured a new duplex downtube front frame, a deeply valanced front mudguard, and full rear enclosure.

1960 was the first year of the duplex front downtube frame. The picture shows the early frame before a lower tank rail tube was added.

A 1960 Thunderbird featuring the new duplex front downtubes.

Twinseat The redesigned seat was hinged on the left hand side giving access to the oil tank filler and the battery. The seat was retained in the closed by a spring-loaded plunger with a plated knob which could be removed to give some degree of security. The twinseat cover was black trimmed with white piping.

Air filter The air filter was changed to a rectangular shape bolted to the seat frame tube and connected to the carburettor by a dog legged-shaped rubber hose.

Electrical A new D-shaped stop light switch was fitted (Lucas No 34181). Operation of the switch was by a small lever contacting the rear brake pedal. The ignition coil was relocated to under the seat, to the rear of the battery.

Speedometer The Smiths speedometer was modified due to the sprocket changes. The 125mph instrument was SC3304/19 and the 190kph SC 3304/20.

Technical development

A radio-equipped 1960 Thunderbird.

The 34 BHP 650cc Thunderbird engine.

1961 Model 6T Thunderbird

Engine prefix: 6T
Engine and frame numbers: D9259 to D15754
Build dates: 05.10.1960 to 22.08.1961

Engine An aluminium alloy cylinder head was fitted to bring the 6T into line with the other 650cc single carburettor models in the Triumph range. Fitting the alloy head raised the compression ratio to 7.5:1, and the head diameter of the exhaust valve was reduced to 1¹¹⁄₃₂in, with an overall length of 3¾in. Inlet remained at 1½in. The oil pressure release valve was fitted with an O-ring seal on the indicator plunger shaft. From 09259 to D11192, December 29, 1960, sports camshafts (E3325 camform as per the Tiger 110) were fitted. Timed dash to dash on inlet and dot to dot on exhaust, they had a running tappet clearance of 0.002in for inlet and 0.004in for the exhaust. These engines didn't carry the spoked wheel (cartwheel mark) stamping alongside the engine number.

From D1193, a redesigned camshaft (E4220 camform) was used for both the inlet and exhaust, and required a running tappet clearance of 0.010in on both. Shorter valve springs were fitted (1⅝in outer and 1¹⁷⁄₃₂in inner free length). From D14438, June 6, 1961, the one piece crankshaft featured straight-sided crank webs, and was fitted with a new flywheel (2¹¹⁄₃₂in as opposed to the earlier 2¼in). The balance factor was changed to 71% using a 540 gram weight. These modifications raised the bhp to 37 @ 6700rpm.

Easily detachable rubber-mounted tank on all 650cc Twins.

The Triumph Speed Twin & Thunderbird Bible

The new petrol tank, with its parcel grid, has a comfortable capacity of 4 gallons, and is easily removed when required.

Gearbox M11121 Torrington roller bearings of ¹¹⁄₁₆ x ⅞ x ¾in were specified for both ends of the gearbox layshaft, replacing the earlier sintered bronze bushes. The layshaft end float was controlled by a bronze thrust washer fitting over the roller bearings. A folding kickstart pedal was now fitted as standard.

Transmission The number of teeth on the engine sprocket was reduced to 22, to give gear ratios of: 11.4, 7.88, 5.55 and a top gear of 4.67. The ⅝ x ⅜in rear chain was reduced to 98 links.

Frame A lower tank rail was added to stiffen the head lug area and to prevent fractures of the twin downtubes, and at the same time revise the steering head angle from 67° to 65°. The fractures had only become apparent when the TR6 Trophy was used in events such as the Big Bear Enduro Race.

Wheels The diameter of the full-width front brake was increased to 8in, and fully-floating brake shoes were fitted front and rear. Front wheelspokes were now 10 x 4⁵⁄₁₆in 78° head, 10 x 4⁵⁄₁₆in 100° head, and 20 x 5¹⁄₁₆in straight. All the spokes were 8/10 gauge butted.

Triumph brochure picture.

Electrical The new alloy cylinder head necessitated a revised sparkplug, so a Champion N5 long reach (¾in) was specified, retaining the 14mm thread diameter.

Speedometer The Smiths speedometer was now specified as a 125mph SC 3304/24 or 190kph SC 3304/25 due to the smaller engine sprocket.

Valve timing the two conditions are:

E3325 form		E4220 form
27°	IVOBTC	25°
48°	IVCABC	52°
48°	EVOBBC	60°
27°	EVCATC	17°

±2½°. Set tappets at 0.020in for timing.

Cam lobe — height from base circle
E3325 form   1.102 - 1.111in
E4220 form   1.123 - 1.131in

1962 Model 6T Thunderbird

Engine prefix: 6T
Engine and frame numbers: 016389 — 01.11.1961 to 020088 — 06.07.1962

Engine A new crankshaft, with pear-shaped crank webs and balanced to 85%, was fitted from D17043, January 15, 1962.

Due to the aluminium alloy pump bodies expanding when temperatures were high, and with the consequent drop in oil pressure, cast iron pump bodies were specified from 017552, February 19, 1962.

Gearbox The unpopular Slickshift auto-clutch was quietly dropped from the specification, the only factory quote being, "It has outlived its usefulness."

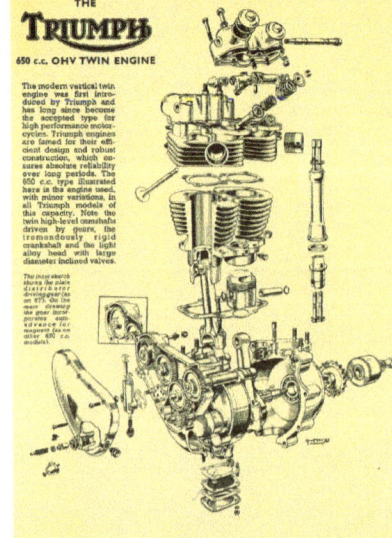

Technical development

The 1961 Thunderbird gained an aluminium alloy cylinder head, and a brighter silver and black paint scheme.

The 1962 Thunderbird still featured full rear panels, but new features were a re-worked seat, with a grey top cover and trim band, and siamese exhaust pipes.

Technical development

Triumph brochure picture.

The 1962 Thunderbird discarded the rear enclosure for the US market.

Petrol tank New petrol taps with flat plate levers were fitted on the left and right hand sides. The left one acting as reserve.

Suspension The Girling suspension units were reduced in length, and there was now 12.4in between centres when fully extended. The spring was also reduced to 5in free length.

Exhaust system The exhaust pipes were 1½in diameter, and were siamesed to run down the right side of the machine terminating in a long, resonator silencer.

Electrical A Lucas RM19 alternator assembly replaced the RM15. A new miniature Lucas rectifier (49072 2DS506) was fitted from D18419, March 15, 1962.

Seat A new seat cover was fitted. It had a grey top with white piping, black sidewalls and grey lower trim band.

The last pre-unit 6T Thunderbird was built on July 6, 1962 (frame and engine number D20088).

1963 Model 6T Thunderbird

Engine prefix: 6T
Engine and frame numbers: DU764 to DU5824
Build dates: 19.12.1962 to 15.08.1963

The 6T received a major face lift for the 1963 season, with a unit construction engine and gearbox, and a new frame with single front downtube. Mini side panels enclosed only part of the rear end, and gave the bike a more pleasing, less ponderous appearance. There were two theories as to the origins of the DU prefix. Firstly, the unit engine was originally fitted to a frame which had twin front downtubes, hence Duplex Unit. Alternatively, since the unit engine had duplex primary drive, DU would seem appropriate. However, I always considered the former to be the origin of the prefix, and it was just that no-one considered it worth changing when the machine went into production.

Engine The flywheel retaining bolt washers were dispensed with, and the bolts retained by 'Loctite Boltlock.' The cylinder barrel featured nine cylinder head fixing bolts, with the ⅜in ones being moved out radially to give more material between the bolt holes and the cylinder wall, so eliminating bore distortion and cylinder head cracking across the bolt holes. Redesigned rocker boxes with horizontal fins and new tappet inspection caps with serrated edges, were retained by short locking clips.

The crankshaft oil feed journal was extended to accept an oil seal fitted in the timing cover. This replaced the bronze bush of the pre-unit models. The exhaust camshaft had an internal taper and a ground journal for an oil seal on the right hand end. The internal taper drove the Lucas automatic advance and retard mechanism as well as the ignition cam for the 4CA contact breaker assembly housed in the timing cover. This advance and retard unit had a range of 14°, so a crankshaft of 7° static and 35° advanced was specified, equating to a piston of ½₄in BTC, fully retarded. Brass-bodied oil pumps were reintroduced to replace the previous cast iron ones.

Wider timing pinions were featured with the aim of giving quieter running and longer life.

Amal Monobloc carburettor settings were revised to 230 main jet, C type needle, and a No 4 throttle valve.

Gearbox Integrated with the engine and primary transmission, the gearbox housed identical internals as the pre-unit machines except for the speedo drive gears, which were changed to 10 and 15 teeth. Due to the different primary drive ratio, a 20-tooth sprocket on the gearbox was specified. A clutch lift mechanism was fitted inside the new gearbox outer cover, and was comprised of three steel balls held between two indented plates. Rotation of the inner plate to which the clutch cable was attached caused the balls to push the plates apart and impart linear movement to the pushrod.

Transmission The new transmission was graced with a three paddle shock absorber unit giving a greater range of movement. A 58-tooth cast iron clutch sprocket housed six plain steel plates and six steel Neo-Langite cork-faced ones. The engine sprocket had 29 teeth, and connecting the two was a Reynolds ⅜ x 0.225in duplex chain of 84 links. Adjustment was provided by a neoprene-lined steel slipper blade with external adjustment at the rear of the primary case). A Reynolds ⅜ x ⅝in rear chain with 104 links was used. Overall gear ratios with the new primary drive and 20-tooth gearbox sprocket were 4th 4.60, 3rd 5.47, 2nd 7.77 and 1st 11.43.

Frame The single front downtube frame carried a new swinging arm lug brazed to the substantial seat tube, and bolted up to the rear engine plates and rear subframe. This, in conjunction with a new, larger diameter tube swinging arm, gave a very rigid mounting, obviating the torsional stress of the previous frames. The anti-theft lock and easy lift centre stand continued as standard equipment.

Suspension The front forks were modified to give a stanchion length of 20⅞in, a damper sleeve of 46in, and a spring free length of 17¹⁄₁₆in with 52 coils of 0.160in diameter. Oil capacity for each fork leg was ¼pt (150cc).

Petrol tank A redesigned petrol tank, but with the same four-gallon capacity, was now fixed to the frame by two bolted fittings at the front and one at the rear. New stick-on knee pads replaced the earlier screwed on ones. Petrol taps, parcel grid, styling badges and petrol cap were as before.

Wheels & mudguards The standard and quickly detachable rear wheels both featured a 46-tooth sprocket.

The large valanced front mudguard was retained, but the rear was a conventional D-shape as the large wrap around full enclosure of the previous year's models was replaced by more stylish quarter panels covering the oil tank and battery.

Technical development

1963 unit Thunderbirds were fitted with special silencers, braced front mudguards, and radio tanks for police use. Note the original footrest mounting position. This was only used on 1963 models.

The Triumph Speed Twin & Thunderbird Bible

A 1963 unit construction Thunderbird for the US market. Mini rear panels gave a less bulbous appearance.

A 1963 UK market Thunderbird. Note the long silencers with integral mounting brackets.

Technical development

Exhaust system Two separate downpipes, of 1½in diameter, terminated into two long resonator silencers which had integral mounting brackets.

Air filter A round pancake-filter with a perforated, chrome plated band was attached directly to the carburettor body.

Speedometer A Smiths SC3304/12mph or a SC3304/15kph with plain dial replaced the engine revolution indicator type.

Electrical A Lucas 4CA twin contact breaker and auto advance and retard unit was housed in the timing cover driven from the exhaust camshaft.

Twin Lucas MA6 6V ignition coils were fitted beneath the petrol tank. Twin Lucas 88SA ignition and lighting switches replaced the combined Lucas PRS8 in the nacelle.

The horn was a Lucas 8H 6V unit and the stop switch (a Lucas 31383 22B) was mounted on the rear chainguard and operated from the rear brake rod via a spring.

Handlebars The 1in diameter handlebar used on Triumphs from pre-war days was replaced by a ⅞in diameter one. Amal clutch and brake levers, which retained the built-in cable adjusters, were used, but now had slots to aid cable replacement. The combined dipper switch and horn push was attached to the clutch lever bracket.

The Triumph twistgrip was replaced by a standard Amal component. Also, the Triumph logo handlebar grips were now standard Amal ones.

1964 Model 6T Thunderbird

Engine prefix: 6T
Engine and frame numbers: DU6329 to DU13210
Build dates: 16.10.1963 to 04.08.1964

Engine The crankcases were modified to improve the oil pick up area around the filter and scavenge pipe. Solid camshaft pinions were introduced from DU1 1482, May 16, 1964, to prevent distortion during manufacture. The engine breather pipe from the crankcase was extended to exit adjacent to the rear number plate.

Gearbox The gearbox outer cover was fitted with an oil seal to prevent oil seepage from the kickstart axle.

Transmission Indents were added to the clutch pressure plates and spring cups to prevent rotation in use.

Frame The footrest mounting points were relocated to the rear engine plates, with the footrests modified to suit. This modification improved ground clearance.

The centre stand operating arm was integrated with the stand, replacing the separate, cottered item.

Suspension The front forks were fitted with external springs in 1964, a first in Triumph's telescopic fork history. Chrome-plated lower spring carriers housed double-lipped oil seals, and individual tubular upper covers shrouded the springs. Fork spring length was 8¾in, with a wire diameter of 0.192in solo or 0.212in sidecar (13 coils solo or 15 coils sidecar).

The loose clips around the bottom fork sliders for the front stay fixing is clearly shown on this 1964 UK Thunderbird, as is the Zener Diode heat sink plate below the petrol tank.

The Triumph Speed Twin & Thunderbird Bible

The 1964 US market Thunderbird featured a sports-type front mudguard and fixing stays.

Right & opposite top: A Metropolitan Police specification 1964 Thunderbird fitted with legshields and a radio.

Stanchion length was 22in, damper sleeve 3⅛in. The brake cable adjustment on the right hand fork slider was deleted, and relocated to the front brake anchor plate fulcrum bolt. Oil capacity was revised to ⅓ of an imperial pint (190cc) for each fork leg.

Oil tank The oil tank was rubber-mounted to insulate it from the frame (and so avoid stress fractures), and was fitted with an oil drain plug.

Mudguards A more conventional front mudguard replaced the large valanced type. It required front stays for support, though, so a fixing-in the form of a loose clip around the bottom of the fork slider was fitted. The integral middle stay and the bottom stay, which could act as a front stand, were still fitted.

Exhaust system A single stay fitted in front of the crankcase joined the two exhaust pipes together, making the whole assembly more rigid. The resonator silencer mounting brackets were now separate items, as chrome-plating the silencers with integral brackets had proved difficult.

Technical development

A Mitchenall full fairing, single seat, sports type front mudguard, and radio set graced this 1964 police model.

The Triumph Speed Twin & Thunderbird Bible

The Thunderbird Police model in its final form. A 1965 model Metropolitan Police specification model.

Technical development

Electrical The entire system was changed to 12 volts, with Zener diode charge control. The heat sink for the Zener diode was an aluminium plate mounted on the front petrol tank retaining bolts.

To provide the 12 volts, two MKZ9E Lucas 6V batteries were fitted in series, with the battery carrier modified to suit. A Lucas 49072A 2DS 506 round-finned rectifier fed direct current through the diode to the batteries.

The high tension for the sparkplugs was provided by two Lucas MA12 ignition coils fitted beneath the petrol tank. A Lucas 8H 12V horn was specified.

Speedometer The Smiths chronometric instrument was replaced by the new Smiths magnetic type.

The dial was light and dark grey with a red indicator needle. Smiths identification for the mph model was SSM5002/00, and the kph SSM5002/01.

Electrical specification

Battery	2 x MKZ 9E 6V
Horn	8H 12V Lucas 70164
Headlight	Pre-focus vertical dip
Bulb main	414 50/40 12V pre-focus
Bulb pilot	222 4W 12V
Bulb speedo	987 2W MES 12V
Bulb tail/stop	380 1W 12V
Tail lamp	L564 Lucas 53432
Zener	ZD 715 Lucas 49345
Rectifier	2DS 506 Lucas 49072
Coils	MA12 Lucas 12V
Fuse	25A

1965 Model 6T Thunderbird and 6TP police model

Engine prefix: 6T and 6TP
Engine and frame numbers: DU 14635 to DU 24874
Build dates: 07.09.1964 to 06.08.1965

Engine A threaded plug was fitted to the rear of the crankcase to provide access for the use of a TDC locating tool, and a slot in the flywheel locked the engine at TDC. For this season only, the crankshaft was located by the engine sprocket clamping the inner spool of the drive side (left hand) ball journal mainbearing. This modification was aimed at countering wear on the drive side mainbearing journal.

The oil pressure indicator button was deleted, and the release valve was fitted with a blind dome nut. This modification required a new $1^{17}/_{32}$in sprocket.

A standard 1965 police model: some forces fitted their own radio and weather protection equipment.

The Triumph Speed Twin & Thunderbird Bible

A redesigned rear light is most noticeable on this 1965 US market Thunderbird.

Gearbox A plain washer was fitted between the kickstart ratchet sleeve and mainshaft bearing to prevent sleeve distortion, thereby obviating ratchet pinion jamming. The gearbox sprocket and high gear splines were modified, so old and new components were not interchangeable.

Frames To improve accessibility, the thread for the swinging arm pivot bolt was moved to the left side. The rear brake pedal mechanism was redesigned by placing a small lever behind the rear engine plate to give a straight pull to the brake rod, which now passed inside the Girling unit.

Suspension The front forks were modified to give greater travel. The bottom sliders were made from extrusions, and were fitted with new wheel spindle clamps. Fork spring free length was increased to 9¾in from 8¾in, and the damper sleeve length was decreased to 2⅛in from 3⅛in. Fork stanchion length remained at 22in. To aid assembly, the damper sleeves now had only one stepped end.

Wheels The quickly detachable rear wheel hub was redesigned and fitted with ball journal bearings of ¾ x 1⅞ x 1⁹⁄₁₆in replacing the taper roller. On both the quickly detachable and standard wheels, the brake cam lever and return spring were modified to accept the altered brake rod operation.

Mudguards The loose clips were deleted on the front mudguard stays. The stays were lengthened and flattened, and two holes in the flattened area provided the fixing by the wheel spindle clamp bolts.

Electrical The US market models were fitted with a new Lucas 679 tail lamp, the lens of which had a protruding central cone.

1966 Model 6T Thunderbird

Model prefix: 6T
Engine and frame numbers: DU25877 to DU44393
Build dates: 23.08.1965 to 28.08.1966

Engine A step was machined in the flywheel periphery to reduce its weight by 2½lb, whilst keeping to the 85% balance factor. The crankshaft location reverted to the timing side (the inner spool of the ball journal bearing was clamped between the crank and the timing pinion by a clamping washer between the pinion and the bearing). The drive side bearing was changed to a single-lipped roller giving a higher load capacity. This roller bearing can be fitted retrospectively if the crankshaft is located by the timing pinion.

Pressure feed to the exhaust cam followers was introduced. The oil was fed through drillways in the crankcase and cylinder barrel to the exhaust tappet block. Oil was then passed through drillways in the exhaust cam followers onto the exhaust camshaft lobes. New cam followers were specified, with a 'flat' of ⁵⁄₃₂in ground on one side of the stem.

From DU42399, a hollow dowel was fitted between the crankcase and the cylinder barrel to combat oil seepage at this point. Aluminium alloy exhaust pipe adaptors were fitted from DU25877, but they weren't very successful so a reversion to the original steel ones was made at DU39464.

Redesigned inlet and exhaust tappet blocks were used with straight tube pushrod covers, flanged top and bottom, which sat on square section O-rings, the bottom O-rings being retained by cupped washers.

Gearbox A longer kickstart lever was fitted to aid starting by providing more leverage. The speedometer

Technical development

drive gears were removed from the gearbox along with the speedo drive cable attachment situated in the inner cover. The speedo drive was now fitted to the rear wheel. The clutch pressure plate central adjuster was increased to ⅜in diameter.

Frame Integral fairing attachment lugs were added to the steering head forging and the head angle changed from 65° to 63°.

A new rear frame with welded pegs to mount the redesigned battery carrier straps was specified. These new battery carrier cross straps had tubular ends to accept spigotted rubber bushes, thereby ensuring a vibration free battery carrier.

To facilitate fitting the rear wheel, the swinging arm was widened by ¼in to 7¾in between the fork ends.

Suspension From DU31119, the front fork damper sleeves were changed from machined aluminium to moulded plastic.

Petrol tank A new design petrol tank badge, commonly known as the 'Eyebrow' or 'Birdwing', replaced the 'basket weave' type.

Oil tank The redesigned oil tank had provision for rear chain oiling via an adjustable metering screw in the filler cap neck. The rocker feed pipe was relocated from below the tank to the top. This modification was not successful, however, as it led to premature wear of the overhead valve gear due to lack of lubrication. A service kit was made available to re-instate the feed pipe to below the tank.

Handlebars/controls White rubber handlebar grips with horizontal flutes were specified.

The final year of the Thunderbird. New tank badges and no rear panels gave the machine an almost retro, late fifties look.

Triumph's modern approach to motorcycle design and production is clearly reflected in the handsome appearance and mechanical perfection of this famous model which is renowned for its smooth, effortless performance – with or without a sidecar.
The Thunderbird's consistent, day-in, day-out reliability makes it the automatic first choice of the fully competent rider who drives his machine hard and expects it to earn its keep. A choice which is endorsed by a long tradition of exemplary service with police forces, military units and other government departments all over the world.

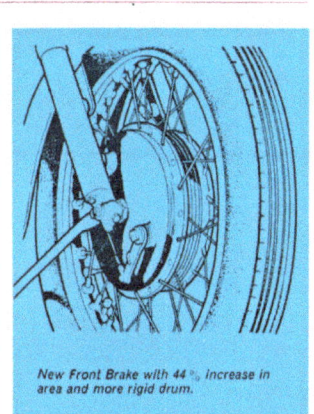

New Front Brake with 44% increase in area and more rigid drum.

The Triumph Speed Twin & Thunderbird Bible

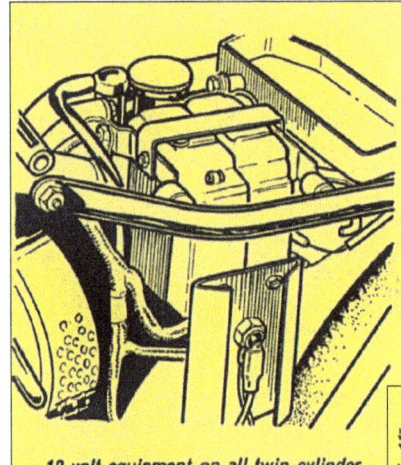

12-volt equipment on all twin cylinder models. Raising hinged twin seat gives easy access to the two 6-volt batteries, and to the neat tool tray.

The new cylinder type Ignition Switch. Warning light fitted in headlamp.

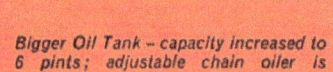

Bigger Oil Tank – capacity increased to 6 pints; adjustable chain oiler is incorporated.

Provision is now made in the frame for the fitting of a "Neiman" anti-theft lock.

Mudguards The front mudguard number plate lost the chrome-style surround, which had been a feature on Triumphs for thirty years. The rear wheel enclosure was discontinued, and was replaced by a shaped side panel matching the oil tank.

Wheels The rear wheel hubs were threaded internally on the right side to accept a slotted sleeve to drive the Smiths speedo gearbox.

The standard rear wheel sprocket reverted to the bolt-on, though the number of teeth remained at 46. The quickly detachable wheel sprocket remained integral with the cast iron brake drum.

Front brake shoes were increased in width, and the brake drum was modified to suit (giving 40% more brake area). The brake drum styling plate was modified to give a plain surface, the radial rings being deleted.

Electrical The Zener diode heat sink was relocated from the front petrol tank to a new alongside the battery carrier. Originally just a flat plate, the heat sink area was increased by substituting a right-angled plate making it L-shaped, from DU40436, May 2, 1966.

From DU32898, January 6, 1966, a single Lucas PUZ5A 12V battery replaced the two MKZ9E 6V ones.

The fuse was uprated to 35A. The horn was a Lucas 6H 12V.

The 6T Thunderbird was discontinued at the end of the 1966 season, and the last off the production line was DU44393, built on August 28, 1966.

Thunderbird 6TP

Although many law enforcement authorities had used the Triumph Speed Twin over the years, as time moved on it made sense to look at the larger-engined Thunderbird as a replacement. At its inception the Speed Twin had probably been as fast and accelerated as well as anything on the road. However, in the 1950s, this was no longer the case.

Originally, many forces were quite happy to take the standard specification Thunderbird, then fitting such items as leg shields and radio equipment themselves. In the 1960s, however, some forces issued their own specifications (and price) which Triumph had to meet. This meant that there was never a lot of profit in these models, but they were always good for publicity. Many overseas authorities took their cue from what the London Metropolitan Police was using, and then ordered the same models.

Up to and including 1964, Thunderbirds built for the police forces carried the letter W after the model, i.e. 6TW. From 1965, though, a proper police model was catalogued, and given the model code 6TP.

When the Thunderbird was finally discontinued, the police models were based on the Trophy TR6, and became known as the TR6P, or the 'Saint.'

Up to 1962, the colours used were the same as those for the ordinary production models. After this

Technical development

date, however, all black became the norm. Around 1965, the Met specified that its future orders would feature white petrol tanks and mudguards.

In 1965, the Met stipulated that the minimum accepted speed would be 100mph. Triumph then had to ship 6TPs to the Motor Industry Research Area (MIRA) near Nuneaton, Warwickshire, where each individual machine was timed electronically and the speed recorded. All exceeded the 100mph minimum but, as I recall, with so many machines around, it was all rather hectic.

The life of a police machine could be very varied; one day escorting a 100-ton load around the outskirts of a city at just above walking pace, and the next day chasing some ne'er do well at over 100mph. As one can imagine, this called for a very tractable but fast machine, and the 6TP was very suitable.

1966 6TP specification

Compression ratio	7.5:1
bhp	40 @ 6500rpm
Camshafts	E3134 form inlet and exhaust
Carburettor	Amal 389 large bore
Gearbox sprocket	19-tooth
Gear ratios	4th — 4.84, 3rd — 5.76, 2nd — 8.17, 1st —11.8.

The illustrations on the following pages are from the Triumph booklet *Motorcycles in Police Service*. The booklet was originally produced to assist chief constables and other officers considering the introduction of motorcycles to their forces.

This is how the Thunderbird would have looked had it been produced after 1966. Shown here is a 1967 police model now known as the TR6P.

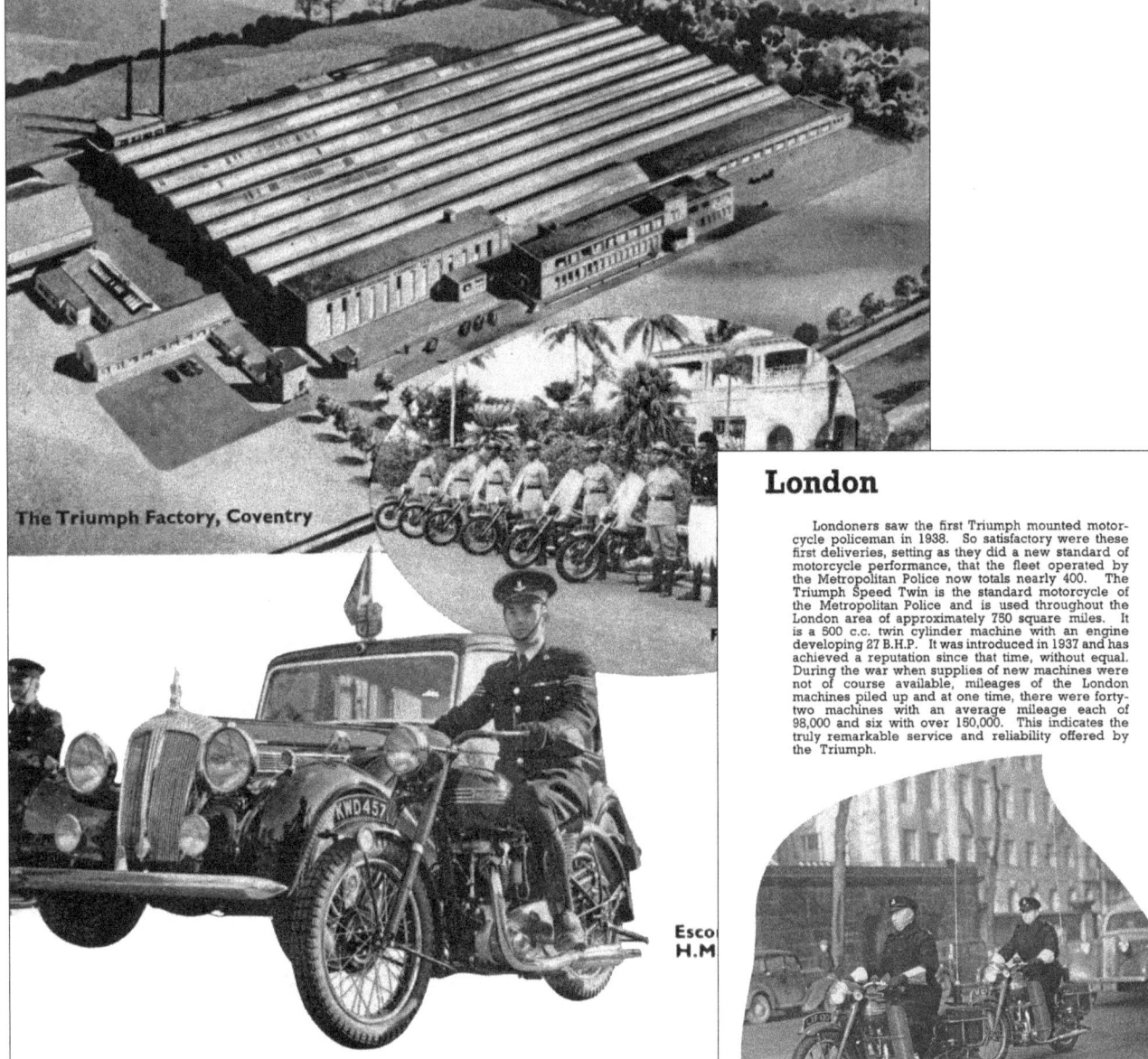

Technical development

The Triumph Speed Twin & Thunderbird Bible

The Olympic Flame arrives in London for the Olympic Games, 1948

BELFAST

TAUNTON

Technical development

Thunderbirds on duty in Paris

A fine line up of Triumph Thunderbirds in South Australia

SIR HAROLD SCOTT, K.C.B., K.B.E. Commissioner of Police of the Metropolis (London), tests some radio equipment on a Triumph Speed Twin.

The Triumph Speed Twin & Thunderbird Bible

Thunderbird colour chart, paint substitutes, show models and carburettor specifications

Colour chart Thunderbird 6T

1950	Petrol tank	Thunder Blue with chrome styling bands and blue insets. The badge had silver lettering on a Blue background.
	Mudguards	Thunder Blue with Gold-lined centre ribs.
	Wheel rims	Chrome-plated with Thunder Blue painted centres, lined Gold.
	Air filter	Gunmetal Grey.
	Voltage box	Black.
	Steering damper	Black.
	Pillion footrests	Black.
	Stand springs	Black.
	Prop stand	Black.
	Battery carrier	Black.
	Choke leve	Black.
	Number plates	Black.
	Rear light	Black.
	All other painted parts	Thunder blue.
	Note. From 10166N (16.06.1950) a lighter shade of Thunder Blue was specified.	
1951	As 1950, but paint changed to Polychromatic Blue.	
	Note. Thunderbirds built from 11130NA to 11166NA (13.07.1950) all had Black finish with Gold-lined mudguards and wheelrims.	
1952	As 1951. Except wheel rims and handlebars were painted Blue.	
1953	As 1951. Optional for USA all Black finish.	
1954	As 1951. Optional for USA all Black finish.	
1955	As 1951.	
1956	Petrol tank	Polychromatic Crystal Grey with chrome styling bands and Grey insets. The badge had silver lettering on a Black background.
	Mudguards	Crystal Grey with Gold-lined centre ribs.
	Wheel rims	Plain chrome.
	Steering damper	Black.
	Brake return springs	Black.
	Number plates	Black.
	All other painted parts	Polychromatic Crystal Grey.
1957	Petrol tank	Metallic Bronze Gold. Badge Silver lettering on a Black background with Black insets on main badge.
	Mudguards	Metallic Bronze Gold with Black centre rib, lined White.
	Front hub	Eggshell Black.
	All other painted areas	Gloss Black.
USA option		
	Petrol tank	Aztec Red.
	Mudguards	Aztec Red with Black centre rib, lined Gold.
1958	As 1957.	
1959	Petrol tank	Charcoal Grey. Badge White lettering on Black background with Black insets on main badge
	Mudguards	Charcoal Grey with Black centre stripe, lined White.
	Front forks/nacelle	Charcoal Grey.
	Oil tank/battery box	Gloss Black, as were all other painted parts except the front hub which was Eggshell Black.
1960	Petrol tank	Charcoal Grey. Badge White lettering on Black background with White insets on main badge.
	Front mudguard	Charcoal Grey.
	Rear panels	Charcoal Grey.
	Front forks/nacelle	Black.
	Front hub	Eggshell Black.
	All other painted parts	Gloss Black.

Technical development

1961		Petrol tank	Black upper half, Silver Sheen lower, Gold line at paint joint. Badge White lettering on Black background with Black insets on main badge.
		Front mudguard	Silver Sheen.
		Rear panels	Silver Sheen.
		Rear mudguard	Black.
		Front fork-upper	Black.
		Front fork sliders	Silver sheen.
		Front hub	Eggshell Black.
		All other painted parts	Gloss Black.
1962		As 1961 except petrol tank badge Black lettering on a Gold background.	
1963		Petrol tank	Black upper half, Silver Sheen lower. (Black now encases the kneepad area) Gold line at paint joint. Badge Gold lettering on Black background, with Gold insets on main badge.
		Front mudguard	Silver Sheen.
		Rear mudguard	Silver Sheen.
		Rear panels	Silver Sheen
		Front fork upper	Gloss Black.
		Front fork sliders	Silver Sheen.
		Front hub	Eggshell Black.
		All other painted parts	Gloss Black.
1964		Petrol tank	As 1963.
		Front mudguard	Silver Sheen.
		Rear mudguard	Silver Sheen.
		Rear mudguard	Silver Sheen.
		Rear panels	Silver Sheen.
		Front mudguard stays	Silver Sheen.
		Front fork upper	Black.
		Front fork sliders	Silver Sheen.
		Front hub	Silver Sheen.
		All other painted parts	Gloss Black.
1965		Petrol tank	Black upper half, Silver Sheen lower, as 1963, with Gold line at paint joint. Badge Silver lettering on Black background with Black insets on main badge.
		Front mudguard	Silver Sheen.
		Rear mudguard	Silver Sheen.
		Rear panels	Silver Sheen.
		Front mudguard stays	Silver Sheen.
		Front fork upper	Black.
		Front fork sliders	Silver Sheen.
		Front hub	Silver Sheen.
		All other painted parts	Gloss Black.
1966		Petrol tank	Black upper half, Silver lower, as 1963. Badge Black lettering on White background.
		Front mudguard	Silver Sheen.
		Rear mudguard	Silver Sheen.
		Front mudguard stays	Silver Sheen.
		Front stand	Silver Sheen.
		Front hub	Silver Sheen.
		All other painted parts	Gloss Black.

Thunderbird paint substitutes

Crystal grey	Citroën silver.
	De Tomaso Grigio Albany.
Charcoal Grey	Jaguar Dark Grey.
Silver Sheen	Vauxhall Sebring Silver.
	Rover Silver.
Metallic Gold	Mercedes Icon Gold No 2 Light Shade.
Polychromatic Blue	Ford Blue Mink or Dupont 202-55824H.
Aztec Red	Dupont 1633H.

The Triumph Speed Twin & Thunderbird Bible

Thunderbird show models

Number	Built	Venue	Number	Built	Venue
6T 1017N	18.10.1949	Earls Court	6T 59964	22.11.1954	Not known
6T 1018N	18.10.1949	Earls Court	6T 71636	13.09.1955	Earls Court
6T 1019N	18.10.1949	Earls Court	6T 71637	13.09.1955	Earls Court
6T 1020N	18.10.1949	Earls Court	6T 71638	13.09.1955	Earls Court
6T 1021N	18.10.1949	Earls Court	6T 71639	13.09.1955	Earls Court
6T 1022N	18.10.1949	Earls Court	6T 71640	13.09.1955	Earls Court
6T 1023N	18.10.1949	Earls Court	6T 71641	13.09.1955	Earls Court
6T 1024N	18.10.1949	Earls Court	6T 72122	22.09.1955	Paris show
16 13727N	19.09.1950	Earls Court	6T 02058	08.10.1956	Earls Court
16 13728N	19.09.1950	Earls Court	6T 02059	08.10.1956	Earls Court
6T 14166NA	21.09.1951	Earls Court	6T 02060	08.10.1956	Earls Court
6T 14167NA	21.09.1951	Earls Court	6T 02062	08.10.1956	Earls Court
6T14173NA	21.09.1951	Earls Court	6T 02063	08.10.1956	Earls Court
6T 15044NA	16.10.1951	Earls Court	6T 02068	08.10.1956	Earls Court
6T 33419	30.09.1952	Earls Court	6T 02073	09.10.1956	Milan show
6T 33420	30.09.1952	Earls Court	6T 03018	09.11.1956	Not known
6T 33421	30.09.1952	Earls Court	6T 020883	08.10.1958	Earls Court
6T 33422	30.09.1952	Earls Court	6T 020889	08.10.1958	Earls Court
6T 33423	30.09.1952	Earls Court	6T 020893	08.10.1958	Earls Court
6T 33424	30.09.1952	Earls Court	6T 020894	08.10.1958	Earls Court
6T 45584	07.10.1953	Earls Court	6T D7712	02.09.1960	Earls Court
6T45585	07.10.1953	Earls Court	6T D7713	02.09.1960	Earls Court
6T 45586	07.10.1953	Earls Court	6T D7714	02.09.1960	Earls Court
6T 45587	07.10.1953	Earls Court	6T D7715	02.09.1960	Earls Court
6T 45588	07.10.1953	Earls Court	6T 07715	02.09.1960	Earls Court
6T 58980	06.11.1954	Earls Court	6T 08327	15.09.1960	Paris show
6T 58981	06.11.1954	Earls Court	6T 08329	15.09.1960	Paris show
6T 58982	06.11.1954	Earls Court	6T DU103	29.09.1962	Earls Court
6T 58983	06.11.1954	Earls Court	6T DU14362	01.09.1964	Not known
6T 58984	06.11.1954	Earls Court	6T DU15353	13.10.1964	Earls Court
6T 58985	06.11.1954	Earls Court			

Thunderbird 6T carburettor specifications

Model	Year	Type	Amal No.	Main jet	Needle jet	Needle	Position	Throttle Valve	Pilot jet	Bore size
6T	1950	276	276FF/1 AT	170	.107	6	2	6/3½	-	1in
6T	1950	276	-	170	.107	6	2	6/3½	-	1¹⁄₁₆in
6T	1951-55	SU MC2	-							
6T	1956	SU 590	-							
6T	1957/58	SU 603	-							
6T USA	1955/58	Monobloc	376/42	270	.1065	C	3	376/3½	25	1¹⁄₁₆in
6T	1959	Monobloc	376/210	270	.106	C	3	376/3½	25	1¹⁄₁₆in
1) 6T	1960	Monobloc	376/246	270	.106	C	3	376/3½	25	1¹⁄₁₆in
2) 6T	1961	Monobloc	376/256	270	.106	C	3	376/3½	25	1¹⁄₁₆in
3) 6T	1962	Monobloc	376/285	270	.106	C	3	376/3½	25	1¹⁄₁₆in
6T	1963/66	Monobloc	376/303	230	.106	C	3	376/4	25	1¹⁄₁₆in
6T Police	1963/65	Monobloc	389	320	.106T	D	2	389/3½	25	1³⁄₁₆in

1) Cable operated chock by handlebar control.
2) Plunger choke lever mounted direct on carburettor.
3) As 1)

Index

Allen, Johnny 89-91
Alves, Jim 40, 89
Ariel Motors 6
Auto-Cycle-Union 87
Automobile Association 9, 45

BSA Technical Director 25
BTH British Thompson & Houston 93, 104
Ballard, Reg 22
Bayliss, Len 89
Bettman, Siegfried 6
Big Bear Enduro 122
Birmingham Small Arm Co 7, 8
Brooklands race circuit 9, 23
Bryants of Biggleswade 22
Bullock, Blackie 91

Campbell, Sir Malcolm 21
Carburettor specifications 80, 142
Catalina grand prix 91
Chain specification 82
Champion sparkplugs 104, 122
Clarke, Freddie 23, 24
Colour chart 79, 80, 140, 141
Customised Speed Twin 37

DTI 8
Dunlop Rubber Co 87, 89

Economy run 90
Engine/frame identfication 10
Eustace, Brian 8

Federation Internationale Motorcycliste 91
Fulton, Walt 91

Gaymer, Albert 40
Gearbox ratio chart 81
Girling Ltd 107, 124

Gover, Kevin 90

Hardwick, Dennis 90
Harley Davidson Motorcycles 87
Headlam, Eric 22, 24
Hitchcock, Jock 40
Hopwood, Bert 7, 8
Horridge & Wildgoose 22

Indian Motorcycles 87
International Six Day Trial 40, 41

Jefferies, Allan 23, 24, 40, 89
Jofeh, Lionel 7
Johnson, Bill 6
Jomo 7, 87

KLG sparkplugs 23, 104

Laird, Henry 23
Lodge sparkplugs 23

Manns, Bob 89
Maudes Trophy 22-24
McCormack, Dennis 7
McIntyre, Bob 62
Meriden 7, 8
Meriden Motorcycles 8
Minerva 2½ HP 6
Montlhéry Autodrome 87, 88

NSU Motors 91
Needham, Mike 7
Nicholls, Bill 22
Norton Motors 22
Norton Villiers 8
Notable registrations 78
Nott, Ernie 87

143

Olympia Show 9
Oxley, Alex 31, 32, 96, 99

Page, Val 6
Paint substitutes 141
Parts serviceability 86
Performance comparisons 78
Pettyt George-Maudes Motor Mart 22
Phillips, Jimmy 91
Police motorcycles 9, 11, 46, 53-55, 61, 62, 70, 114, 115, 117, 119, 125,129-132,135-139
Poore, Dennis 8
Prototype Speed Twin 12

Race successes 24, 25
Raleigh Cycles 6
Reynolds chain 126
Richards, Rich 91
Royal tour 26

San-Remo 40
Sanders, AA 40
Sangster, Jack 6, 7
Scobie, Alex 87, 89
Shawcross, Lord 8
Show models 83-85, 142
Shulte, Mauritz 6
Speed records 9, 23, 89-91
Speed Twin 1949 Road Test 20
Speed Twin 1953 Road Test 52
Speed Twin 1959 Road Test 68

Speed Twin Early Road Test 20
Speed Twin, new model described 17-19
Standard Motor Co 6
Sturgeon, Harry 7
SU carburettor 90, 102, 104, 105, 110, 112, 115, 142

T50WD 75
Taylor, Harold 87
Thomas, Jess 122
Tri-Cor 7, 87
Triumph Engineering Co Ltd 6, 7, 9
Turner, Bobby 90
Turner, Edward 6, 7, 25, 26, 28, 33-35, 77, 87, 88, 90, 91
Turner, Eric 78
Tyrell-Srnith, HG 87, 89, 90

Umberslade Hall 7, 8

Vandervell bearings 109
Victory Parade 34, 137
Vincent Motorcycles 91

Wallis, Tommy 24
Ware, EB 22, 24
Whitworth, Dave 23, 24
Wicksteed, lvan 23, 24
Wood, Ginger 90, 104
World speed record 89, 90
World travellers 57

www.ingramcontent.com/pod-product-compliance
Lightning Source LLC
Chambersburg PA
CBHW040740300426
44111CB00026B/2989